LIGHT BLUE

SYDNEY T. SCOTT

ACKNOWLEDGMENTS

This book of memories could not have been achieved without the help, comments and guidance of many people including those whose tales are intertwined with the hardships of the keepers and the reality of 'Bobbys on the Beat'.

My heart-felt thanks extends to those who have read varying draft copies:

Morag Sinclair (RIP) a friend from Orkney; my daughters, Hannah Stringer and Sharon Scott and her partner, Lasse Jensen who organised the publishing; Alison Scott, my niece, whose proof reading and punctuation amendments and suggestions were invaluable.

My gratitude to Tony Moore,(TM), ex Chief Superintendent, who relates his All Saints Road experience.

I must mention the contributors to the Scallywags' Tales who gave permission for me to name them are:-

Frank Bottlander (FB), John Bowden (JB), Stuart Campbell (SC), Paul Coventry (PC), Graham Hamilton (GH), William (Geordie) Johnson (WJ), John Kenny (JK), Stuart McIvor (SM), Anthony Moore (AM), Tim Redmond, (TR) , Roy Skinner (RS), Frank Wilkinson (FW), Brendan Brett (BB) and Arthur Hornblow (AH) who supplied me with the synopsis re the driving school.

Arthur is about 6'5" and it was a comical sight when he and I walked the beat together.

He is a Triple 1 product of the Hendon Driving School: Class 1 vehicle driver, Class 1 motor cyclist and Class 1 motor maintenance. He was a member of the Royal Protection Special Escort Group (SEG) motor cycle contingent and when he was in hospital he was visited by Princess Diana several times. He was the lead motorcyclist at her funeral.

I am grateful to all those who have allowed their names and / or photographs to be used and Natalie Jones @ Reach PLC (Daily Mirror), John Macinnes (Fraserburgh Herald), Craig Kitson for 'Dunnet Head' image, Andrea Thrussell for Douglas Head image, Ian Cowe for Muckle Flugga, North Ronaldsay and Skerryvore images, Chris Foster for Collators' reunion photo, Stuart McIvor for 'Noddy' and 'Panda', Johnny (Geordie) Johnson for Rillington Place, Terry Arthur for the cartoons, John Davidson, John O'Groats Journal (Text) and John Adams (RIP) photo from the book, 'HM The Queen Mother in Caithness', my trusty Ipad for various photos and anyone else whom I may have missed out.

I have used some other newspaper entries and photographs. I have tried to contact each individual distributor of the entries but, despite repeated attempts to gain their permission, they have not replied. I trust they will make allowances for my presumptions.

I must pay homage to my wife, **Phill**, whose patience and support was immeasurable,and my children: **Sharon, Ian, Hannah and Philip.**

They all had to endure the tribulations of being a policeman's family.

Long and unsociable hours were the norm for officers which obviously impacted on family life. They knew not what I was doing. I hope they forgive me.

My grandchildren, **Loke, Viggo, Caelan, Eden, Eimer, Rhea, Ellie and Isla** who have suffered grandad's jokes and tickles and their other parents, **Lasse, Gemma, Gareth and Maiken** who joined the family for 'better or for worse'.

GLOSSARY

These are the acronyms, initialisms or abbreviations used during my period of service. Some may have been changed or made redundant.

MPD – Metropolitan Police District (covers Greater London) except the City.

The Job – The Police Force (now Service).

B Division – The MPD division covering Chelsea (BD), Kensington (BK) and Notting Hill (BH) / Nottingdale (BN).

X Division – I also served at two of its sub-divisions – Hayes (XY) and West Drayton (XE).

Beats – Each sub-division was divided into smaller patrolling areas and called 'Beats' patrolled, usually, by an individual foot officer.

Reliefs – The number of personnel were divided into four and nominated as A, B, C or D relief, each one, of course, claiming that it was the best and there was a healthy rivalry between them.

Hours of Duty – Beat officers were paraded for Early Turn (6am – 2pm), Late Turn from 2pm – 2opm or Night Duty (10pm – 6am). The Area cars started an hour later to cover the change-over periods.

Area or RT car – A fast response car equipped with a radio linked to Scotland Yard.

Bravo 1, 2 or 3 – The call sign for the Area car covering the respective sub division usually crewed by an authorised Hendon trained driver, a front seat radio operator and a rear seat plain clothes officer. Bravo 1 – Chelsea. Bravo 2 – Kensington. Bravo 3 – Notting Hill.

Bravo 4 – The call sign for the spare car that covered the whole division and crewed from an officer from each station.

Bravo 5 – The two man crewed spare RT car used on Notting Hill section during night duty.

BH2 – The Notting Hill station van. (Black Maria and then Ford Transit).

BN2 J4 van – A light Commercial vehicle with the engine between the two front seats. There was little protection between the front of the vehicle and the foot wells.

GP car – An unmarked general purpose car.

B23 / B24 – Noddy bikes covering Notting Hill and Notting Dale respectively.

I.B. – Instruction Book.

SQ23 – The designated identification term for the building, called a Section House, located in Hammersmith with individual rooms for single officers.

NSY – New Scotland Yard.

TDA – Taking and Driving Away (a motor vehicle). It was not classified as 'theft of a motor vehicle', until it had been missing for a month.

Suddeath – Sudden Death (Covered all deaths, really, whether sudden or not).

Ceremonial Uniform – A uniform made from heavy gauge material and in the styled in the old-fashioned way with a high collar and multiple silver coloured buttons down the front. It was worn with white gloves and actual medals, rather than just the ribbons.

Arm Band – A striped, removable, striped band worn on the left lower arm denoting that an officer was on duty.

Dedicated to all those stalwart men who kept our seafarers safe and the men and women who, daily, cross the thin blue line and put their lives in danger.

NORTHERN LIGHTHOUSE BOARD

NOTTING HILL AND NOTTINGDALE

Hazelwood Crescent

Barlby Road

Golborne Rd.

Trellick Towers

The Eagle PH

St. Charles Square

St Quintins Ave.

RR

TC

Notting Hill Area (BH)

RP

LancR   HaP   WPR   PG   LeR

Warwick Castle

Westway

BN and BH are roughly split by Ladbroke Grove

CM   CT

Blenheim Crescent

Elgin Crescent

Ladbroke Grove

AG   VY

Henekeys

Westbourne Grove

SG

Portobello Road

Ken. Park Rd

BN   WR

LC

KPG

LS   LG

HiP

Clarendon Rd

Lansdowne Rd

Ladbroke Arms

LT

PR

FR

LR   NHG   PGT

PL

BH

The Mitre PH

Nottingdale Area (BN)

Shepherds Bush

KCS

Campden
Hill
Square

NR   AA

RC

Holland Park Avenue

AA=Addison Ave. AG=Arundel Gdns. CM=Codrington Mews CS=Colville Sq. CT=Colville Terr. FR=Freston Rd HP=Haydens Pl.
HiP=Hippodrome Place KCS=Kensington Church Street KPG=Kensington Park Gardens LC–Lansdowne Cres. LR=Ladbroke Rd
LS=Ladbroke Sq. LT=Ladbroke Ter. LancR=Lancaster Rd LC=Lansdowne Cres. LansR=Lansdowne Rd LeR=Ledbury Rd
LG=Linden Gdns NR=Norland Rd NHG=Notting Hill Gate PGT=Palace Garden Terrace PR=Pembridge Rd PL=Pottery La.
PG=Powis Gdns. RR=Raddington Rd RP=Rillington Place. RC=Royal Cres. SG=Stanley Gdns TC=Tavistock Cres.
VY=Vernon's Yard WR=Walmer Rd WPR=Westbourne Park Rd

I, AYE, 'TIS ME
& T'OTHERS' SNIPPETS

I make no apologies for using the pronoun, *I*, throughout this book. After all, *I* know more about myself than anyone else. In my anecdotes I do not intend to name either the police officers or the victims, criminals or any other person involved in the incidents, unless necessary or permitted. The officers will know who they are and I believe the others deserve their privacy. Their identities are marked by X's for the number of letters in their names.

All the incidents are true, based on my memory. (No, Your Worships, I did not make notes at the time or as soon as possible afterwards – a question inevitably asked by the defence counsel to ensure that your recollection of an incident was accurate and relevant). If my memory has tricked me after so many years, please forgive any slights or slight errors. All mistakes are mine and, if anyone wishes to correct me, please do so and let me know (for the revised edition...!)

Some of the police incidents are horrific, some humorous, some are not politically correct according to today's standards and some are just the ordinary stories that reflect the traumas that officers face each and every day as seen by the eye of I. The reflections may upset many people but, as is often said about people working in stressful situations, humour is the relief from tragedy and often black humour is necessary.

Please forgive what you may believe to be the unforgiveable and indefensible. The opinions are my own and you are entitled to disagree.

This epistle started off as a tribute to my Police Service but it seems to have morphed into a 'Brief Encounter' of the family circumstances affecting my life so please excuse the interruptions. The story begins before I was born, as you will see...

PS 1 The book was written over a period of time so some date reference may be out of sync.

PS 2 It is sad to see so many RIPs within the text.

CONTENTS

CHAPTER 1

IN MEMORY OF MY FATHER, JOHN ROBERT SCOTT, PLK

John Robert Scott was born to John and Anne Scott nee Tulloch, on 12th January 1900 at North Manse, North Ronaldsay, Orkney and the eldest son of a family of eleven. Having attended school on the island he served as a ploughman and as a boat-hand – from the age of 14 years to 17 years – on the 'Foam' of Kirkwall, whose skipper was William Tulloch. Much of his early life would have been helping his parents on the croft but, presumably as the small farm could not sustain such a large family, he decided to join the Lighthouse Service.

P1. John Robert Scott

He served initially at Auskerry in the Orkney Isles as an assistant light-house keeper (ALK) from 16th October 1920.

P2. Muckle Flugga

He was transferred to Muckle Flugga (the most northerly tip of the British Isles lying off the North coast of Unst in the Shetland Isles) on 25th August 1924. On this most inhospitable outcrop of rock it was said that no-one could build a lighthouse, but Thomas and David Stevenson did. The structure is made of brick since the raising of granite blocks onto the rock would have been impossible. On Unst he met his wife, Rose Sutherland Fordyce, and they married on the 29th September 1927. She and 'Jock' were together for over 50 years until his death on the 11th of February 1979.

Their first son was born on Unst in 1928. His father was on the rock and he was notified about the birth by semaphore. When asked to name him, he signalled back, 'John Harold Fordyce'.

Hens were kept in wired chicken runs on the rock for fresh eggs. A Supernumerary, an apprentice keeper, felt sorry for them and let them loose. With a following wind, they were last seen 'winging' their way towards Norway!

His next posting, on 20th July 1929, was to the other end of Shetland – Sumburgh Head – where their first daughter, Norna Rose, was born in 1929.

On then, on the 30th of March 1932 to Stroma – 'The Island in the Stream' – battered but unbowed between the notorious Pentland Firth on one side and the North Sea on the other. Sigurd Gordon Sutherland was born there in 1936. Rose said:

"I think this was the happiest time in the Lighthouse Service."

There was a move by the family on 14th June 1937 to Stromness where John was posted to Suleskerry. On the 10th October 1939 he was promoted to Principal Lighthouse Keeper. (PLK).

The long trek then, via ferry, train and ferry was to the Isle of Erraid. It nestles off the Ross of Mull just south of Iona, separated by a splash of the Atlantic Ocean which subsides twice a day enabling people and beasts to cross the gleaming, white strip of sand to the mainland of Mull. The sand is the dross of billions of seashells pulverised by the ocean's rollers. Erraid was the shore station for the Dubh Artach and Skerryvore lights. John was stationed at the latter; its construction is credited to Alan, a member of the Stevenson dynasty.

Here another two children were born: June Sunniva in 1942 and Sydney Tulloch (myself) in 1943.

P3. Sydney and June Scott

Because of the need for Rose to have recourse to readily available medical facilities, the family were moved on compassionate grounds on 13th December 1943 to Douglas Head lighthouse on the Isle of Man. Over eight years were spent there before all chattels had to be packed and crated by the 16th February 1952 and the journey to Dunnet Head lighthouse (the most northerly point on the mainland of Britain) began. The family, June, Sydney and parents, travelled from Douglas to Ardrossan in Ayrshire on the lighthouse tender 'Hesperus', and then by train from Glasgow to Thurso, Caithness.

Dunnet Head to Kinnaird Head in Fraserburgh, Aberdeenshire was the next long journey, the family arriving on the 20th November 1957. The reader ought to be aware of the logistics of such monumental moves. All belongings, furniture, bedding, crockery, toys, household goods - everything - had to be packed in boxes and then crated for transfer by many different means of transport. The lighthouse tenders, Hesperus and Pharos, were in constant use. Trains, lorries, buses, cars and, of course, manpower, were used at various stages.

An extract from a letter dated 4th November 1957 from the Northern Lighthouse Board, 84 George Street Edinburgh, 2, addressed to John Scott states:-

"Sir,
The Commissioners have decided to order your transfer from Dunnet Head to Kinnaird Head Lighthouse.
You were instructed by telegram on Friday 1st November to pack your effects for transfer. I have now to instruct you to arrange to leave Thurso on Tuesday 19th November by train at 3.40pm for Inverness. On the following day you should proceed by bus leaving Farraline Park Bus Station, Inverness at 10am arriving in Banff. At 2.52pm you should leave Banff by bus to Fraserburgh.
Your furniture and effects should be forwarded in advance by good's train addressed to Kinnaird Head Lighthouse, Fraserburgh, Aberdeenshire."

One may note that the keeper not only had to pack and crate everything, but arrange for his family to be ready to move at very short notice. Changing schools was always a disruptive problem.

John was a highly intelligent, compassionate, well-read and self-educated and was always concerned with the welfare of his fellow man. He instigated in the mid-1930s, with others, including John. R Miller, PLK, Hon President and George McKenzie, ALK, Hon Treasurer, the first Lighthouse Keepers' 'union'. It was entitled 'The Scottish Lighthouse Keepers' Association', whose motto was 'Unity is Strength'. The Objects and Aims, as described in the Constitution and Rules were:-

"The Association shall aim at advancing the status of Lightkeepers and improving their conditions of service by all Lawful and Honourable means. It shall, at all times, be the object of the Association to preserve and increase the efficiency of the service."

John was the first Hon. Secretary and ultimately the Chair, serving for 34 years up to his retirement. With patience and foresight and in the quiet and efficient manner in which they conducted dialogue with the Northern Lighthouse Board, the Association members negotiated many improvements for the men. Without their input, no doubt, the lot of the keepers may have been a sorry one.

Wages, in general, in the 1930s were fairly low, but in 1937 an Assistant was earning about £84 per annum and a Principal about £150, rising to £156 after four years. This was £15.17.1d less than they earned in 1924.........

On the eve of an Industrial Court Action, agreement was reached and an increase of £5 for Assistants and £7.10/- for PLKs per annum was agreed. They also had free accommodation and free coal.

John retired from active service on 31st October 1964 after 44 years of 'Long and Faithful service', as the Commissioners acknowledged. He continued assisting as an Occasional keeper for several more years.

In a letter from the Commissioners in acknowledging his retirement an extract says:-

"The Commissioners are also mindful of the fact that for over 34 years you have acted as a representative of the lightkeepers during which time your wise counsel has contributed in no small measure to the friendly relations which exist today and to the steady improvement which has taken place in the Service."

During his service John had the honour of meeting many dignitaries including the Queen Mother, on several occasions, and Princess Margaret when they visited Dunnet Head with their guests. The Queen Mother spent her summers at the Castle of Mey and on one occasion my sister, June and I, were introduced to her. He appeared on the BBC radio programme 'Town and Country'.

He was a family man who, with his wife, imbued honesty and a sense of justice to all his children, one of whom, June, described him at his funeral as being 'A Gentleman's Gentleman'. He treated all he met as equals. His upbringing on an island stood him in good stead for the vagaries of a hard, and often lonely, life. He will long be remembered by many.

P4. Lighting the lantern at Kinnaird Head

John was not the only man from North Ronaldsay who served the Lighthouse family so well and each should be saluted in his own right for spreading his island heritage, humour and dedication to an outside world.

Many anecdotes could be related about the lives and times of light-house folk who were a close knit family. There were many hard and tragic times, but through it all, a humour and fellowship flowed which, sadly, with the automation of the lights, is gradually passing away. But those who lived through that era will never forget the comradeship of the Service as a whole. This includes the Commissioners and their staff at head office, the artificers, the engineers and the sea men who tended the boats. Their traditions still flourish.

The lighthouse motto is 'In Salutem Omnium' (For the Safety of All) and these men and their families were certainly proud to live up to that saying.

Compiled in 2004 by Sydney. T. Scott,

- (John Robert passed away on 11th February 1979 – aged 79)
- (Rose passed away on 28th December 2005 – aged 96)
- (Sigurd passed away on 15th May 2013 aged 77)
- (John Harold passed away on 24th November 2017 – aged 89)
- April 2021: Norna is now 91, June is 78 and Sydney is 77 – long may we three live.

This is the only known photograph of all the family together.

P5. L – R Standing: Sigurd, John Harold & Norna. Seated: Rose, June,
John R. & Sydney

For those who may be interested in Scottish lighthouses I would recommend a very interesting, informative, impressive, fascinating and spectacular series of programmes on BBC ALBA: 'Lighthouses of Scotland'. The episodes are regularly repeated. The four lighthouses mentioned above are featured: as are Muckle Flugga, Stroma and Sumburgh Head which are three of my father's other postings. Another one is on North Ronaldsay, the island in the Orkney islands on which my father was born.

The flag of the Commissioners of Northern Lights is interesting. It depicts in the canton the pre-1801 Union Flag and is the only British flag which incorporates it. It is flown at the Northern Lighthouse Board (NLB) Head Quarters at 84 George Street, Edinburgh and on vessels with Commissioners aboard. The NLB was formed in 1786 before the union with Ireland. Basically it is the Union Flag or Jack, minus the red saltire which signifies Ireland (the whole of Ireland, not just the North). Wales is not represented on the Union Flag.

CHAPTER 2
THE LAND OF MY FATHER
(SORRY CYMRU)

The island of North Ronaldsay (NR) on which my father was born, is the most northerly of the Orkney islands. It is approximately 3 miles long and 2 miles wide, very low lying, sitting like a far flung stone in the North Sea separated from the nearest island, Sanday, by the North Ronaldsay Firth.

When living at Dunnet Head in Caithness in the 1950s I had several memorable summer holidays on this treeless windswept islet. A trip on the MV St Ola from Scrabster harbour, near Thurso, across the tempestuous Pentland Firth to Stromness was required. From there the steamer, either the Earl Sigurd or the Earl Thorfinn, sailed only once a fortnight to NR so sometimes we had to go ashore at Sanday. An overnight stay at the Kettletoft Hotel was usually necessary and I remember having to hunker down between two armchairs. The following day would incur having to wade into the sea at the disembarking place called 'The Black Rock' and suffer an often sea-sick induced passage in the 'peedie' (small) motorised mail boat manned by wizened and intrepid seafaring islanders. Thankfully I was not afflicted.

NR is famous for its unique breed of ancient sheep whose main diet is the seaweed, washed inwards by the incoming tide but laid bare in the ebb. A dry-stone built dyke, 5–6 foot high, was built within the perimeter of the shoreline. It stretches for some 12 miles and is the longest such wall in existence. This method was adopted to preserve the inland grazing/cultivating fields for cattle and crops although pregnant ewes are allowed 'in-by' for lambing purposes. Wily sheep have learnt to jump up and over the wall. The colloquial name for them is 'loupers'. The more persistent have to be shackled to stop them and so as not to teach others. The ravages of the gales and insurgence of the sea often breaches the defences and continuous reparations are required. Traditionally they were carried out by the sheep owners. Shoreline stretches are allocated, but with a dwindling and aging population this task has become burdensome. Recently, a paid dyke builder has been procured.

There are now only 6 sheep owners when there used to be up to over 70. Each house owner had a distinctive mark which was cut into each sheep's ear/s. The silhouette can be seen at a distance so that the owner can command his trained dog to target a particular beast. The dog will then chase it, grab it by the wool around its neck, and haul it to the ground. Interestingly, the Eveny reindeer herding tribe from Northern Siberia mark their animals the same way to identify their owners. Despite objections from interested animal cruelty factions, this regulated method is still used alongside the replacement coloured identification tags. However, the latter become loose and fall off thus making the said sheep unidentifiable. These somewhat feral sheep are corralled each year in a method called 'punding'. The sheep are rounded up by families, friends and trained dogs by herding them into stone enclosures called 'punds'. There they are sheared and the lambs ear-marked.

As I grew older (and bigger) I had the opportunity to ride, bareback on one of the last horses. Lily was a grey, elderly and placid which was just as well. Trips to the shop and the lighthouse were interesting because when I dismounted I had to find a suitable mound to climb back on. Whenever I visit I am always reminded of my exploits by my few remaining contemporaries.

The lighthouse, distinctive in its red and white livery, is the tallest land-based one in the UK. The ex-keepers living accommodation has been converted into self-catering cottages.

There is a most successful bird observatory on the island. A multitude of migrating species take refuge on this speck of land along with those that have been blown off course. The variety is astounding and many 'twitchers' visit to try to get a glimpse of some rare feathered friends. Budding ornithologists and zoologists spend weeks and sometimes months studying here and help out at the internal restaurant.

There is an archive within the church which depicts a social history of by-gone days which visitors always find intriguing and informative; well worth perusing. There are now several 17 minute daily scheduled flights now from Kirkwall to NR - determined by the weather. Fog is a continuous hazard. The ferry now sails once a week bringing in necessary food supplies, equipment etc.

CHAPTER 3
MY EARLY LIFE
BORN FREE

My upbringing may explain some of the naïve and foolish decisions I have made throughout my career. I was born on a wee island, Erraid[1] which is off the west coast of Mull in Argyllshire, Scotland when my father was the Principal Lighthouse Keeper (PLK) at Skerryvore lighthouse which is some 14 miles offshore in the tempestuous Atlantic.

P6. Erraid

P7. Skerryvore lighthouse

It is the tallest in the UK and has been described as the most beautiful one in the world. Erraid, was mentioned in Robert Louis Stevenson's book, "Kidnapped". The hero, David Balfour, was shipwrecked there. He thought he was unable to leave the island until some Gaelic speaking fishermen indicated that he could walk across the sand and shell strewn isthmus between it and the Isle of Mull when the tide receded twice a day. (See Appendix 1 for further information) The Stevenson dynasty built many of the iconic lighthouses in Scotland and the Isle of Man, both places being under the jurisdiction of the Northern Lighthouse Board (NLB) based in Edinburgh.

Mona's Isle

When I was two months old the family was relocated to Douglas Head Lighthouse on the Isle of Man because my mother was so ill after my birth that she had to be near a hospital and medical assistance.

P8. Douglas Head lighthouse

A foghorn was essential at most lighthouse sites and the one here, which was referred to locally as 'Moaning Minnie', was not far from the Assistant Lighthouses Keepers' (ALK) cottages. Its mournful and haunting sound wafted over a sea mist enshrouding an otherwise silent Irish sea. One could almost imagine a 'ghost' ship suddenly appearing out of the fog. If you have ever heard the continuing thundering blast of reverberating air which can exceed 140 decibels, you will begin to understand the agony of the families. The crockery used to shake on the shelves which, like a Welsh dresser, had lips to prevent the dishes falling off. Even the residents of Douglas town itself complained of the ear-splitting cacophony of sound. The last one to be decommissioned was at Skerryvore in 2005.

What a Wretch (sic)

Access to the lighthouse was by a series of wide stone steps which led steeply down from the road from Douglas town. A path beside a small beach called Port Skillion was negotiated and then more steep steps led up to the main complex. Aged about 6 years I began choking on a piece of raw carrot or turnip which would not dislodge. My father, with me face down over his shoulder, ran down and then up the steps to a waiting ambulance. Apparently I was blue in the face. All I can remember was being in a cubicle in the hospital and hearing my father and doctor discussing the dilemma when I suddenly gave a violent cough and the obstruction was ejected. Panic over.

Look Out!

Interestingly, in a round building near the top of the headland is a Camera Obscura. It shows 360 degree contemporaneous far-reaching images of the surrounding countryside and pedestrians were unaware that they are being viewed in real time. Near it, a funicular railway, now defunct, ran to the foot of Douglas Head and my contemporaries and I would sometimes sneak under the seats to experience the short ride. I think the ticket collector just turned a blind eye.

Small Memories

Those formative years are a bit sketchy. I attended a school in Tynwald Street until the age of 7 years and then transferred to Demesne Road before the family's move to Scotland. I remember attending my brother, John's, wedding to Betty Mills in 1950. I was dressed in a 'Hunting Scott' tartan kilt (which I still have but it doesn't fit anymore!) and wearing shiny patent leather shoes with silver buckles. Betty's mother ran a fish and chip shop on the pier at Douglas and the fare was most welcome.

Lobsters were caught from the rocks at low tide when a fire-side ash rake was poked into crevices to which the crustaceans would pincer and be hauled out. Great care had to be taken to prevent being the victim of their vicious claws. They were sold to the hotel on top of the Head. At Port Skillion we 'bairns' found a thick rope leading across the sand into the sea. When, with a struggle, we hauled it in there was a very large conger eel writhing at the end of it. They are very dangerous and, even when their heads are cut off, they continue to squirm in their death throes. The cats were well fed for weeks.

On the Move

On 16th February 1952, the day after H.M. King George VI's funeral, we boarded the Northern Lighthouse vessel, Hesperus, (the flags aboard were at half-mast) and sailed for Ardrossan in Ayrshire. It anchored outside the port awaiting a suitable tide. The next morning I woke up, and looked out of the porthole to a magical view. The sea was as placid as a millpond, sea birds were bobbing or diving in the crystal clear waters and the bulk of the volcanic island, Ailsa Craig, dominated the ocean. I was mesmerised. This isle is always seen on television when major golf tournaments are held at Turnberry. Quarried granite from there is the only stone engineered into curling stones.

Upon docking our entourage took a bus to Glasgow and the following day a train to Thurso.

On Top of the World

So, after living for eight years in the Isle of Man we were moved to Dunnet Head Lighthouse (my spiritual home) which is in the county of Caithness, Scotland, and is the most northerly point on the British mainland (not, despite common assumption, John O'Groats).

P9. Dunnet Head by Craig Kitson

Exposed atop a 300 foot cliff, Dunnet Head is three miles across open, rugged, and undulating moorland, from the nearest village, Brough. The incessant battering of the precipitous cliff face by the relentless Atlantic and the fierce winds and the rain, continually eroded the escarpment. Exacerbated by the vibrations and reverberating sound waves, two successive foghorns sounded their own death knell as they plunged to their watery graves. The third of these warning sirens has been erected and it still stands today. It has been silenced so may last longer than its forebears. No wonder the parental warning at most remote lighthouses to their children was, "Don't go near the cliffs."

Myriads of seabirds festooned the craggy landscape, clinging to their own plot of real estate surrounded by their squabbling neighbours. Puffins (locally known as Tammie Norries), razorbills, kittiwakes, and fulmars were incessantly harassed by arctic skuas, herring gulls and the occasional peregrine falcon. The master of all was the great skua (Bonxie) which was ferocious and often attacked the unwary ramblers if they came near to its ground nesting site. Their talons were vicious.

There were two other families at this lighthouse so we did not have many neighbours. A taxi (a very draughty Austin 10, as I recall), driven by Johnnie Sinclair (RIP), was required to take my sister, June, and me to Crossroads primary school 5 miles away and subsequently by taxi and bus to secondary school in Thurso some 13 miles away. During heavy snowfalls and subsequent drifting, we were often unable to attend school and sometimes a helicopter was deployed to bring us necessary provisions.

Our primary school consisted of two classrooms. The 'upper' school catered for the 8 – 12 year olds seated in year columns. Our class contained 8 pupils progressively moving across a row at the beginning of each new academic year. In many ways the lack of space was a good idea as you could listen to the previous years' teaching, thus revising your depleted recollections. Some of the older readers may remember the free third-of-a-pint bottles of milk which were issued at break-time. We left there at the age of 11 or 12 after taking the 11+ exam. In 2017, (63 years later), I organised a class re-union. All my peers were still alive, aged 74, and six of them were available. I drove from London but the other five were still living in the local area. A right fine blether was held over lunch and, as the photo suggests, we don't look a day over 50...! Sadly, Jocky passed away about two months later and George passed away in 2019.

P10. School reunion From L around the table: Catherine Nicholson nee Robertson, Margaret Andrew nee Bain, Sydney Scott, Jocky Sutherland (RIP), George Douglas (RIP) and Moira Land nee McKay. Unable to attend were David Farquhar (lives in USA) and my sister, June

All Grown Up

Herewith is a photograph of our class at secondary school, Thurso Miller Academy.

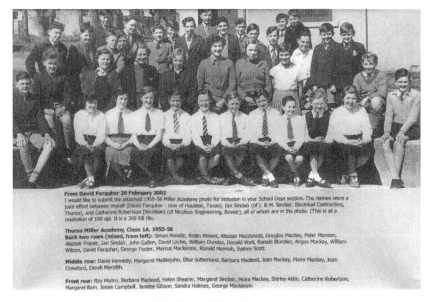

From David Farquhar 28 February 2002
I would like to submit the attached 1955-56 Miller Academy photo for inclusion in your School Days section. The names were a joint effort between myself (David Farquhar - now of Houston, Texas), Ian Sinclair (of J. & M. Sinclair, Electrical Contractors, Thurso), and Catherine Robertson (Nicolson) (of Nicolson Engineering, Bower), all of whom are in the photo. (This is at a resolution of 100 dpi. It is a 308 KB file.

Thurso Miller Academy, Class 1A, 1955-56
Back two rows (mixed, from left): Simon Moodie, Robin Mowat, Alastair Macdonald, Douglas Mackay, Peter Manson, Alastair Fraser, Ian Sinclair, John Gallon, David Lockie, William Dundas, Donald Watt, Ronald Blunden, Angus Mackay, William Wilson, David Farquhar, George Foster, Marcus Mackenzie, Ronald Hannah, Sydney Scott.

Middle row: David Kennedy, Margaret Meiklejohn, Elise Sutherland, Barbara Macleod, Joan Mackay, Maire Mackay, Jean Crawford, Derek Meridith.

Front row: Roy Munro, Barbara Macleod, Helen Shearer, Margaret Sinclair, Moira Mackay, Shirley Atkin, Catherine Robertson, Margaret Bain, Jessie Campbell, Janette Gibson, Sandra Holmes, George Mackenzie.

P11. Thurso Miller Academy

You may note the names: Catherine Robertson, Margaret Bain, Moira Mackay, David Farquhar and myself. On 11th August 2017 I met up with Simon Moodie and Ian Sinclair.

It's a Small World

When the lighthouse was automated the living quarters and the ancillary buildings were up for sale. My wife was waitressing in a friend's restaurant in Twickenham, London, when she overheard someone mention a lighthouse. "Which one?" she enquired. A man replied that she wouldn't know it as it was Dunnet Head in Caithness and that he owned it. My wife said, "I've been there. My husband was brought up there."

The man lived just around the corner from the restaurant. Weird!

I wrote the following poem, inspired by my sojourn at Dunnet Head:

Thoughts of Yesteryear

Have you ever sat alone upon a cliff top
And watched the terns go screaming overhead
And seen the rock below you
Where the fulmars make their nest
And spit at any stranger they detest?

Have you ever watched the fulmars play the upstream
In the currents that sweep up from down below?
They move into position
But never flap a wing
They are smiling, you can almost hear them sing.

Have you ever seen the multitude of puffins
The razorbills, the guillemots, the gulls?
They screech at one another
A cacophony of sound
In an orchestra it never could be found.

Have you ever watched the gannets at their diving
Gleaming white with creamy coloured heads?
Their wings are folded inwards
Like arrows straight and true
They slide into the water – azure blue.

Have you ever watched the sea in all its fury
Smashing on the beach and rocks below?
The ships are making headway
But at a pace so slow
You wonder what the sailors do not know.

Have you ever felt the sting of salted water
Upon your face when turn'ed to the wind?
You can smell the tang of seaweed
You can see the spuming foam
You would never wish to change it or to roam.

Have you ever sat upon the mounds of heather
And watched the campions swaying in the breeze
Ate berries sweet and juicy
Blew whistles with the rye
And watched the skylark spiral in the sky?

Have you ever heard the soughing of the wavelets
As they gently massage pebbles on the beach?
They seep into the rock pools
They sink into the sand
If only you could catch them in your hand.

Have you ever crunched among the shells at ebb tide
Or left your sunken footprints in the sand?
And watched the waves devour them
And your presence disappear
You can either give a smile or shed a tear.

Have you ever seen the sun drown in the ocean
And felt the darkness creep up finally?
The stars and moon peep out then
So shy throughout the day
And spend the night just twinkling cross the bay.

Have you ever watched the flashing of the lighthouse
Its beam of light spread finger-like to sea?
It stands in all is glory
With head so proud and high
'A saviour in the night' the sailors cry.

Have you ever seen the mist coming rolling shoreward
And listened to the foghorn's deafening roar?
When the safety of the seamen
Will always be the test
If they're coming from the East or from the West.

Have you ever sat alone upon a cliff top
And seen and felt and heard this wondrous world?
If you say you have been there sometime
Then my friend, 'tis what I'll say
You've never been alone there; I've been with you all the way.

(Sydney T. Scott, November 2000).

Near self-isolation was mandatory. People often ask me if I was ever lonely. My reply? "How do I know? I didn't know anything else."

Keepers' Keep

The standard practice within the service was to move families after a few years so, at the age of 14, we moved to Kinnaird Head Lighthouse.

P12. John and Rose Scott at Kinnaird Head lighthouse

Built on the top of a castle, it is the first substantive lighthouse on the mainland of Scotland. Now, the museum of Scottish and Manx Lighthouses is located there. It is on the outskirts of Fraserburgh, a town, then, of about 10,000 souls, in Aberdeenshire. Colloquially it is called 'The Broch': spelt differently but pronounced the same as Brough (rhyming with loch).

This period of my life was fairly unremarkable. I spent two years as a milk-boy, the milk supplied by a farm called, Cairness. The farmer's son joined the Metropolitan Police and became a firearms' instructor (mentioned later). The milkman was called Jim Lawson whose daughter, Jane, also, incidentally, joined the Force. Delivery during winter was not pleasant. It can be very, very cold in the North East of Scotland and the numbness of fingers wrapped around freezing bottles, where the cream had expanded and was protruding maybe an inch above the rims, was almost unbearable. Gloves were useless, becoming quickly saturated. A 6.30am start did not improve the learning process at school, especially when I fell asleep during lessons.

The money and tips from this enterprise were squandered in the local snooker hall where a Woodbine cigarette could be purchased for six pence.

The owner of a large drapery store who lived in, what we would have called a mansion, asked me if I wanted 6p a week tip or a £1 at Christmas. Naturally I said, "The pound". It was only later that I worked it out! He actually proffered a £5 note, which, in those days, was an absolute fortune. I rejected it and said that his wife had already given me that amount the week before. He told me to keep it as I was so honest. More clicks of balls ensued through the thick smoke haze!

When I left secondary school I joined the National Commercial Bank of Scotland which my parents considered to be a worthwhile career. I saved up and bought myself a BSA 125 Bantam motorcycle much to the chagrin of my parents who were concerned with my safety. However I still had the smell of Castrol motor oil in my nostrils, reminiscent of the TT races in the Isle of Man. C-c-c-cold again with no proper motorcycle gear. Fun days.

At one stage in the bank, when there was a shortage of staff either by sickness or holidays, I was seconded to the branch in Thurso. Remarkably a few of the customers were teachers who had previously taught me many years beforehand. Some even recognised me.

However, after working in various branches for five years, I was getting restless and yearned for a bit of excitement so I applied for the police service. My parents were not keen on the idea and my mother thought I would not have the courage, but I had been taking judo lessons and my confidence was high. They did not try to stop me.

Suffice to say that I was brought up in lighthouses for 22 years so my view of the big wide world was limited. Is that an oxymoron? Before joining the MET (The Metropolitan Police Force affectionately known as 'The Job'), I had only met two different policemen when stopped, twice, whilst riding my motorcycle.

P13. Syd on Motorbike

1. For those interested I would recommend a book 'Erraid' which can be obtained by emailing 'Leen' at Erraid@live.co.uk. The cost is £25 + postage. It depicts the

history of the island and includes the current life style of a remote isle in the Inner Hebrides Scotland and is illustrated with magnificent photographs.

CHAPTER 4
OFF WE JOLLY WELL GO

Why the Metropolitan Police (The Met)?

At the Age of 14 years I joined the Fraserburgh (1383) squadron of the Air Training Corps (ATC) eventually becoming a Cadet Warrant Officer. I cannot remember why – it may have been the lure of a uniform or a pal of mine may have been a member. The cadets enjoyed flight training in Chipmunks flying out of Dyce airfield, visits to various RAF camps each year and I attended a radio operators' course near Weston-Super-Mare. Two of the varied disciplines were .22 and .303 rifle shooting. I and my fellow cadets were fortunate to have an enthusiastic commanding officer and, through his tutelage, using old fashioned .22 rifles, we won the Battle of Britain postal shooting trophy in two successive years. It is awarded to the most successful ATC squadron in the country. This qualified us to shoot in the inter-services competition (the Punch Trophy) involving the Royal Naval cadets and the Combined Cadet Force cadets who had been equivalent winners of their respective competitions. These competitions were held in the shooting range below County Hall at the southern end of Westminster Bridge so we twice took the 'Flying Scotsman' train to London and were billeted at RAF Uxbridge. Unbelievably we travelled via public transport and walked through the streets with our rifles strapped to our backs; we were only between 14 and 17 years of age.

Although we did not win either time I achieved the highest score (99/100) on the first occasion. My overall prowess was rewarded when, in 1960, I was awarded the 'Sportsman of the Year' trophy for Fraserburgh and District.

P14. Arms full of silver

Big night for Fraserburgh A.T.C. corporal

Sharpshooter is Broch's Sportsman of the Year

Last night was a wonderfu night for Cpl. Sydney T Scott, of the 1383 (Fraser burgh) Sqdn., A.T.C. In the first of three presentations in the British Legion Hall Fraserburgh, he is pictured receiving, on behalf of the squadron, the Battle o Britain Trophy from Grou

P15. Sportsman of the year

The .303 rifle was a different beast altogether with a vicious kick-back. The nearest shooting area was within sand dunes at the Black Dog range at Balmedie just North of Aberdeen. Donald Trump created an International Golf Links there, much to the consternation of several residents and environmentalists. I have twice shot at Bisley, the home of the National Rifle Association, and gained my crossed rifles badge proudly worn on the forearm of the uniform.

On one such trip to London I saw about 20 police officers in full uniform coming out of an Underground Station. The image impressed me so, in 1965, I applied to join the police in Edinburgh and then Aberdeen but was rejected by both because I was too short. (One had to be 5'10" in Edinburgh and 5'9" in Aberdeen). However, both recruit-ment officers suggested I join the best police force in the world: London. On application I had to attend the Metropolitan Police recruitment centre in Borough High Street, where I sat tests in written English, mathematics and general knowledge and was subjected to a medical. "Strip off, turn around and touch your toes" was one of the orders of the day. A stern but 'friendly' searching interview by three senior officers followed. One asked what my parents thought about me joining up. I told them honestly and I saw him make a note of my answer. I passed but felt sorry for other applicants who were rejected for various reasons and whose prospects of another job were limited. Some cried.

After some badly needed dental treatment, aged 22, I arrived at King's Cross on 25th October 1965 at 5'8' (1m 72.7 cm) weighing about 10 stone 4 lbs. (65.3 kilos). A wee wisp of a laddie.

The Following is a 'Shaggy Dog' Story

Lost and confused at 7.30am at Kings Cross I had to take the Underground to Victoria on the way to Peel House, Beak Street. Emerging into a crowded commuter stream I began wandering and wondering when I spotted a large policeman with a very tall helmet. (You will note that everyone in my tales was larger than me - except the dwarf). I was saved.

"'Could you tell me how to get to Beak Street please?" I tentatively asked him in my modified Scottish brogue.

He peered doon (down) at me with disdain and said, in a strong Scots accent, "'You're nae thinkin' o' joinin' The Job are ye laddie?"

A Scotsman. I was definitely saved. "Aye, I am."

"Son, I wouldna' bother, The Job's 'f----d." (TJF)

Has anything changed? No. The phrase is still standard within the Service.

CHAPTER 5

TRAINING SCHOOL

"What has happened here sir (or madam) please?"

This is what we were taught at Training School to say to victims, spectators or witnesses when coming across an incident.

Having been measured for their uniform, helmet and boots, and issued with their accoutrements, (truncheon, whistle, armband and torch) recruits were inducted into the regime of either Peel House (Central London) or Hendon, the training school at Aerodrome Road, Colindale, where I was sent. Thirteen weeks of classroom training at Hendon included learning by rote the I.B. (Instruction Book), a large book on the law and regulations. The first dogma that we had to memorise was written, in 1829, by Sir Richard Mayne, one of the first two Commissioners of the Metropolitan Police:

"The primary object of an efficient police is the prevention of crime: the next is that of detection and punishment of offenders if crime has been committed. To these ends all the efforts of the police must be directed. The protection of life and property, the preservations of public tranquillity, and the absence of crime, will alone prove whether the objects for which the police were appointed have been attained."

Many Acts and Sections were drummed into us, interspersed with role play, physical training (especially of containment and disablement holds) and the inevitable discipline and uniform cleaning and pressing. Competence in swimming and jumping (sometimes 'forced') from the top board was required. It still amazes me how virgin recruits soaked up (pun not intended – I promise) so much information in such a short space of time and were then let loose on an unsuspecting public. Strangely, and to me unfathomably, the art of interrogation was not one of the disciplines.

Our boot camp, consisting initially of 17 callow all male recruits, took place during the winter months of November and December 1965 and January 1966. At times it was very, very cold and, despite wearing our greatcoats and gloves, role play outside (standing in snow and freezing temperatures) was 'unpleasant' to say the least. At one stage the instructor made us run through the snow and ice around one of the Nissan huts to warm us up (nice chap). Arriving back with rasping breaths and billowing hot air, he made us run around again (not such a nice chap). We then gathered around in a semi-circle for the next lesson.

After a few minutes the instructor enquired, "Where is Xxxx?" Not to be seen. He was a very large and unfit gentleman (and he was a gentle gentleman in both senses). We all trudged around to the back of the hut and there was the unfortunate 'Lurch' (nickname) collapsed in the snow, having succumbed to the cold dry air. He was quickly revived and suffered not from his unexpected 'snow bed'.

Footprints in the Snow

...and talking about beds. Most rooms had two beds and I was billeted on the ground floor with Xxxxxx (who has since sadly passed away). There was a strict curfew (10 o'clock?) and the large grounds were allegedly 'patrolled' by staff. Temptation can be very powerful. There was a hospital with nursing quarters nearby and, having visited there, a few of us used to return after lights out. We had found a way to climb the outer perimeter wall, sneak back to our room and climb in through the window. When it snowed it added an extra challenge, but we used to climb into an adjacent room thus leading our tell-tale footprints to an unsuspecting snorer. Whether anyone was ever caught I do not know. My best friend, who became my best man, often wonders how I passed any exam as I kept falling asleep in class.

(No change there then).

Boxing Training

Each year there was a novice boxing competition with the Metropolitan Police Boxing Club for a trophy called the 'Lafone Cup'. It is the oldest Police boxing competition in the world. The training school always entered a team and, of course, we were all fairly fit (except for 'Lurch'). One of the perks was that you were excused many of the daily uniform inspections by the 'Guvnors' and, at lunch time after training, steak was served to the volunteers. The down side was that you had to do a three mile run (a mile, more likely) first thing in the early morning, even through the snow. With the training I was down to 10 stone (63.5 kilos). Prior to the competition, which was refereed by Amateur Boxing Association (ABA) members, you had to be weighed and examined by a doctor. On fight night, they could not find anyone light enough to be in my category and no-one to face a heavyweight who was over 20 stone (127 Kilos). So, all my weeks of training and deprivations were in vain.

Having passed the necessary exams we were taken to Scotland Yard where we were inducted and sworn into the office of police constable, issued with the ubiquitous warrant card (which gave us almost unbridled and powerful authority concerning the upholding of the law) and allocated to our individual stations.

P16. Hendon Training School – I am top right

Reunion

I managed to contact five men who were in my class at Hendon and, on 11th May 2016, we had a 50 years reunion at The Nelson Public House, Whitton. From L – R: Malcolm Boother, Dave Hemley, John Boorer, Jim Boocock, Sydney Scott and Michael Cavalini.

P17. That Was the Class that Was

Memories were distant but I think my poem sums it up for all:

Memory

Memory stays in the past
We try and try to make it last
But often in that little brain
We have to strain and strain and strain.

We try our best with A B C
To find the words we cannot see
Our minds are blank, we can't recall
Anything, at all, at all.

The more we think the worse it gets
Why is it that we forgets?
A simple word or well-known name
Escapes from us just all the same.

We know it's there and get frustrated
Our memory banks just need updated
Ah! What was that, a passing thought?
It was the word that we had sought.

But gone again in just a flash
That spark of light just had to dash
We strive to get another glimpse
Surely we are not all wimps.

Forget it, we will not remember
That simple word, until September
Between us now we try to think
There it is, just on the brink.

I've got it now, I don't know how,
Just before we start a row
The word we needed was so clear
It only took a little beer.

(Sydney T. Scott – 15th November 2018)

CHAPTER 6
STEP WE GAILY ON WE GO...
(SCOTTISH DANCE SONG)

In January 1966 I was posted to Notting Hill Police station. Notting Hill is synonymous with the Race riots of the late 1950's, the Notting Hill Carnival, Rillington Place and Portobello Road. All four will be mentioned later.

P18. Notting Hill police station

On my first day at about 9am, proudly wearing my pristine uniform, I entered the station that, unknown to me, would be my 'second home' for the next 23 years. Entering through the front door I came to the public side of the counter to be faced by an irascible Chief Superintendent sitting at the Station Officer's desk, checking the Occurrence Book (OB).

"What do you think by coming in the front door?" he angrily shouted at me.

Unfazed I explained that this was my first day and I knew no other entrance. No apology was forthcoming, but he did get off his arse and opened the side door for me. I did have further contretemps with him as will be explained later. Those who knew him will remember him as 'Slippery Xxxx'.

A tour of the station ensued and the next day I was allocated my shoulder identification number (519B), introduced to members of my relief ('C' relief), and allocated an experienced officer (changed regularly - they hated 'puppy walking') to teach me three weeks of learning 'Beats'. So my journey began. The whole sub-division area was divided into smaller geographical areas called 'Beats' to which you were posted on a daily basis. There were four alternating reliefs, usually with their own dedicated personnel.

Quick Change Overs

A typical rota at Notting Hill for patrolling beat officers was defined in a nine week cycle. There were three continuous weeks of night duty (10pm–6pm) followed by six weeks of alternative late turn (2pm–10pm) and early turn (6am–2pm) interspersed with a few days off. Because of the lack of work force we had to work our additional rest days. There were four sets of officers called Reliefs (A, B, C & D) who worked rotating shifts. When you finished at 6pm after 3 weeks of nights, you had to be back on duty by 2pm the same day. Similarly, when you finished a late turn at 10pm and the rota demanded it, you had to be back on duty at 6am the following day for early turn. The Area car (fast response car equipped with a Force radio) crew started an hour later to cover the change-over of Reliefs. If you had a custody arrest you had to be at court at 10.30am (at the latest) so you can imagine that on night duty (off at 6am or 7am if you were on the Area car) and to be at Marylebone Magistrates Court by 10.30am, you did not get much uninterrupted sleep. They were hard times but good for overtime.

Throughout my time on the streets, I was a foot officer, Home Beat officer, pedal cyclist, Noddy bike[1] rider, car, van and Area car driver, and occasionally performed plain clothes duties. The latter included surveillance: at one time sitting on top of the gasometer at the north end of Notting Dale. With binoculars there was a panoramic view of not only the local streets but also the skyline of London. I dressed as a hippy with a wig, kaftan and open-toed sandals and wasn't even recognised by my colleagues as I 'begged' at Notting Hill Underground Station.

Herewith, John Bowden's reminiscence. He was a Police Officer on BH/BN section,

The Noddy was, in my mind, a rite of passage for young male PCs (not suitable for WPCs as they would have to sit side saddle) who were able to escape from foot patrol and have mains R/T (radio), a PR (Personal radio) and wheels. I had a choice at Notting Hill, call sign either Bravo 23 at BH or Bravo 24 at BN. It gave you the ability to go all round the ground and many other places besides and not really explain why you were there. I chose Bravo 24.

The training Noddy-bikes at Hendon (Driving school) bore no resemblance to the battered bikes on Divisions but on one of the days on the course through the water splash near Ember Court was always the event. On a Noddy it allowed you opportunities for traffic process, hence overtime in due course, and also crime arrests by, hopefully, being first on the scene due to your mobility in traffic. Parked up watching traffic was a deterrent, and waiting up around the corner for the pub traffic to leave and then pounce was a bonus. You always beat a Trafpol (Traffic Patrol) to an RTA (Road Traffic Accident) to keep you busy and in the dry for a few hours. All the above allowed you to meet and speak to people of all persuasions and make decisions, and, in today's speak, interact and 'up-skill'.

It was good going off the ground to get petrol or maintenance at Barnes: this was where the Traffic Patrol garage was based. It was also used to take blood samples to the Lab at Holborn, or acting as courier of messages between stations. Many years later the Lab moved and this was the home of SO6 (a New Scotland Yard department) where I ended up. The main event at that time was the construction of the Westway A40. There were many opportunities to attempt to go the full length whilst under construction until I succeeded one dark night into Paddington. Noddys could cover any obstacle. The panniers were also handy for shopping. When the Westway was fully open, did I establish the land speed record off the flyover approaching Marylebone flyover at 56 MPH +? No speedo on a Noddy was that accurate so that is history.

Thoroughly enjoyed the Noddy, great experience, and today a similar type would still be useful, no doubt with an electric starter, satnav, cruise control etc. etc.

P19. Noddy bike

The First Tentative Steps

Many of the following incidents occurred at Notting Hill (BH), Nottingdale (BN) - a satellite station to BH - or Hayes (XY) / West Drayton (XE) sections unless otherwise stated. BH, BN, XY, and XE were the designated identification letters for the individual stations and used for internal communication.

The reputation of BH still revolved around the Notting Hill riots of 1958 whereby some of the black immigrants rebelled against their treatment by the local population and the police. In my ignorance I was unaware of the previous history. No-one enlightened me.

As mentioned, each new officer spent three weeks learning beats accompanied by a seasoned officer. Then you were your own. On parade everyone had to shew their appointments: pocketbook, incident books, accident books, whistle, truncheon (the only 'weapons' we had – no handcuffs) and torch on night duty, and of course Form 29. This was a form you filled in if you came across an injured animal and they always quoted an injured horse. I carried my first form for the rest of my 33 years' service. The instruction we had to deal with for a runaway horse was to run in the same direction as the horse and grab its reins. This came in handy when I was later posted to Hayes and West Drayton. Two skewbald ponies had escaped from a field and were cantering down the middle of a normally very busy road. Fortunately it was early morning and traffic was light. My colleague and I managed to stop the horses. They were a bit skittish and had no halters but I managed to conjure up two with some rope, having recently having learnt the skill during a recent visit to Ireland. Jogging beside them we returned them to their field. I think my colleagues were surprised.

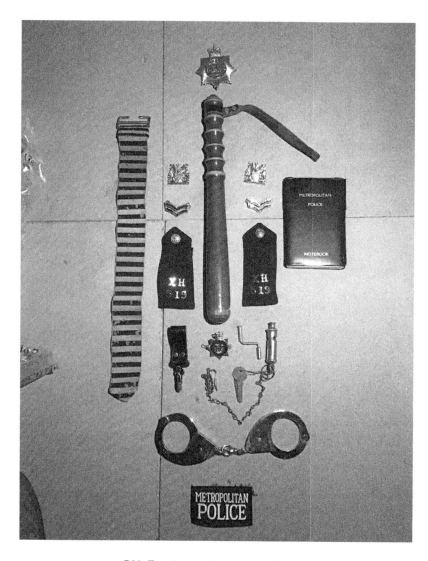

P20. Truncheon, whistle, handcuffs etc.

P21. Incident and accident books etc.

1. These were small grey two-stroke Velocette motorcycles featured in the ITV
programme 'Heartbeat'- which had running boards for one's feet and two panniers
at the back. Their maximum speed, downhill with a following wind, was about 50
mph and they were used for general patrol and for delivering messages across
    London. They were virtually silent and very manoeuvrable in a tight space. I
remember one officer on early turn (6am to 2pm) was practising to see how tight a
circle he could turn in. He nodded off and fell off in the communal area of a block
of flats. Was he ribbed? Was he ever? I guess that he 'nodded' off in more ways
than one. When meeting/seeing a senior officer, Inspector or above, one had to
salute. Allegedly this was deemed a bit dangerous on a motor cycle so they were
given the permission to just 'nod'. Hence the term.

CHAPTER 7
NEW BOY ON THE BLOCK
SO, AS JULIE ANDREWS SANG IN THE SOUND OF MUSIC, "HERE ARE A FEW OF MY FAVOURITE THINGS"

My first solo outing

At the beginning of February 1966, with a map and a torch to show me the way on night duty (10pm to 6am), I ventured into the unknown wilds of Notting Dale. I certainly needed my map so that I could find my way back to the station (no lighthouse flashing beacon to guide me home). This was one of the less salubrious parts of the area. There were some expensive large Victorian houses to the south owned by the very rich, but moving further north, Notting Dale gradually became more 'middle class', creeping into more deprived areas. Many of the large houses had been converted into individual flats with multi-occupancies, including a basement which the servants would once have occupied. Large estates and tower blocks (including Grenfell Tower, the scene of the horrendous fire in June 2017) were being built.

Two of the streets here are called Pottery Lane and Hippodrome Place. The first reflects the use of the area where there were several kilns (a token one still stands today) for the making of bricks. It was a slum area inhabited by a very low class of society whose living habits were less than wholesome. The latter, (in ancient Greek, 'Hippo' means horse and 'drome' means running), reminds us of the only race-course ever to be situated in London. It surrounded the hill of Notting

Hill and some of its location is still visible, consisting of the private gated gardens of the wealthy starting at Ladbroke Square then towards Pottery Lane and beyond and back behind those gardens in Elgin Crescent and Kensington Park Road. The carriage entrance into the course was from Kensington Park Road where there is now a taxi stand with a small green refreshment hut at the entrance which is now a Grade 11 listed building. This facility was very handy on night duty when a bacon or sausage sandwich and a hot drink were required. The running track did not last long because of the presence of the locals who frequently crossed it, disrupting the races, mingling with and aggravating the gentry.

Although the following accounts are not in chronical order, this neatly brings me to my first story.

Alleged Rape or Larceny?

In April 1966, I had been given an assignment to investigate the breaking into of a gas meter in a house in Clarendon Road. A shilling (5p nowadays) had to be placed in the meter to access the gas. It was not unusual for false reports of theft/burglary from these machines to be made, especially if the occupants were desperate, and it was difficult to prove that an actual burglary had not occurred. Fresh-faced and naïve, I knocked on the basement door and was shown in by a fairly heavy woman, probably mid-twenties with dyed blonde hair and very poorly dressed. In the main untidy room was an unmade bed on which three very young mixed-race children were frolicking, each wanting to try on my helmet. Being my first investigation I treated it very seriously and came to the conclusion that it was an 'inside' job. From her answers I suspected the occupant was involved and when I returned to the station I entered my thorough findings and suspicions on the crime sheet. House break-ins were dealt with by the CID and I was soon told that I should not have named a suspect but should have left it for the investigating officer to decide. A tap on the wrist but a lesson learnt.

On 26th May 1966 I was called into the Detective Chief Inspector's (DCI) Office. He handed me a Form 163 which is used to inform that an allegation has been made against you. The accusation read:

It has been alleged, in a letter to the Home Office, from some woman at present unknown that a police officer number 519 'B' entered her premises at *** Clarendon Road, W,11. on or about 24th April 1966 and had intercourse with her without payment.

He intimated that it was 'rape', not 'failing to pay for a service'. Knowing I was not guilty and that some mistake must have been made, I smiled. The DCI was very upset and told me in no uncertain terms that it was a very serious allegation and should not be taken lightly. I agreed with him, of course, but then said that I knew who the anonymous woman was. This interested him. I guess he was waiting for a confession.

He said, "How do you know who it was?"

"I have only been in the Job for 4 months and in that time I have only dealt with one woman," was my reply.

I named her. She was, of course, the burglary suspect. It was clear that he did not believe me. I then told him it would have been almost impossible for me to rape her.

"Why is that?" he asked.

"I am only 10 stone and that woman was nearly twice my weight."

After the interrogation, as I left the room, his parting words were, "Keep it in your pocket, son."

There was no substance to the allegation although I was never served with a withdrawal form which states that an allegation is unsubstantiated. I found out later that the premises were a brothel, that the woman had been arrested the day before I was called and that she had made a similar allegation against the Sergeant who had charged her but who had not even left the station. It didn't take me long to recognise the typical prostitute (I had not knowingly met one before – honest) and to heed those oft repeated wise words:

"Beware of Property, Prisoners and Prostitutes"

There were many prostitutes and pimps in Notting Hill which led, in part, to the riots of 1958. Another alliterative mantra was that the only things that should be out at night should be:

"Cats, Crooks and Coppers"

Allegations, many of them false, were, and still are, directed at officers trying diligently to perform their duties. I have had five in my career, none of which was substantiated. It is, I'm afraid, one of the hazards of doing one's job whereby arrested persons try to wriggle out of a charge by 'muddying the waters', often on the advice of their legal representatives.

CHAPTER 8
GORY, GORY, JUST TO SCARE YAH
THE SEEDIER SIDE OF LIFE

Gruesome

Inevitably a policeman has to come across some sights which the majority of the public never see. The result can be devastating to some officers who never really recover from the horrors experienced or injuries received. Post-traumatic stress disorder (PTSD) did not seem to be the convention of the day. It was probably not understood properly by some senior officers and the macho 'Get on with it' was their preferred response to any sign of weakness. Many of them were World War 2 veterans so there may have been a 'Hey Ho' attitude residual to their military service.

High Jump

In, 1968, being a Scot I had been out on Hogmanay and remember returning to the Section House in Hammersmith, designated as SQ 23 (a large building holding about 150 police officers in individual rooms), at about 6am on New Year's Day. I was on duty at 2pm and was not feeling in the best frame of mind. My condition deteriorated throughout the afternoon. At about 8pm a sad soul decided to leap off the roof of Hazelwood Towers which is off Golborne Road in North

Kensington. He landed on his head on top of a Vauxhall car (I haven't forgotten the make) and made a large dent on the roof. A Sergeant was first on the scene and he asked for immediate back up. I was the young recruit and passenger in the Black Maria police van, call sign Bravo Hotel 2 (BH2).

When we arrived the Sergeant was very pale and kept asking for a cigarette. Thankfully he had covered the remains of the head with a blanket. Because the person was dead the ambulance would not take him away and nor would the fire brigade help except to loan us a rubber sheet on which to transport the body. Four officers, one on each limb, then began to lift the body onto the sheet. I held an arm which came away as it was broken. Nevertheless we managed to carry the corpse into the van and drive to Horseferry Road Coroner's office. We transported him into the morgue and I was left alone to search the body. Obviously this was an initiation for me. Suffice to say that I began to lift him gently, piece by piece, onto the slab and in so doing I accidentally bumped the head against the block on which it would be laid. I remember saying "Sorry, mate" which was incongruous in the situation.

Transsexual Encounter of the First Kind

This tells of how I missed arresting a murderer. The spare Area car (call sign Bravo 5) was utilised on night duty. I think it was introduced when Oswald Mosley, who was the leader of the British Union of Fascists, opened offices in Kensington Park Road and serious distur-bances followed. After they closed, however, the extra car was still employed. It usually dealt with the more serious incidents leaving the mundane (is there such a thing?) call to the foot officers, van or the GP (General Purpose) car. The vehicles were equipped with radios connected to Information Room at Scotland Yard and often the message was just, 'A disturbance at…', especially if the dispatcher could not make out the reason given by the caller, some of whom were very incoherent for various reasons. Just before 11pm a call came for a disturbance at the Warwick Castle Public House, Portobello Road/Westbourne Park Road. We were in Portobello Road just approaching the pub. I was driving Bravo 5. I looked in the rear view mirror and saw the van coming up behind us. We in the car were a bit annoyed as we had dealt with all the calls so far that evening so I decided to let the van deal and I circled the block to back them up.

The story unfolded. A white transsexual had entered the pub the clientele of which was predominately black. She had been pestering one of the customers to such an extent that he had returned home, taken a large knife, gone back to the pub and stabbed the lady once, in her chest, puncturing her lung. The assailant had run out right in front of the van and the van passenger, the first black officer at Notting Hill, chased and arrested him. I suspect that this is the only time, in the UK, that a black officer has arrested a black man for the murder of a white transsexual. We, in the car, were left to deal with the victim who was still alive but oozing blood. The bar staff had utilised some bar towels to attempt to stem the flow.

The nearest ambulance was in Chelsea so it took some time for it to arrive. I went in the ambulance and held the oxygen mask whilst the ambulance man tried to treat the wound. The ambulance driver did not know where to go and I suddenly told him to turn left. He took a sharp left turn which caused the injured party to roll over and land on top of the ambulance man and me which meant that we were now spattered with blood. Unfortunately the injured person died as she was being treated by the doctors. Continuity is essential and next morning I had to attend the morgue where the unmistakeable smell of death and antiseptic is overpowering. I identified the person to the pathologist. Having never seen an autopsy I stayed to watch. I have great admiration for those who attend and perform such a task. At the subsequent trial there was a conflict of evidence. Witnesses had stated that the assailant had stabbed the lady only once but there were two entry holes. It was established that the second one had been made by the doctors at the hospital as a drain hole. A little anomaly such as this can jeopardise a trial.

The Armless Man

One night, a homeless man, very scruffily dressed and unshaven, walked into St Charles Hospital demanding to be seen by a doctor as his arm was badly affected and Jesus had told him it was diseased. The night duty doctor was called, thoroughly examined the man but could find no physical impairment. The man was adamant, shouting and swearing at the nurses insisting that his arm be removed. When he realised that no treatment was forthcoming, he left. Sometime later he returned minus an arm (the left one, I think) demanding to have his other arm removed as it was also diseased. We were called and asked to see if we could find the arm with a view to stitching it back on although I do not think that nerve surgery was very far advanced in those days.

We followed the trail of blood along Barlby Road and onto the railway line which was adjacent to Wood Lane. This was a distance of about three-quarters of a mile and I am still at a loss to explain how the man had walked that distance, having lost so much blood with the main arteries severed. It was very dark. However, we scoured the area with our torches being mindful to step back as trains passed by. I found a depression in the gravel beside the track where the man had lain down and I asked my colleagues if that was what was called an "armpit." (They threatened to throw me under the next train). In the event we did not find the limb but we came across a very small derelict signal-man's hut which was where the man had been 'dossing' down. The walls were covered in religious artefacts - crosses, religious writings, bible extracts etc. The poor man had obviously been afflicted by his religious beliefs. I cannot remember what happened to him.

Underground – He Should Have Been

The Central Underground Line runs through Notting Hill Gate and Holland Park Avenue. We received the call, which every officer dreads, that a man was under a train at Holland Park Station. We rushed to the scene expecting the worst. The man was under the stationary train and the driver, who had been unable to stop in time, was in an agitated state. The train had been emptied of passengers, many of whom were 'rubber-necking'. Having ensured that the electricity had been cut off, we climbed down onto the track and, peering under the carriages, we saw the man. He was fast asleep. He had been drinking heavily and somehow he had either fallen or just lain down between the tracks and the train had run over him. He was unharmed, much to the relief of us and the train driver.

CHAPTER 9

SUDDEN DEATH

Suddeath

This was the abbreviation of 'Sudden Death' which again was not a word that officers wished to hear. It was inevitable that you had to deal with a deceased person in your career because people die in a variety of circumstances.

I was directing traffic in Earls Court Road outside the Exhibition Centre on Kensington section: we were occasionally sent as aids to other stations if they were short of manpower. I was approached by a social worker and a caretaker who informed me that they could not get a reply from an elderly lady who lived in the top floor of an old Victorian row of houses. I had been in the Job for less than a year and this would turn out to be my first Suddeath. I was on my own, in a strange location and we did not have radios in those days. I followed them to the top floor where the door was locked and we were unable to open it. It took some time for the caretaker to find a duplicate key.

As we opened the door the stench was unbelievable. The lady had quite a number of receptacles dotted around full of excrement and urine. The smell was enhanced by the aroma of rotting vegetables. All the windows were shut and curtains drawn. The lady was slumped across the table with her head on her arms and her breathing was staccato and laboured. It was obvious that an ambulance was required so I left the social worker to take care of the lady and I went down to the ground floor where there was a pay-phone. Having dialled 999 I awaited the arrival of the ambulance which took some time. I escorted the medics upstairs to find that the lady had passed away. I often wondered if her sudden demise was caused by the cold wind coming from the window that the social worker had opened (and I couldn't blame her for that). I was then left alone to try to find details of relatives and secure the premises.

At times like this you remember what you have been told at training school: 'Take your time, don't panic, the deceased is not going anywhere'. Phew! – in both senses of the word.

A Charred Life

The two worst incidents were very gruesome. The first one was in Codrington Mews, a small turning off Blenheim Crescent. A van was on fire and when it was doused the charred body of a young man was found in the back.

Ironically, if I remember correctly, the band 'The Police' had their recording studios in Codrington Mews (perhaps Sting, the lead singer, can confirm) as did The Sex Pistols. Virgin Records eventually had large premises at the corner of Blenheim Crescent and Ladbroke Grove. Sir Richard Branson started selling second-hand records, with his mother, in the early 70's from a stall in Vernon's Yard just off Portobello Road. I often wondered why he called them Virgin Records. I seem to remember reading somewhere it was because he was still one at that time.

A Lonesome Life

The second, another 'suddeath', and probably the most gruesome, was in Linden Gardens off Notting Hill Gate. Another elderly woman had not been seen for some time and there was a distinct evil odour coming from the letter-box. There were a number of dead-locks on the thick security door and it took us some time to smash it in. We didn't have the 'Enforcer' - a designed manual metal battering ram in those days. The lady was lying in the hallway with her dress above her waist and she wasn't wearing any lower underwear. She had been there for some time and bluebottle maggots had been eating away at her. Again, the smell was atrocious.

When bluebottles grow to nearly three times their normal size and are seen congregating at a window inside premises trying to get out, you can be sure that there is likely to be a dead body, human or animal close by.

I have only mentioned a few incidents but they emphasise what police officers (and other essential service personnel) have to cope with during their careers. One cannot afford to be too squeamish.

CHAPTER 10
LIVING THE HIGH LIFE

To Jump or not to Jump, that is the question

'B' Division in the Metropolitan Police covered Chelsea, Kensington and Notting Hill. An Area car, a fast response car with horns and a flashing blue light on the top and called an RT (Radio Transmission) car, was assigned to each with calls signs: Bravo 1, Bravo 2 and Bravo 3 respectively. They were crewed by a Class 1, Class 2 or (occasionally) a Class 3 driver, a radio operator and a plain clothes observer who may be required to either carry out surveillance or follow a suspect. An additional car, Bravo 4, was crewed, on rotation, by a driver from one station, a radio operator from another and a plain clothes officer from the other. This vehicle was assigned to cover the whole of 'B' Division. On 26th March 1968, I was the observer on the latter when we were called to the Park Royal Hotel in Cromwell Road (on Kensington section).

A domestic employee had allegedly been caught 'in flagrante' by the management. She had climbed out of a top floor window and was standing on a very narrow ledge (about a foot wide), nearly 100 feet above the ground, threatening to jump. (When I look at the newspaper cuttings I notice the point of my shoe is over the ledge and I am only a size 8). She was standing rigidly with her hands flat against the wall, clearly very frightened. We tried to persuade her to come back inside but her only response was to sidle along the ledge away from us. I thought that she might respond better if I joined her so I climbed out.

Being familiar with lighthouses I had little fear of heights – or so I thought. When I had an occasion to look down, vertigo set in and I had to consciously look at the horizon otherwise I felt that I was being lured downwards. I can still imagine it and shudder to think what would have happened if I had succumbed. Ludicrously, in retrospect, my driver took off his belt and wrapped it around my ankle. What good that would have been if I had fallen, goodness knows. I talked to her gently, trying to persuade her to come back inside but she just kept shaking her head. I even lit a cigarette for her and pretended to smoke it (I didn't smoke) but to no avail. She kept edging away. I have no idea how long I was there – 3 hours according to newspaper reports.

The fire brigade arrived and people began gathering in the street below. An extended ladder was raised and it just reached below the ledge. A fireman climbed up, at one point slipping as he neared the top. A more substantial ladder with side railings was also raised and it was at the far end of the ledge preventing the girl moving any further. Eventually a rope was passed to me from the window and I tied it around my waist. If I had fallen at least I would only be dangling about 10 feet from the ledge. Yippee-I-Ay!

Some firemen and others had climbed on to the roof and another fireman had climbed up the second ladder. The girl had now moved further along the ledge. One of the firemen on the roof then dropped a looped rope to try to harness the girl but she struggled. The fireman on the second ladder and I tried to get it over her but we abandoned the idea as I was in a very precarious position. A senior fire officer replaced that fireman and a man, who said he was a Samaritan, came to the window and suggested that he took over from me. I came in and he sat on the window sill.

By this time the street below was crowded with spectators, fire engines, ambulances and police cars. Traffic along the Cromwell Road had been stopped both ways and this was during the rush hour. The girl said that if the street was cleared she would come in so I went downstairs and found the police Duty Officer (Inspector) and conveyed this to him. Just at that time, however, the fire officer had grabbed hold of the girl and was pulling her towards the ladder. He was hooked to the ladder but he had to bodily lift her over the side railings. He managed to do so. He then began coming down, hooking himself to each rung as he did so. The girl began struggling again and another fireman went part way up the ladder to assist him.

They managed to get her down safely to a waiting ambulance and she was taken to St Mary Abbotts Hospital in Marloes Road nearby. The Duty Officer, who was from Kensington and did not know me, (I was in plain clothes remember), suggested the car crew go to the hospital to speak to her but I declined as we had not even had a break since starting our shift at 2pm. Subsequently, as is required, he wrote a report of the incident. There was no mention of our involvement and most of it was about the efforts that had been made to re-route traffic around the area. The daily papers next morning had dramatic pictures of the rescue and I am featured in most of the photos. However, I was named in only one newspaper. The Samaritan, who worked in the West London Air Terminal opposite, was named several times as they thought he might lose his job.

The senior fireman on the ladder was awarded the BEM and the man who went to assist him was awarded the Queen's Commendation for Bravery. Me? Nothing. No doubt, if I had been in uniform or if the Police Inspector had known me, the outcome may have been different.

P22. Ledge photo

P23. Roof newspaper cutting

CHAPTER 11
GOING EQUIPPED TO FEEL
(SOME PEOPLE ARE VERY TOUCHY)

Inkling (Unexplainable)

Stop and Search (Sec. 66 Metropolitan Police Act, 1829) was a powerful tool. It became known as the 'Sus (Suspect) Law' and was eventually repealed in 1981 and partly replaced by the Criminal Attempts Act, 1981). Without it, there is no doubt that many serious offences would have been undetected. I seem to remember that 10%[1] of all stops resulted in an arrest which, to me, was a very fair average.

It is often said that there was an abuse of random checks. But were they random? Often it was that inkling, that innate instinct, that something was not quite right. It may be the attitude or actions of the person when they see a police officer, their furtive movements, the suspect being in the vicinity of a recent crime, or other quirky characteristics that triggered a subsequent stop. Trying to explain it to a non-police officer could be, and still is, very difficult and even when you explain your sixth sense they are still mystified. I think this comes from experience dealing with criminals and their wily ways. Very few ever told the truth when first stopped and questioned even if there was 100% evidence of their guilt.

That was the challenge for the interrogator. Beat officers were not given any training in interrogation techniques which I always thought was incongruous. Incidentally, it is quite easy to give a false name when stopped but difficult to give a false date of birth spontaneously and being able to repeat it a short time later.

The oft used phrase 'Once a policeman, always a policeman' rings true because one never loses that acquired sense of intuition. My, perhaps biased, view is that the increase in knife crime correlates with the reduction of this power. The black minority and their supporters demanded that the Act be repealed. I would hazard a guess that most knife crime happens between black on black which should make their parents, who were vociferous in their demands to repeal the Act, think of the consequences. By November 2021, it has been reported that there have been more murders by knife crime than ever before in London. The majority are black on black. I believe that stop and search, which has increased in London, is one of the necessary tools to try to reduce these incidents. Studies by eminent researchers suggest that despite this there is no significant evidence that this has reduced this type of crime. However, if you take it to its logical conclusion, if no-one was stopped it would be a licence for anyone to carry weapons. Think of gun crime in America.

There are no Government statistics regarding knife crime but in London in 2019 it was established that 50% of murders were committed by BAME which is three times more than that of any other ethnic group. They consist of only 13% of the population. It is estimated that 10,000 young people carry knives/weapons. In my opinion, if you want to stop knife and gun crime, stop people.

A favourite 'wind up' question by members of the public was, "Do I look like a criminal?" I usually answered in the affirmative. The disbelief on their faces was a joy to behold. I would then say, "If you know what a criminal looks like, you should be doing my job." Enough said.

You've Got to Hand It to Them

Interestingly, in March 2020 I read an article in which a black girl postulated that knife carrying youths often used children/girls/young women to carry their weapons when a police presence was suspected, as these people were seldom stopped or searched by police. She said that they were sometimes coerced or intimidated with the threat of force or assault if they refused. There was a dearth of women police officers in the late sixties/early seventies and they were not usually on regular patrol. Females were seldom searched (they could not be physically searched by a male officer) in the streets and it may have taken an age to contact a WPC. Unless there was direct evidence e.g. theft/shoplifting/assault/ weapons etc. women were often let off even if they had been in cahoots with their male accomplice(s). Even at the station, if there was none available, one had to await until a WPC was traced at an adjacent station.

There now seem to be more incidents of women involvement in crime generally. My perceptions again? There are far more WPCs now who have successfully integrated with their male counterparts. A recent straw poll survey of women officers suggests that they would prefer to retain the 'W' rather than being a plain PC. After all, it does describe them more accurately - or is that not PC?

Perhaps someone could invent a light and inexpensive, handheld body scanner (or even a magnet?) capable of detecting any concealed metal weapon/object and producing a digital display. This may obviate the necessity of a pat down or physical search of the person. Where the modern police officer carries it amongst his other 'weaponry/paraphernalia' might be the problem........ A complication would obviously occur if suspects started carrying plastic weapons.

Is Education the Key?

I left the police force/service in October 1998 after 33 years. On 1st September 1999, I began employment as a Commissionaire and subsequently as the Community Liaison Officer, in a further education college of about 4,500 students in Twickenham, a large proportion of whom would be classed as black and lived within boroughs south of the River Thames. Naturally, there were rival gangs from their own turf or postcode area with scores to settle usually for the most innocuous reasons e.g. for 'dissing' (disrespecting) someone by just looking at them in a certain way. In the 10 years I worked there we knew of 10 blade related weapon murders, outside the college, by students who either committed or were accessory to them. The majority were black v black and all but one (in Shepherds Bush) of the incidents happened south of the river. Knives, machetes, swords and other deadly weapons had been used. The college was very aware of the potential for violence so it was important for the security staff to be cognisant of the different gangs and so curtail violence within the college.

One can only speculate on the reasons why knives are prevalent as a favourite weapon: easily available, easy to carry, easy to conceal, inexpensive and a status symbol. Who was responsible for the proliferation of evil intent? Should one lay the blame on the inefficiency and/or apathy of government, the perceived inadequate and reduced powers of the police, the lack of parental control (my little Johnny wouldn't carry a knife), fear of ridicule, the PC and Human Rights brigades, the failure of the education system and the proliferation of the 'gang' culture – or even a combination of several of these? The youths themselves apparently have little concept of the misery and heartache they cause, not only to the victims or their families but also to their own families and acquaintances. They are undaunted by the consequences of the prospect of incarceration.

Many are teenagers and Section 141a of the Criminal Justice Act 1988 makes it an offence to sell or let or hire certain bladed items to a person under the age of 18 years. Similar to the Metropolitan Black Museum which houses artefacts from unusual and serious crimes, a separate museum of the extraordinary diversity of knives and related unnecessary weaponry would fill one with horror. Sadistic manufacturers and unscrupulous retailers must hold a large proportion of the blame. Why are these weapons manufactured in the first place? Why are outlets allowed to sell them with no practical use except possibly for martial arts? There are many Acts and Sections which cover bladed items in a public place. Images of these armaments are readily available on the internet.

------

1. 2021 – apparently this has increased to 14%.

CHAPTER 12

KNIVELIHOOD

The sight of blood, of course, is an occupational hazard. Every officer had to be trained in basic first aid and be re-assessed triennially. However, there was no more pleasing and relieving sound than the "hee haws" of an ambulance approaching a scene. Road accidents, fist fights and broken glass were obvious locations where blood may be found. Knives were not so grisly or as predominant as a weapon then as they appear to be today. That is not to say that they were not being carried but usually as a 'defence weapon' rather than an aggressive one. The following are a few incidents in which I was involved.

Thank You

One afternoon, I was standing in Kensington Park Road at the junction with Westbourne Park Road when a black cab drew up opposite. A young man emerged, went up the steps of a house and rang the bell. The door opened, the man went in for about 30 seconds and when he came out he got back into the taxi. I thought this was unusual and, knowing that drug-dealing was prevalent in the area, I stopped the cab. The man was just putting a package down the front of his trousers. When asked what it was he readily admitted that he had just bought some cannabis. I asked the cab-driver if he could drive us to the police station to which he agreed.

As we drove down Ladbroke Grove and approached the lights at Ladbroke Road where the police station was situated, the youth said he had something else. He pulled a very large knife with a blade about 12 inches long from the side of his trousers and handed it to me. He was carrying it for protection.

Cabbies

Many taxi drivers, who were generally very helpful, were ex-police officers, having learnt 'The Knowledge'. It takes between 2 to 4 years to learn the highways and by-ways of London and its suburb and these were the days before the invention of Satnav. Gaining a green badge allowed the cabbies to operate in the Central London area and beyond. Earning a yellow badge for only the outer areas provided them with less lucrative custom.

Always Watch the Hands

On another occasion, whilst standing at the same junction with another officer, we saw a man walking down Westbourne Park Road crossing the junction with Kensington Park Road. He was carrying an empty milk bottle in his hand. We followed him and saw him go up the steps to a three storey house and enter. We then heard shouting and by the time we reached the ground floor corridor he was struggling with another man. He had the bottle raised but the other man, who had a cut to his head, was stopping him hitting him again.

We separated them and the injured man said, "He's got a knife in his pocket", whereupon the assailant reached for his jacket pocket. My colleague (sadly now deceased) and I put arm-locks on him and, sure enough, there was open-bladed knife there. One can never be sure what one might encounter.

Not Always for Protection

There had been a spate of thefts of radios from soft-top vehicles where the roofs had been slashed to gain entry. I was the plain clothes officer on Bravo 3. We saw a youth, aged about 15 or 16, wandering apparently aimlessly in Lansdowne Crescent. From the description received over the personal radio, the Duty Officer (Inspector) and Section Sergeant said they had stopped and searched him earlier and that he had a small knife with him. The area car dropped me off and I followed the youth at a distance.

There were a couple of soft-topped sports cars in the street and he stopped beside each of them and kept looking round but he did not do anything. He continued walking around the Crescent and crossed Ladbroke Grove into Kensington Park Gardens. He stopped at the first building which had a series of steps to the front door with pillars either side (coincidentally, where my cousin worked). He started up the steps which were flanked by a low wall. As he did so an ambulance, which had been coming up Ladbroke Grove, suddenly put its sirens on.

The youth, in panic, ran back down the steps and along Kensington Park Gardens away from me. I noticed he now had something in his hand. I gave chase and luckily he slowed to a walk and I managed to reach him as he walked down Kensington Park Road towards Notting Hill Gate. I stopped him and saw that he had a full bottle of milk in his hand. I took it and he agreed that he had just stolen it. I did not have a personal radio with me. It was not far from the police station so I decided to walk him in. He came very peacefully. He was very thin and his complexion was very white. I would call him emaciated.

In the charge room at the station he was told he was going to be searched. In his pocket I found the small folding pocket knife. He then took a bread knife from his shirt sleeve and handed it to me. Again, was it for defence or slashing car roofs? I never found out. Was there a red-faced Inspector and Sergeant? However, it transpired that he had run away from Eton where he was being bullied and had lasted for days without any proper food or drink. He said his parents had forced him to go to Eton against his will.

I subsequently gave him a cup of tea in his cell. He asked what that was for and I said it was because he hadn't stabbed me. His bullying father, who was a high ranking military officer, (Brigadier, I think) arrived and shouted and yelled at his son for a) running away from Eton and b) stealing a pint of milk. I could see why the son was terrified. Unfortunately he had to be released into the custody of his father. I often wonder what happened to him.

The Woolly Jumper

Again, whilst in Bravo 3, we saw a stolen car in front of us containing two black youths. As we went to stop them they braked and jumped out of the car and ran in different directions. I ran after the driver who was faster than me. (Who wasn't?). I lost sight of him as he turned into Powis Gardens but when I got there and was searching the area bystanders pointed to the basement of a house. Steps led down to the basement and as I reached the top of them the youth was coming up towards me but had changed his top clothing. When he saw me he ran back down and into the house closely followed by me. Directly ahead of him was the kitchen area where he grabbed a large bread knife and waved it towards me.

I drew my truncheon and wondered what I could use as a shield. These decisions have to be made in seconds. Hanging on the coat hooks in the narrow hall was a soaking wet jumper on a metal coat hanger. I grabbed this and advanced towards him telling him not to be silly. Other officers were now behind me so there was no escape (for me). Again, luckily, he put the knife down and put his hands in the air. He was charged with the TDA (Taking and Driving Away a motor vehicle) but I took no action regarding the knife as it was obviously just a spontaneous reaction of a frightened youth.

The Hells Angels

During the week there is a fruit and vegetable market in Portobello Road stretching from Colville Terrace northwards. Additionally on Saturdays, throughout the area, the antique shops are fully open and there are antique stalls scattered around the surrounding streets. There are then estimated to be 300,000 to 400,000 people milling around.

At the corner of Portobello Road and Westbourne Grove was a large pub known as Henekeys. It was fairly respectable being on the outskirts of the mainly deprived streets. However, drug-dealing also occurred there. There was a time when the Hells Angels decided they would frequent it as it would be a lucrative place for their dealing. It was impossible to police the inside of the pub or the near vicinity, but one could watch from a distance and when likely punters were seen leaving the pub they could be stopped at a short distance away without causing a disturbance or alerting the dealers that the police were close by. Such was the scenario when a colleague and I saw two teenage lads leaving the pub. We stopped them and they readily admitted that they had bought drugs – cannabis. While searching them I found one had a lock knife on him which was, per se, an offensive weapon. Asked why, he said he wanted to become a Hell's Angel and that you had to go through certain initiation ceremonies before being allowed to join a Chapter. These two were very respectable and respectful boys.

At court they pleaded guilty to the possession of drugs but the possession of the knife as an offensive weapon was contested. I had carried out a bit of homework (not usual for me) and had read about the Hell's Angels and their initiation rites. Some involved stabbing people or even murdering them to show bravado. The bench consisted of three lay magistrates. The youth's barrister persisted in asking me about the initiation rites which, thankfully, I was able to answer. He kept saying he did not understand - to try, I guess, to confuse the bench. I was trying to think of how I could say it succinctly bearing in mind one is under a lot of pressure in the witness box.

Finally I said, "They were "Fledgling Angels".

This caused merriment throughout the court and the barrister asked no further questions. Found guilty, of course: the youth, that is, not the barrister.

Back Stabbed

On 25th May 1971 an incident occurred whereby two black youths were
chased by police and took refuge in the Metro Club (Youth Club) on
the Harrow Road division side of Ledbury Road. The police were
refused entry and a stand-off occurred between them and the organisers. These types of incidents often led to a volatile situation, and so it
proved. Police reinforcements were called and Notting Hill officers,
me included, went to the scene with the task of preventing the ever
growing number of bystanders from reaching the club.

I was standing facing the crowd when a large black man leant over and
hit me behind the left shoulder. I did not want to be the spark to start
off an incident but I said to him that if he did it again I would arrest
him. He hit me in the left shoulder again. I went to arrest him and he
ran down Tavistock Crescent chased by me, some other officers and a
crowd of black people. As we were catching up with him he turned
around. He had a knife in his right hand and, what turned out to be a
police truncheon, in his left hand. He lunged at us. He was very large
and extremely violent. We drew our truncheons and began hitting him
with a view to disarming him and defending ourselves. We were
surrounded by a large group of people who began throwing bricks,
sticks, stones and whatever material came to hand. One item that was
thrown was a wooden trestle. This was about two and a half feet high
consisting of three pieces of 4 x 2 timber. There were two pieces either
side of the third piece which could be folded between them so that the
trestle was flat. When opened up it was often used to hang a work-
man's safety lamp on and they were usually placed beside builders'
skips at night to warn motorists.

I faced the crowd with my truncheon raised to try to protect the other
officers. I was hit on both upper arms which eventually resulted in
heavy bruising. The other officers were unable to contain the man and
he escaped. One of the other officers received a stab wound to the
back.

Other officers came to our assistance and the crowd dispersed. As I
walked back up Tavistock Crescent two officers from a Traffic Patrol

(TrafPol) car approached me and asked what was dripping from under the left arm of my tunic. It was blood. Unknown to me the man had actually stabbed me twice in the shoulder. They immediately put me in their car and took me to St Charles Hospital. As I lay face down on the trolley awaiting medical attention one of the officers took hold of my blue police issue shirt and began ripping it up the back. I remonstrated with him as I thought that I would have to pay for a replacement. He intimated that with two holes and blood all over it, it was unlikely that I would be wearing that shirt again. I was placed on sick leave for some time and, as I was affected by the trauma, I spent a week at the Police Convalescent Home in Hove where I was visited by my future wife and my parents from Scotland who were obviously anxious. A suspect was later arrested and charged but subsequently acquitted.

Too Close for Comfort

During his trial and four others at the Old Bailey, it was put to the other stabbed officer by a Barrister, that it was not his client that had stabbed him but it could have been the person who threw the trestle who must have been pretty close to him. The officers denied that this was the case. The Barrister persisted and made him describe the trestle to the jury. The officer having done so, the Barrister suggested that the trestle was fairly heavy and so the thrower must have got close to him. Again the officer denied it.

The Barrister said, "Come officer. How far do you think you could throw that trestle?"

Now, the witness box in No. 1 Court at the Old Bailey is raised quite high. The Barristers are about 15-20 feet away. The officer eyed him up and said, "I think I could hit you with it from here, sir."

At which point not only did the Judge laugh but so did most of the people present, including the five suspects in the dock.

Be Precise

It was the practice to write some notes as soon as possible after an incident when the recollections were fresh in one's memory. If a suspect decided to plead not guilty then a full statement was made from those notes and a type-written copy handed to the defence. On this occasion I was asked by the defence counsel if I had written in my statement that items had been thrown at me by the crowd and that I had been hit with bottles, bricks, stones, trestles etc. One always addressed one's reply to the Judge.

"'No, M'Lud," I said.

The Barrister consulted his notes and asked me the same question.

Again I replied, "No, M'Lud."

The Barrister was perplexed. "Did you write a statement regarding this incident, officer?"

"Yes M'Lud."

"Did you make this statement as soon as possible after the incident?"

"'Yes M'Lud."

"Where did you write this statement?"

"In hospital, M'Lud." (Sympathy vote).

"Would the usher please hand PC Scott his original hand written statement? Now officer, is that your writing?"

"Yes, M'Lud."

"I put it to you that in your statement you have written that –"I was hit with bottles, bricks, stones, trestles etc."

"No, M'Lud."

By this time the Barrister was exasperated. The Judge, however, suspected that I had an explanation and he asked me to tell him what it was.

"Certainly, M'Lud. Mr ...... keeps repeating that I mentioned the word trestles. If one reads my statement it clearly says 'trestle' in the singular. I know that another trestle had been thrown that night but not at us."

The Barrister slammed his papers on his desk and said, "If you want to be pedantic, PC Scott."

Knowing that if I had agreed to the word 'trestles' the Barrister might have turned that to his advantage later in the dialogue, I said, "I just want to be right, M'Lud."

The Judge said, "Quite right, PC Scott. Any further questions?"

"No further questions", answered the Barrister, grumpily, as he smashed his papers on the desk, swished his gown and sat down.[1]

---

1. Ah! The trials and tribulations of being a Barrister. This was not the only time that I challenged a Barrister. (See Chapter 21).

CHAPTER 13

AKIN TO KIN – OR FAMILY MATTERS

(AN INTERLUDE)

Hello Mother, Hello Father.

As I mentioned previously my parents had not been keen on my joining the Force. After my stabbing they came down to visit me when I was at the Police Convalescent Home in Brighton and also spent a few days in London. Subsequently, after I was married, my mother visited several times. One time I was standing outside Buckingham Palace in my ceremonial uniform at the Trooping of the Colour when I heard my wife and mother behind me. How they found me amongst the crowd and numerous other officers on duty that day I do not know.

One day they were shopping in Notting Hill Gate when we were passing in the police car. I jumped out, grabbed my mother and wife and put them in the back of the car. Bystanders stood in amazement seeing them 'arrested'. We gave them a tour of Portobello Road and surrounds.

Ambiguity is the Enemy of Precision

When we arrested someone the everyday expression used was we had "nicked a body." When I went home to visit my parents in Scotland

and related some of my escapades, my mother suddenly said, "There must be a lot of people dying in London." I then had to explain what the saying meant.

A White Wedding

My wife (Bridget Philomena nee O'Driscoll) and I were married on 29th January 1972 on one of the coldest days of that winter with heavy snowfalls. I had permission to marry in my ceremonial uniform (called No 1s).

P24. Wedding photo

My best man, John Boorer, with whom I joined the Job, also wore his and we were glad of the warmth. The uniforms were made from a very heavy and warm material and buttoned up to the neck. After the reception, a police officer friend drove us through deep snow and continuing snowfalls to Gatwick where we had booked in for the night. After a quick meal our driver had great difficulty identifying his car in the car park as it and others were covered with a thick blanket of snow. Ours was the only aeroplane to take off that morning and we landed in

Majorca where it had also been snowing. So much for a hot Spanish holiday!

More Snow

Got the drift?

My daughter, Sharon once lived in a tower block in the French Alps at a ski resort called Avoriaz and previous to that in another winter destination, Morzine, where we attempted to cross-country ski around Lac de Montriond. The following two poems may resonate with some of you but, if not, feel free to use your imagination.

~

Impressions in the Snow

I looked out from the tower block
From the window way up high
The snow was falling softly
And blotting out the sky.

And far away below me
The seats swayed in the breeze
Empty now of travellers
The workings start to freeze.

The rooks flew round in circles
Black wings against the white
Back and forth they sallied
For ever gaining height.

The cliff face is so close now
An avalanche did fall
The noise was that of thunder
As it smashed against the wall.

Faces turn'ed upwards
With wonder in their eyes
Saw the beauty of the maelstrom
As the dust began to rise.

The many different footprints
Of mammals of the night
Disappeared for ever
Ne'er again they'll see the light.

Skiers shrug and glide now
Down freshly covered slopes
Like ants far in the distance
In their multi-coloured coats.

Clinging to the rock face
Are trees with needles green
The weight of snow upon them
Just makes them weep and lean.

These are my first impressions
And not a sign of grass
On the first day that we stayed there
In the town – Avoriaz.

(Sydney T. Scott - 19th April 2001)

And...

~

Happy Landings
(or the day we fell in line)

'Twas on a Thursday morning
That we landed in Morzine
It's just as well we had some fat
And weren't too thin or lean.

We clipp'ed on our walking skis
And hoped we were not seen
I stood up on the glistening snow
And landed in Morzine.

The three of us, my wife and I
My daughter, too, I mean
Went slithering, sliding down the track
And landed in Morzine.

We walked along at steady pace
And forward we did lean
With sticks we pushed and pushed so hard
We landed in Morzine.

We stopped a while to have a drink
And ate the salad green
But stepping sideways up the slope
I landed in Morzine.

Around the lake we puffed and shoved
The snow was crisp and clean
When down the hill, we bolder got
And landed in Morzine.

With me in front, the wife behind
Our daughter in between
We both, with laughter, then did sit,
And landed in Morzine.

She said to us, and so she should,
'I am a human bein'
I can't look after both of you
As she landed in Morzine.

This tale I tell to warn you all
If thinking you're a 'teen
Think twice before you try to ski
Or you'll land up in Morzine.

(Sydney T. Scott 30th January 2000)

~

Mother Sledge

As previously mentioned Dunnet Head Lighthouse was three miles from the small village of Brough. The single track road wound its way through hilly moorland and passed several lochs. Heavy snowfalls and blizzards would block the road and a sledge was required to acquire groceries etc. from the local shop/post office. A looped piece of rope was put over your neck and then under your armpits – harnessed like a horse. On one occasion my mother and I cut across the moors using a walking stick to gauge the depth of the snow. Alas, my mother fell into a World War 2 bunker hidden under a snowdrift. She and I were laughing so much that it took an age to pull her out using the walking stick.

Prickled Ma

Drifting snow on the headland was usually very deep and ideal for sledging. On another occasion my mother was travelling so fast down a slope, she couldn't stop and ended up on top of a gorse bush.

CHAPTER 14
BURGLARY

False Alarms

Burglary was a common problem and still is throughout the country. Notting Hill, with its affluent southern half, was no different. Portobello Road was a Mecca for Metropolitan burglars and those from 'the sticks' (anywhere outside Central London) where stolen goods could be distributed amongst the numerous premises and stalls within the antique market. It was a Marché Ouvert (Open market) whereby goods could be sold between the hours of sunrise and sunset and their proper provenance could not be questioned. Caveat Emptor (Buyer beware) applies.

Despite the efforts of advertising, seminars, and advice from crime prevention officers and others on how to prevent these crimes many people were either indifferent, lackadaisical or could not afford the anti-burglar alarms or the equipment required to make their property safe. Burglar alarms were not, and still are not, fool-proof. Thieves were usually one step ahead of the game and soon learnt how to by-pass those original unsophisticated systems. Sometimes dummy boxes were installed on the outside walls to try to deceive the criminal but they soon learned the difference between that and a genuine alarm.

Alarms, both burglar and vehicle ones, were the bane of a policeman's life: they were often set off accidentally, developed faults and were loud and strident. Residents would go off on holiday and if the alarm went off it could be days before it could be reset. Some neighbours have resorted to smashing the alarms off the walls or trying to disable vehicle alarms. The police had to answer every call and sometimes weather conditions would set quite a number of them off at the same time.

"Do You Remember 1976?"

(I know, it was That Carnival)

It was one of those years when very high and sustained temperatures were recorded. It was the first year in living memory that officers were allowed to take off their uniform jackets and roll up their shirt sleeves on night duty. I was seconded to Kensington's area car, Bravo 2, for one night and it was the busiest night that I ever had in the Force.

I had just got into the car and was running through the obligatory vehicle checks when the young operator appeared. I had never met him before but as he got into the car there was a call to a burglary, 'Suspects on Premises'. I had no idea of the location so followed my operator's instructions. Blue lights on but no horns - a silent approach. We drove South down Earls Court Road and left into Cromwell Road. The traffic lights at Marloes Road were just changing to green with three lanes of traffic just starting off. On the offside, three lanes of traffic had just started coming from the junction of Collingham Road. I judged that I could go down the outside and cross over between the two lines of cars.

Unknown to me there was a raised central reservation which I hit at about 50 MPH and casually drove over it with the other officer bouncing in his seat. He looked quizzically at me but I continued as if nothing had happened. Was there any damage to the car? I have no idea. I never had the time that evening to check anything. What happened on arrival? Thereby hangs an untellable tale......

Artful Dodgers

'Suspects on premises', again. A very expensive three storey building in the Earls Court area was occupied by a dentist who was on holiday. A young lad was staying there and he had been awakened by a man standing over him reaching for his radio. Half asleep he had called the police. The place was like a fortress with all windows barred, security locks everywhere and an alarm which hadn't activated. When we gained entry we began a search of every room. We were fascinated by the dental surgery which had an electrically controlled chair and curtains and doors - very chic. We searched every room bar one which was locked. Suspecting that the burglar(s) was/were still in the house, with permission from the Duty Officer, we decided to smash the door down. No-one was there but there was a very large water bed and the ceiling was a mirror. I say no more.

No suspects were found. We were called back about two hours later and when we arrived this time two men were coming out of the front door carrying very expensive paintings and there were other pictures already out in the street. Having chased them they were cornered in the back garden where, apparently they had been hiding previously. A great arrest.

The above describes just two of the incidents of that sweat-soaked night.

An Alarming Story

There was a friendly bakery on Notting Dale section. The alarm often went off at night so the key-holder had to be called. Each time he gave the attending officers a cake for their troubles. Unknown to me (see, I told you that I was naïve), whenever there was an officer's birthday a stone was thrown onto the roof of the factory thus setting off the alarm.

The Mica Man

As previously mentioned, most police officers develop what one could call a sixth sense or a nose/instinct for detecting offences. With a colleague I was patrolling Stanley Gardens when we saw a man acting suspiciously coming down the steps at the front of a terraced house. He was 'out of place'. On stopping and searching him we found a piece of mica (flexible clear plastic) which was often used as a tool to gain entry to Yale locks. It was very easy to slip the mica between the tongue of the lock and the door jamb thus negating the lock altogether. Yale eventually changed the structure of the lock by reversing the tongue so that it was more difficult to 'slip' it. He readily admitted that he was 'equipped to burgle' and he was arrested.

We treated him very fairly and when asked if he wished to take any other offences into consideration (TICs) he willingly co-operated. TICs were a legitimate method of allowing the arrested person the chance to admit to any further offences that he may have committed and the Judge/Magistrate would give him a lesser sentence for those offences that were admitted. Our man started talking and he would not stop. He admitted over 90 burglary offences on Notting Hill and Harrow Road sections. He was a prolific burglar and wanted to wipe the slate clean.

We, of course, were delighted and we handed him over to the CID. He also gave us an insight as to why he seldom got caught. He said the police were stupid because when a burglar was at a burglary or was disturbed the police arrived with their sirens blaring, allowing the suspect to hide or decamp. Another lesson learnt. He was granted bail.

Know Your Man

A few weeks later a burglar alarm was set off at premises on Harrow Road section adjacent to our area. We approached (quietly). The other officers spread out and I stayed with the police car. Suddenly a man jumped over the high wall beside me carrying stolen property including pieces of silver. Guess who? He was about to run off but recognised me and stopped and gave himself up. He then took a long pair of scissors from his sleeve and handed them to me. I was glad that we had been friendly with him previously.

Take This into Consideration

Sometime later, as we had set up a rapport with him, we thought he may provide us details of any local receivers so we authorised to interview him in prison having been convicted of the offences for which we had arrested him. He refused to co-operate, and when we asked him "Why", he said that the CID who had been assigned to the case had not mentioned the TICs to the Judge so he felt that they were still hanging over him and that the officer would use that as leverage in the future. We were astounded and no information was forthcoming.

Drop Inn. Why didn't They?

Bravo 3 again, no observer, night duty. As we drove at the end of a short street we saw two men climbing over a wall at the side of a pub, carrying property. I jumped out of the car to chase them. They ran back along the top of the narrow wall followed by me wearing slippery shoes. It was pretty dark. They disappeared to my left and when I reached there they were just disappearing through a window into the pub. Did I follow them? Did I what? They had run across two planks of wood which they had obviously used to get into the pub in the first place. Why didn't I follow? These two narrow planks were just resting on the edge of the wall at one end and the window sill of the pub at the other and they were bowed. There was a drop of about 30 feet into the basement of the pub. They must have been mad – I wasn't. The pub was surrounded. One of the men was caught immediately but there was no sign of the other one and he could not have escaped. He was eventually found in the false ceiling of the toilet.

"Stop. Who Goes There?"

Night Duty. 10pm – 6am - Bravo 4 Operator – Wise old driver-
Portobello Road.

We had been quite busy but we were on the lookout for a drink driver.
A car in front seemed a likely suspect so we decided to stop it.
However, as we approached the junction with Lancaster Road, a silver
BMW sped through the traffic lights and we decided to stop it instead.
It was in a hurry. It turned left into Ladbroke Grove and right in to
Blenheim Crescent where it stopped on our signal. The driver was
aged about 25 years old, suave, confident and very well dressed in a suit
and tie. His two rear seat passengers were obviously prostitutes and
they sidled out of the car and disappeared into the distance. Whilst my
driver questioned the young man and examined his driving licence, I
took a wander around the car and noticed that the registration mark
on the Road Fund Licence (RFL or Tax disc) did not correspond to
that on the car. He stated that the car was his but could not explain
the discrepancy in the numbers so I arrested him. As we awaited transport, my driver lifted up the boot lid. Lo and behold! It was full of
silver items. It turned out that the car had been stolen from the car
park of the Kensington Gardens Hotel and the driver was a prolific
burglar of expensive houses.

Questioned by the night duty CID he not only admitted many
burglary offences but he gave them the details of an unoccupied house
in Hampstead. Aladdin's cave would not have been big enough: each
room was completely full of stolen expensive property mostly silver-
ware. This was a tremendous haul. As a result I received a good arrest
commendation, dated 27th June 1968, from the A /Chief
Superintendent of 'B' Division. It read as follows:

Dear Scott,

*Superintendent Xxxxxxxx has told me about the recent arrest of xxx xxx xxx.
My congratulations and thanks for the vigilance you displayed and the thor-
oughness of the 'stop' which resulted in this very useful arrest.*

High Jinks

A burglar was disturbed. He evaded capture by climbing out of a window, three storeys up, and then jumping from balcony to balcony or by grabbing down pipes. The area was surrounded and a stalemate ensued but he eventually climbed down some scaffolding. It is amazing what dangers some people will endure in their effort to escape.

He Took the Lead

On the Area car we took an emergency call to suspects on the roofs of a long row of three storey high buildings due for demolition. We managed to scramble up through the empty and dangerous structures and found two men stripping lead from the roofs. A short foot chase over holey, slate-less rafters with 100-foot drops, ensued. When I arrested and cautioned, one he said, "Come on Guvn'r, I am on bail for the same thing at Shepherd's Bush." This 'confession' I duly recorded in my arrest details – as is required.

At Magistrates court the suspect pleaded guilty and I gave the brief facts including his reply to caution. It was not practice to unduly prejudice a case and the magistrates looked up sharply. He pondered and then asked the defendant if what I had said was true.

"Yes, your honour," he replied and so my reputation was unimpaired.

Fear is an Innate Instinct

Despite being involved in many dangerous situations, as were the officers at Notting Hill on a daily basis, I was only genuinely 'frightened' twice.

The first time was:

Cat Burglar?

I liked night duty. This was a three week tour from 10pm – 6am. It was usually pretty busy until about midnight (pubs were closed at 11pm) and then it was fairly quiet, certainly for the walking beat officer. One often wandered along day (or should that be night) dreaming. I was in such a trance at about three in the morning dawdling down Portobello Road when, all of a sudden, a screeching cat jumped out of a metal dustbin in front of me clattering the lid onto the ground. I don't know where my heart or my helmet went.

The second time was:

Don't Asp Me Again

An armed robbery with a sawn-off shotgun had occurred in Queensway which was only about a mile and a half from Notting Hill. A description of the car, a mini, was given but no index plate details. I was patrolling Colville Terrace when I saw a car matching the description and there was something wrapped in cloth on the back parcel shelf. I went around the corner and discreetly called for assistance. Bravo 3 arrived. We had a discussion and my idea was to enter the car and retrieve what I perceived to be the shotgun from the back of the car before the robbers returned. With the car crew watching I sauntered nonchalantly to the car, glancing around. There was no one in sight so I tried my own key in the lock. Minis were very easy to open in those days. Suddenly the car alarm went off. Did I jump? Over the Eiffel Tower if it had been there! I quickly came to my senses, reached in and grabbed the object on the parcel shelf. It was a snake draught excluder......

The car owner did not arrive despite the blaring alarm. Having secured the car I crept (slithered) quietly away. Why the car crew were sniggering I do not know.

CHAPTER 15
GUNS AND THE AXE MAN

Gun Law

Firearms are manufactured or adapted to kill whether it be humans or animals. There may be exceptions - stun guns, tranquiliser guns, Very pistols (flair/distress gun) or similar - but basically they were invented to kill. To my mind anyone carrying a gun (in the UK) illegally or for an unlawful purpose has no given right to expect sympathy and, if the consequences are that they are killed or wounded whilst in actual or constructive possession, then so be it. Anyone who sells, adapts, supplies, harbours (either on person or elsewhere) an illegal firearm or sometimes even a licensed firearm, should, in my mind, if convicted, be automatically jailed for a substantial time. It matters not who they are - be it any dealer, wife, girlfriend, or gang member: the possibilities are endless. Coercion and fear could be mitigating circumstances.

One wonders about the mentality of the populace who defend the killers or prospective killer (because that is what they are) who go on a rampage of wilful destruction. If they carry a gun to commit a robbery they are likely to use it if challenged. Likewise if it is carried for protection during a drug deal, they should not have been dealing in the first place. Please don't blame the police when they are trying to

protect the general public and themselves when faced with a potentially fatal outcome of anyone carrying a gun for illicit motives. Who
would these so called 'vigilantes' call on when their lives are in danger?
Riots and fervent demonstrations, stirred up by hostile anti-establish-
ment figureheads, reflect badly on the democracy of this country.
Many of the relatives start off a lawful peaceful demonstration, which
is their right, but their protest can be usurped by those who wish to
turn it into a cause celebre and inveigle others, who may not even be
aware of the legitimate circumstances, to join in the mayhem.

I Will Never Know

Guns used to be used by villains - real villains. Armed robberies and
the occasional gangland shootings were usually the extent of weapons
on the street. One must never forget the shooting dead of three plain
clothed unarmed police officers which occurred in Braybrook Street,
Shepherds Bush in August 1966. Having only been in the Job for eight
months I was still counting paving stones but I was aware, as every
police officer was, of the tragedy that had occurred. I was called to
Notting Hill Underground Station to a man with stomach pains. I felt
that he was drunk but he kept complaining and was on the ground,
doubled-over. I called for an ambulance and escorted him to St Charles
Hospital.

Whilst awaiting treatment he asked me how long I had been in the
police and when I told him it was 8 months he said, "Do you want to
make a name for yourself?"

"How do you mean?" I asked.

He told me that he knew who had shot the coppers and knew the car
they had used. I, of course, was sceptical (and naïve, I guess) and
thought he was just saying this so that I didn't arrest him for being
drunk. Whilst he was being treated I contacted the station and told
them what had been said. I was told to arrest the man immediately and
bring him to Notting Hill, which I did. I never saw him again.
Whether or not he was telling the truth, I have no idea, but one of the

murderers, John Duddy, lived in a block of flats off Ladbroke Grove, and, as the man was from one of those blocks, it is possible.

You Can Fool Some of the People......

Trellick Towers is a block of flats in Golborne Road, W.10. It is considered an innovative, design by Erno Goldfinger. It has a tall thin profile with a different lift and service tower linked at every third storey to the access corridors in the main building: flats above and below the corridor levels have internal stairs. The concrete corridors run along lengthwise on one side of the building with the doors of each flat opening directly from the corridor. At the time I mention, the lower part of the doors were very flimsy, almost like plywood, with a square frosted wired-glass insert in the top half.

I was the operator on Bravo 3 and we were called to a flat where the white male tenant had allegedly assaulted his wife, who had a small babe in arms. An ambulance had been called and the man had assaulted one of the ambulance personnel. All innocent parties had fled the flat and the man had locked himself inside. My driver and I were told that the man had a gun and a knife and he had threatened the ambulance crew with them. On our arrival, his wife was very distraught, as can be expected, and the ambulance crew were shaken. The shadow of the man could be seen through the opaque glass. He had a rifle in his hand and was indiscriminately shooting towards the door. At one point he shot out the internal hall light. It was impossible to know what kind of weapon he had as, miraculously, none of the bullets had hit the glass. We subsequently found out that the surrounding frame was peppered with air pellets, but without knowing the type of weapon at the time it would have been foolhardy to shoulder in the door.

Although we had obtained a key from the caretaker, the man had locked the door from the inside. The caretaker told me it was just a small catch. I tried, with a metal coat -hanger to release the catch, but the man realised what was happening and prevented me from doing so. By this time, two Inspectors had arrived along with dogs and a posse of other officers. No-one possessed firearms in those days although there would have been one available at the station. The siege mentality had not developed so wits were the only alternative. Having been trained to handle and fire rifles whilst in the Air Training Corps, I knew that the man had to reload each time he fired a shot. I instructed all the personnel present to hide behind a jutting out wall where they would be safe.

I then knelt down and lifted up the letter box and suggested to the man that he should shoot us through the letter box. Foolishly and obligingly he pushed the barrel through and fired one bullet (actually an air pellet) against the concrete of the corridor. I immediately grabbed hold of the barrel of the gun and pulled the gun as far as I could until it jammed in the letter box. The man tried to retrieve it but by that time I had kicked in the door. Luckily the weapon was a high powered air rifle which meant that the barrel had to be broken before inserting another pellet. It was comical as I had to bend back the barrel to allow the officers to run past and up the short flight of stairs. My driver was first in and he was slightly cut by the knife the man brandished. The man was arrested. We found that he had shot and smashed the huge plate glass in the lounge and there was about a 100 foot uninterrupted drop to ground level.

The wife was still distraught and the baby was crying with hunger. As I had a very young baby myself I was able to heat up some water, make a bottle and feed the baby.

Interestingly, and inexplicably, the Duty Officer (Inspector) who was present, refused to nominate my driver or myself for a commendation despite being asked to do so by the Divisional Commander. The man eventually appeared at the Old Bailey (Central Criminal Court) on 23rd July 1973 where the driver and I were commended by the Judge and were each awarded a Commissioner's Commendation with the citation:

"for courage and determination leading to the arrest of a mentally deranged man in possession of a firearm".

Unbelievably, the Inspector was also commended. He had done absolutely nothing except to criticise me for allegedly putting myself in danger. Strangely enough, despite my suggestion that he hand the commendation back as John Lennon had recently done with his MBE, he decided not to...![1]

Sniffing out the Trouble-Maker

Back to Trellick Towers. This time a black woman and child had come to the Police Station alleging that her husband had gone out to the pub but had threatened that, when he returned, he would shoot her and their child. Although she had not seen a gun it was decided that we would deal with the situation as if he had one. At that time I was an authorised firearms officer and I booked out a revolver from the station safe. With the Section Sergeant and a young probationer we went to the flat and entered using the woman's key. This time the stairs led from the corridor down to the living area. I took a position in a bedroom directly opposite the bottom of the stairs, but before doing so I took the bulb out of the downstairs hallway so that the suspect would be silhouetted against the light but I could not be seen. The Sergeant positioned himself in the bedroom behind but adjacent to the stairs and the probationer was in the living-room to the left of the bottom of the stairs. Our plan was that if the man had a gun in his hand I would deal with it and if he didn't the Sergeant would detain him.

In the event, the man came in and started to slowly descend the stairs. The house design was such that I could not see his hands until he was half way down. The Sergeant suddenly rushed out and pinned both the arms of the suspect behind him. I was taken by surprise and could easily have pulled (squeezed) the trigger.

I stepped out into the light, assumed the standard crouch position with both hands on the gun, and said, "Where's the gun, mate?"

The man, who had obviously been drinking, was completely shocked and he emptied his bowels at both ends causing an almighty smell. (You usually hear in movies that they 'emptied both barrels' but this was a bit different). I started to laugh with the tension and the gun was wavering up and down.

Our job now was to search him and the premises. The probationer asked what he should do and I nonchalantly suggested he search the small bathroom as stolen goods are often found behind the bath panel. Whilst the Sergeant kept the suspect secure I made a thorough search of the flat including the air vents but found only a toy gun. The probationer asked me to come into the bathroom. To my surprise he was standing there with a brown briefcase in which there were many cheque books and cheque cards. He had unscrewed the panel at the back of the toilet cistern where the pipes were and found the briefcase amongst the piping. A great find by a persistent officer. The suspect subsequently appeared at court charged with fraud and possession of stolen property.

Back to the U S of A

A black man, his wife and two young children came into the station at about 11pm and alleged that they had been threatened by a big black man with a gun who demanded money. He stated that when he sheltered his family, the suspect went off and then into a basement in Raddington Road. We took him there and he pointed out a basement where he thought the man had gone. As we were quietly scouting the basement for a suitable entry point, the door opened and an elderly white couple peeked out so we apologised and left.

About half an hour later the man returned to the station and said he had now identified the correct basement. We were a bit sceptical but when we got there he was certain because of a 'For Sale' sign outside. Again we had no access to a gun. We had been joined by several other officers. We crept around the back and the basement window was slightly open. We started silently to push the window up. There was a bed with two people in it – a black man and a white woman. Two or three of us managed to get in the room before the woman, who was stark naked (she was a prostitute) jumped up. Those officers still trying to get in were goggle-eyed. However, I and another officer were watching the man and we saw his hand go under the pillow. We pounced on him and pulled him away from the pillow, under which was a gun. He was a very big man, dressed only in his underpants. He was arrested.

One other officer had been on a firearms course so the gun was handed to him. He immediately identified it as a starting pistol and he pulled the trigger in this tiny bedroom. How so many policemen squeezed out of the window at the same time I shall never know.

It turned out that the man was a serving USA serviceman based at Lakenheath and so the Snowdrops (American Military Police) were called. We thought our suspect was very big but these guys were even bigger, especially with their white helmets on. He eventually appeared at the Inner London Quarter Sessions where he pleaded guilty. His counsel made an observation to the Judge that, despite the many rumours that abounded at the time that black prisoners were beaten up by the police at Notting Hill, his client would like to express his gratitude for the way he had been handled in a dignified and humane manner by the Metropolitan police officers. Unfortunately for the man he would always be classed as a second-class subject and would never be able to hold a decent job in America again.

Extract from Metropolitan Police Orders 13th November 1970

The Commissioner has commended the following officers:-

B. Stn.P.S. Shaw and PCs 218 Ramsay and 519 Scott for determination and ability leading to the arrest and conviction of a man for possessing an offensive weapon and attempting to make use of an imitation firearm with intent to resist arrest. Also commended at the Inner London Quarter Sessions.

There was a newspaper article in the West London Observer of Thursday November 5 1970 under the heading 'He Hunted Gunman', regarding this matter. The local police Commander gave the Informant a cheque and praised him for his courage and sense of duty. He was also given a letter of appreciation from the Assistant Commissioner Crime (ACC)

A sequel was that the victim invited my colleague and me to a party in Brixton which was the first time we had eaten goat curry. It was very surreal being the only two white people there and we were police officers from Notting Hill whose reputation was not exactly rosy at the time. We didn't stay long.

Threats to Kill

The issue of firearms was never taken lightly and had to be authorised by the Duty Officer (Inspector). A call had come from children who had been playing football in the street stating that a man had come out of his house and threatened them with a gun. I drew a revolver from the safe at the Station and climbed into the back of an unmarked car driven by a uniformed officer.

As the vehicle was being driven fast down Ladbroke Road towards the junction with Lansdowne Road I prophetically said, "Don't have an accident on the way!"

Sure enough, against the give way lines, an American tourist drove straight out into the side of the police car. The Duty Officer and another authorised shot were behind us so I transferred to their car and we drove to the incident. The children pointed out the address to us which was a three-storey high Victorian building with a basement. Stone steps led up to the front door flanked by two pillars.

Since an incident in Kensington some years previously, when a police officer had disturbed an armed gang holding up a bank with sawn-off shotguns, we had been trained to shoot with either hand. He had been on his way to or from an armed post and carried a gun which he drew. He was shot, injuring his right arm so he transferred the weapon to his left hand and shot one of the robbers who subsequently died a short time later on the roof of a building off Kensington High Street. So I stood to the right of the door with gun in my left hand and my colleague stood at the other side whilst the Inspector rang the doorbell.

I lifted the letter-box (You see, I had learned from my previous experience) and saw a man walking down the internal stairway. He was not carrying a gun and he opened the door to be faced by two armed policemen pointing their weapons at him. The Inspector repeated what the children had said and asked if it were true. The man said it was. When asked where the gun was he started to put his hand into a jacket which was hanging in the hallway but stopped when, in no uncertain terms, I told him that if he pulled out a gun and pointed it at us he would be shot. He was very surprised saying he had just threatened the children in fun. The weapon was a replica firearm which, to all intents and purpose, was identical to a real gun.

He was arrested but I cannot remember the outcome.

Gun g Ho!

This incident did not happen in Notting Hill but in West Drayton where I had been transferred. On 1st February 1993 I was driving the police van with another officer as radio operator. We received a call that a man was at a burger stall, that he had a gun tucked into the front waistband of his trousers and had a black dog on a lead with him. We were very close by and the burger man pointed down the road saying the man had just left. We could see him a short distance away. My colleague jumped out of the van to follow him discreetly until assistance arrived. However, the man glanced round and saw the police van.

It was all or nothing. I drove past the man and leaped out. The man had turned and the other officer was running towards him when he tried to pull the gun from his belt. The other officer grabbed the gun and I managed to pin his arms and throw him to the ground and a struggle ensued. We commandeered the gun and other officers arrived. The gun was examined by an authorised officer and it was found to be a .177mm air pistol with the appearance of a 9mm automatic pistol. It was loaded. He was found to be a person prohibited from carrying a firearm as he had recently served a prison sentence, and was wanted on warrant in Brighton. We received a 'Good Work Report' dated 1st March 1993 from the Superintendent of Hillingdon Division which read:

PC Jones and yourself approached this dangerous situation with restraint and acted in a courageous manner to disarm this person.
This was an excellent piece of police work and worthy of the highest possible praise.
Well done!

The Sweeney

A radio call came through from Scotland Yard (call sign 'MP') asking for assistance for a uniform car to stop a Rover vehicle being followed by a Sweeney (Flying Squad) 'Q' car on Hammersmith section. The 'Q' car (unmarked) was crewed by a male driver and a woman radio operator in plain clothes. Foxtrot 3, the Area car from Shepherds Bush, responded. I was acting sergeant that day being driven in a Hillman by a colleague and we decided to wend our way to the vicinity. A commentary stated that the 'bandit' car had entered Elsham Road, which is a one-way street, and had stopped. We were in Holland Road, which ran parallel to that road, so we continued and turned right into Russell Gardens. We then heard that the 'bandit' car was being chased by Foxtrot 3 and a gun was mentioned. We turned into Elsham Road against the traffic flow. The 'bandit' car was speeding toward us followed by Foxtrot 3, also a Rover, with its blue lights flashing. My driver managed to pull in and both the other vehicles hurtled past us towards the 'T' junction.

The road surface was wet. The 'bandit' skidded and stopped at an angle against the kerb. Foxtrot 3 drove in front of it to try to stop it escaping. The operator from Foxtrot 3 and a police cadet, who was a rear seat passenger, got out, but the 'bandit' car reversed back into Elsham Road. By that time we had reversed and were parallel to it. I got out. The passenger pushed down the door lock preventing me from opening it. I took out my truncheon and attempted to smash the windscreen and then the passenger's window with it: neither broke. The car was an automatic and the driver was panicking and wrestling to put it into drive mode when Foxtrot 3 drove diagonally in front of it again. However the suspect managed to get it into gear and drove straight at Foxtrot 3 forcing it aside. He then sped off down Russell Gardens. Foxtrot 3, with only the driver aboard, chased it, giving a running commentary, via a hand-held microphone, as he went. We scrambled back into the Hillman almost leaving the police cadet behind. He had not completely got into the car.

When the 'bandit' reached Hammersmith Road it turned right towards Olympia closely followed by Foxtrot 3. The traffic lights at the junction with North End Road were just turning to red and traffic was stopping. The 'bandit' went down the outside in to the fast lane of oncoming traffic and then swerved back in as it entered the junction and continued towards Hammersmith hotly pursued by Foxtrot 3. We intended to follow but just at that time, a chauffeur-driven Rover (another one) turned right out of North End Road and remained in the fast lane. We were now heading for a head-on collision (bear in mind that we did not have blue lights). My driver braked hard but in the wet conditions began sliding towards the nearside. Unbelievably, the chauffeur quickly sized up the situation and calmly mounted the kerb outside Olympia and carried on his way. I will never forget the reactions of the limousine rear seat passenger. There were none. He was sitting reading his newspaper oblivious of the drama around him.

The 'bandit' car was being held up in traffic so it took the outside again and smashed headlong into a J4 van coming in the opposite direction and swung around parallel to it jamming in the Rover's passenger. The J4 van hit a taxi which mounted the pavement knocking down a woman with a child in a pushchair (thankfully not injured). The Foxtrot 3 driver then drove straight at the driver's door preventing him from exiting. I arrived and saw that the 'bandit's' car had a smashed windscreen so, with my truncheon still in my hand, I dived across the bonnet, through the windscreen and pinned the driver's arms against his seat.

"What are you running from?" I demanded.

He said, "We have escaped from prison."

The incident happened opposite the Albion Public House and some CID officers, who were drinking there, came out to help. When searched, the 'bandit' car had two guns under the front seat and others in the boot. The driver and passenger in the J4 van had their legs broken. I'll never forget that they came from Yateley in Hampshire.

The sequel to the story was that the suspects appeared at The Old Bailey where they eventually pleaded guilty (after some horse-trading) to something like 140 serious offences, some of which are too gruesome to mention. They were sentenced to only 10 years' imprisonment, concurrent: that meant at the same time as the 10 years they were serving before escaping so, technically, no additional punishment. This was a surprisingly light sentence as, apparently, the Judge's brother had been shot by a burglar.

Seemingly, when the 'Q' car had originally tried to stop the 'bandit', they had drawn parallel to it whereupon the 'bandit' driver had pointed a gun at them and then sped away. Naturally the 'Q' car occupants received commendations. There were no such accolades for us uniformed officers. Such is life.

If I remember correctly, the driver of Foxtrot 3 was reprimanded for failing to stop and inspect his vehicle after the first collision, but no action was taken. When it was put to him that he had damaged the police car at the second accident, he defended this accusation by stating it wasn't an accident - he had deliberately driven in to the 'bandit' car.

The Mad Axe Man

In the early 1970s, Roy Jenkins MP was the Home Secretary in a Labour Government. 'Mad' Frankie Fraser, who had been deemed insane on a few occasions, had escaped from Dartmoor and had allegedly threatened that he would attack Mr Jenkins with an axe because he had refused him parole. As a result an armed officer was posted outside Mr Jenkins' house in Ladbroke Square. This is a slight misnomer as there is only one street and no square). Very expensive and fashionable houses lined the south side of the square whilst an iron railing ran along the North side bordering the large communal garden area, (which, incidentally, had been part of the Hippodrome).

There were parked cars on either side of the road. One night when I was posted there I decided that I would not stand outside Mr Jenkins' front door to be a target for the Mad Axe man so I stood opposite between the cars and the railings. It was winter and bitterly cold and I was wearing a greatcoat. A rapid response was not the order of the day. The gun was worn in a holster on a belt under the coat which was cumbersome and heavy. To undo the coat, draw the weapon and be in a position to fire would have taken – I estimate – probably about two minutes, hence my reluctance to stand in the street.

In the early hours of the morning the only sounds to be heard were the distant rumble of traffic and, I guess, an owl now and again. I heard a car coming along Ladbroke Terrace which joins Ladbroke Square at a right angle/T junction half way along the street. I could see two men in it as it turned towards me and stopped in a gap between some cars. The men got out and began looking and breaking into parked cars. I called for assistance on my personal radio and asked for a quiet approach. As I mentioned, it was peaceful and, although they tried to be as silent as possible, you could hear a car coming from Ladbroke Terrace and another coming along Ladbroke Square. The two men saw the cars approaching. They split up and ran in different directions, one of whom was running toward me. To his surprise I stepped out of the shadows and grabbed him. Both were taken to the police station.

I was happy. I was off the fixed post and in the warmth of the station for the rest of the night. I took off my greatcoat revealing that I was carrying a gun. One of the men immediately jumped off the bench where he had been sitting and stood strictly to attention. It transpired that he had been in the military and said that if he had known I was armed he would never have run away. A search of the car revealed that it was packed with stolen property from cars including radios, handbags, wallets etc. They had been on a spree throughout the night in Chelsea and Kensington and were just starting their crime wave in Notting Hill. They were given bail the next day at court but the 'soldier' agreed to accompany me (an officer had to get permission to meet someone on bail) and he showed me where they had been stealing and many offences were TIC'd (Taken into Consideration) when he was sentenced.

Look Behind You

Police firearms officers are very highly trained. Within the history of firearms' courses they practised using indoor and outdoor ranges and were regularly sent on refresher courses. As mentioned previously we had to learn to shoot with both hands. How the West was won! The idea, of course, of shooting accurately with a revolver from a moving horse was ludicrous. Even standing and with support, it could be difficult to hit the target of a man at 25 yards. Modern firearms and dedicated firearms officers have improved the probability of successfully hitting the intended target.

One of the training establishments was at the Royal Woolwich Arsenal where there were many derelict buildings which had various hidey holes. An alleged armed suspect, or suspects (firearms officers), were hidden in different rooms or corridors and it was the task of the trainee officers to flush them out or 'die' in the attempt.

On one occasion I saw the target carrying a sawn-off shotgun dart between rooms in a corridor about 20 yards ahead of me. I ran down and crouched behind the jamb of a door. Unknown to me the villain had climbed between two rooms and was now behind me. I heard a

noise, turned around and was 'shot' with a hard pellet from the gun –
and it hurt. No bullet-proof vests in those days.

On another occasion the bandit was allegedly in a room which had to
be searched. Four men were assigned to each team and, after discussion of tactics, a search began. The recognised entry into a room was
conducted by a team, each one of whom was given a number. When all
the officers were in their designated position the leader (No. 4) would
shout loudly, "All right No. 1?"

"Yes."

"All right, No. 2?"

"Yes."

"All right, No. 3?"

"Yes."

Then the action began. (I won't give details of the manoeuvres). This
was to ensure that all personnel were in place and also to disorientate
the hidden man (always men in those days).

One team leader, however, kept shouting,

"All right No. 4?" (He repeated the calls up to No. 7)

When the room was entered the man, who had been hiding in a roll of
carpet, said he was getting very worried as he was only expecting four
armed officers to enter so the psychology worked. Needless to say that
nearly all of us were 'shot' at some stage. They were really fun and
exciting days but essential for exposing the pitfalls that could occur if
you were not 'switched on'.[2]

Have a Heart guvn'r.

If a weapon was carried, authorised firearms officers used to be issued
with a card which fitted inside the warrant card holder and when
flipped open, was slid into the top pocket of uniform or civilian jacket
to inform other officers that they were armed. It had two broad orange

reflective horizontal stripes on it. What an ideal target for a sniper. They were later withdrawn.

-----

1. The man was sentenced to 18 months imprisonment suspended for 2 years.
2. Coincidentally, one of the firearms' instructors was the son of the farmer for whom I used to deliver milk as a milk-boy in Fraserburgh. As I was such a good shot he suggested that I become an instructor but travelling from Twickenham to Loughton each day was not an appealing prospect.

CHAPTER 16

BOMBS AWAY

During the 1970s and 1980s, bombs and the threats of bombs were prevalent. Hoax calls were always a worry for officers attending the scenes as they literally took their lives in their hands. They had to make calculated decisions and treat each incident circumspectly. With the best will in the world the 'bomb squad' could not be called on each and every occasion so, with a wing and a prayer as they say, many executive decisions were made on the spot.

Handle with Care

One late evening a detective sergeant (DS) offered to drive me home but just as we were about to leave the station a call came in that a taxi-driver had found what he thought was a bomb. It was in the doorway of a shoe-shop in Kensington Church Street (which was actually on Kensington Section) about 20 yards from a very busy Notting Hill Gate. A few years previously a bomb, planted by the Provisional Irish Republican Army (PIRA) with an anti-handling device, had detonated in that doorway causing not only extensive damage but also killing the senior bomb-disposal officer, Roger Goad, GC. BEM. Where do these men get their courage? The cab-driver knew of this.

When we met him at the scene and asked him where the suspect parcel was he pointed to the middle of the road. When asked how it got there he said he had moved it to prevent any serious damage. I know, I know, one couldn't make it up. Suffice to say that the area was sterilised and the bomb squad was called. Initially the robot was sent in with little positive success. Subsequently the bomb-disposal officer, who was unsure of the nature of the parcel, thought it was realistic. He decided to instigate a controlled explosion – only the second time he had ever done so. Thankfully it was a hoax. Deep breathing ceased and peace was restored. Or so we thought.

Two in One Night

Having returned to Notting Hill Police Station and recorded the details on a crime sheet, we then made our way to our homes. Again, I was given a lift by the DS. It was now late evening and it was dark. Our route was down Holland Park Avenue. At the junction with Clarendon Road there is a set of traffic lights which were turning to red as we approached. We noticed two youths, one in a kilt, placing an object about a foot square, on top of a green traffic control box. They then walked west towards Shepherds Bush carrying a bag. The DS and I looked at each other and discussed whether the first one had been the hoax but this might be the real thing. Nah! Too coincidental but, just in case, I got out of the car to inspect the object.

Unbelievable! I could see two strange looking batteries. They were green and rectangular, about nine inches high by four inches square each and were joined to their terminals with red and black electrical wire. What to do? We shouted to a passer-by to call the police and we drove down Holland Park Avenue and stopped the youths. They had been drinking but were not drunk. In the bag was similar electrical wiring, pliers and insulating tape and other paraphernalia which could have been used to make a bomb. There was also a quantity of clothing. They were arrested and taken to Notting Hill Police Station. The bomb squad were called and declared it another hoax.

The scene was attended by the Duty Officer (Inspector) and the Section Sergeant. Whilst the youths were being processed they returned with the batteries, having carefully avoided putting their fingerprints on them. When asked what had happened they told us that the bomb squad officer had examined the batteries. He had said that he had never seen anything like them before but thought they may have been of a German make. He had then snipped a piece from each of the two wires that had been joining the terminals. When asked where those pieces now were, the Sergeant questioned why we needed them. In no uncertain terms he was told they were required for evidence as, without them, the terminals could not be joined together to make a circuit. They sheepishly went out to find them but did not do so. Perhaps the bomb squad officer had taken them.

When listing the youths' property on the custody sheet the custody Sergeant took hold of one of the batteries. I immediately shouted 'Fingerprints!' whereupon he quickly put that battery down but then grabbed the other one in his panic. If it hadn't been so serious it would have been a comedy of errors. It transpired that the suspects were students at a school/college in Campden Hill Road and were studying science. Despite our evidence they denied planting either bomb. The equipment, consisting of batteries, wires from both devices (not much left from the first one), pliers and other paraphernalia, was sent to the Police Scientific Laboratory. I cannot remember if they were ever charged with any offence/s but there is no doubt that they had been responsible for the hoaxes. The batteries had come from the college science lab. C'est la Vie!

The Sandman Cometh

A call had been received that there was a suspicious parcel on a 52 bus in Pembridge Road.

The bomb squad was called and discounted it as being a bomb or even a hoax bomb. They had just driven away when a Sergeant and I were told that there was a suspicious parcel in a yellow sand-bin in Kensington Park Road. The sand is used when the roads are icy. It was almost opposite a block of flats where high ranking military personnel lived. Was this one genuine? We lifted the lid and, on top of the sand, was a cake box with string tied around it: the type of string that was used by bakeries in those days and was not stretchable. Should we call the bomb squad back? No, it would mean disrupting the traffic again with the Land Rover and the police escort having to come back with horns blaring.

The Sergeant gingerly tried to ease the string off without success. What did he do? Again, you won't believe it. He took out his lighter and started to burn the string off. I was behind the biggest tree by this time. (Not that it would have done much good but that is all that was there.) 'Light the blue touch paper and stand back', was the phrase that sprang to mind. Thankfully it was a hoax as the box contained old screwed up newspapers. Breathe again!

Bravery or Stupidity

I was called to an abandoned, old-fashioned and dilapidated brown suitcase in Blenheim Crescent. I gingerly opened it up. It was empty. It was clearly 'a case for the police'. Similar 'cases' were being dealt with, daily, by officers throughout the UK. There is no doubt that their individual judgements saved the lives of many people. With the upsurge of the suicide bomber throughout the world, security men and women everywhere have to be extra vigilant and they patrol with trepidation daily.

Gordon Hamilton-Fairley

On 23rd October 1975 a bomb exploded in Campden Hill Square on Kensington Section about 200 – 300 yards from Notting Hill Police Station. The intended target was the Tory MP Sir Hugh Fraser. It had been placed under his XJ6 Jaguar car but a dog, being walked by its owner, Gordon Hamilton-Fairley, triggered the device. Sadly both he and the dog were killed. The members of the IRA Active Service unit were arrested two months later at the well documented Balcombe Street siege.

A Panda (small police car painted light blue and white) with two officers (JH & MH) was sitting in Campden Hill Square at the time. A police van, driven by (RS) was at the junction of Ladbroke Grove and Holland Park Avenue. As these three rushed to the scene having heard a big blast, the petrol tank of the XJ6 exploded and the car began to run downhill towards them. They found the bodies of the dog and the victim in a garden. Danger was never far away. (RS)[1]

"I Was There"

This is an account by an Inspector regarding the above incident.

"Longstanding information suggested that drugs were being supplied from a house near Ladbroke Grove Station. The front door was particularly secure as they had been raided before and there was only one entry point. A postman's hat and jacket were obtained and an officer, so attired, knocked on the door to deliver a package which required a signature. The ruse worked and peaceful entry was obtained. During the extensive search a call came through that there had been an explosion not far from Notting Hill Police Station – Camden Hill Square. A bomb had been placed under the wheel of a car with the intention that when the car was moved it would explode killing the occupants. Professor Hamilton-Fairley, a cancer expert, was walking his dogs before work when one of them disturbed the bomb which exploded killing the Professor and one of the dogs. Thankfully no-one else was injured. Sizeable bits of the car were found 100 yards away." (FW)

Bombs threats were prolific.

---

1. Images of the incident can be found at 'Campden Hill Square IRA Bomb Photos – Campden Hill Stock Photos, Royalty free photos and images.

CHAPTER 17

LAUGHING MATTERS (OR DOES IT?)

Not PC but WPC

When I joined the police force in 1965 the traditional role for uniformed women police officers (WPCs) was to deal with children, young persons and aliens (immigrants or overseas visitors who often failed to report changes to their visas/conditions of entry) and, I guess, any situation where a sympathetic ear was required. We male officers were very pleased and appreciative of their expertise. There were exceptional cases, of course, who joined the CID or drove the MG sports car for the Traffic Division (Some were called 'Fly Girls' because the index of their MG was 'FLY 106'). WPCs were seldom, if ever, allowed in the fast response or Area cars as they were called.

One day I was driving Bravo 3 down Holland Park Avenue. Parked on (what was then) a grassed roundabout at the junction with Holland Road, watching the world go by, was the Area car, Foxtrot 3, from Shepherds Bush, it being the adjoining division. I was very surprised to see a WPC as the radio operator. I drove around and drove onto the roundabout adjacent to Foxtrot 3 with my driver's window close to its front passenger's window. When asked how a WPC was posted as an operator she said that they were very short of male officers that day at Shepherds

Bush. We chatted for a wee while. A call came from MP – the call sign for the radio dispatch room at New Scotland Yard. The call was to the van that covered Oxford Street – Charlie Bravo 2. The message was:-

"Charlie Bravo 2, Charlie Bravo 2, 300 Oxford Street, man through a plate glass window."

The WPC immediately said, innocently, "Why would he want to throw a plate glass window?"

I am sorry to say that all those present began to laugh, much to her annoyance. She did, however, laugh when it was explained to her.

Expect the Unexpected but Not a Laughing Matter

There are times when one should not laugh but, as everyone knows, if you start laughing under tension it is almost impossible to stop.

My colleague and I were on foot patrol in the early hours of the morning making our way back to the station for refreshments along Ladbroke Grove. As we passed the end of Arundel Gardens a call came over the personal radios to a disturbance at an address there. We waited a few minutes to see if any of the patrolling cars or van would answer the call but none of them did. We volunteered. As mentioned previously a call to a 'disturbance' could mean anything and this was no exception.

The Victorian houses in Arundel Gardens are three or four storeys high with a basement which would have been used by the servants. Most of them have been converted into flats with a row of individual bells – sometimes with the name of the occupier, adjacent. Being unsure where the disturbance might be I remained on the pavement in case the basement flat was involved. My partner went up the steps to the front door and rang the bell for the named occupier.

A young girl, aged about 19 years, opened the door. She was in a terribly distressed state. She was crying and her eye make-up was streaking down her cheeks, her hair was dishevelled and her blouse was torn down the front revealing bare breasts. That made us blink.

The other officer said to her (and I remember the words exactly), "What's wrong love?"

"I have just been raped." was her tearful response.

Naturally, this was not an expected response and, in my mind, the tension started to rise. Flashing through my mind were the instructions from training school - console the victim, preserve the scene, preserve the bedclothes, preserve the knickers and other clothing, arrest the offender, inform the Duty Officer, inform the CID, inform forensics, call a woman police officer etc. - all in a split second. Back to the scene.

My colleague asked, "Where?" He was expecting to be taken to the venue. However, the girl was so confused that she lifted up her skirt to reveal bare thighs and not much else. It was so unexpected and, with the tension, I started to have a suppressed laugh. Unfortunately it was infectious and my colleague started to try to smother his laughter but the situation was so incongruous that we couldn't contain our mirth. The poor girl was crying and we had tears in our eyes. Were we unprofessional? Of course, but it was certainly memorable!

She then showed us down the internal staircase to the basement and the suspect was still there and, having investigated the incident, we arrested him. Major and most criminal incidents were dealt with by the CID and we, in uniform, just wrote out our evidence, gave it to the CID and then moved on to the next incident.

Update. After writing the above, coincidentally, I spoke to my colleague of that night who filled me in with the facts. The man was an American Service man who had picked up the girls in Bayswater Road, one black and one white. The girls were prostitutes and they took him back to their flat. After 'servicing' the black girl he 'serviced' the white girl. He then went back to the black girl for a second 'service' and the white girl took exception so she decided to cry 'wolf'. When we entered the basement he was, in fact, in bed with the black girl. At the station all three were examined by the Divisional Surgeon (doctor) who stated that the man had got more than he had bargained for as both girls had syphilis. He was discharged...... No further action......

(No, it wasn't intended as a pun – or was it?)

Little and Large

I cannot remember the reason but I think they were involved in a fight. I had been the operator on the Area car when I found myself chasing two men along Westbourne Park Road towards Ledbury Road. One was tall and well-built but the other was a dwarf. It turned out that they were brothers. The tall one was well ahead of me. Chasing the dwarf I started to laugh to see his little legs pounding up and down. He was fast and the soles of my shoes were loose and flapping (we didn't earn too much in those days). I eventually caught him at the junction with Ledbury Road where the building had a large plate glass window. His upper body was very well-developed. He was tremendously strong and I had difficulty holding him. Suddenly his brother appeared and tried to pull him free but desisted when I pointed out that we might fall through the window. Help arrived and they were arrested. I have never forgotten the image of the dwarf's little legs which moved like pistons.

Boy Oh Boy

In 1972 all street lighting was extinguished, not because of a war but the effect of the miners' strike, to conserve energy. On our way back to the station, my colleague and I were walking along Ladbroke Terrace when we heard the noise of the rattling of coins. From where? It seemed to be coming from the other side of a high wall which backed on to private gardens. It was pitch black. Everywhere else was silent. Our strategy was to climb up the wall and then shine our torches into the darkness. We did so and saw two teenage youths rifling through some monies which were strewn on the lawn. Beside them lay a collecting box which had been broken open. On our demand they climbed back over the wall and were taken to the police station which was a short distance away.

As is the custom, I related the arresting facts to the custody officer (Sergeant) stating that we had found the boys in the garden. They told us they had smashed the head of a defenceless crippled (in callipers) boy and were in the act of stealing his money when we had arrived. The Sergeant was apoplectic, ranting and raving at the youths. He was incensed. The boys hung their heads in shame knowing that their parents would be called and that more chastising would be forthcoming. As he booked in the boys the Custody Sergeant was still seething. The door of the Custody Suite opened and another officer came in carrying the severely damaged St Barnardo's advertising effigy (remember this design?) with the collecting box smashed. The Sergeant stared. It was only then that the penny dropped (pun intended). He then started ranting and raving at us. The subterfuge was worth a laugh.

Beware of the Dog

As we were driving along Walmer Road in the Area car an attractive woman waved us down. She said she had been robbed of her handbag and contents. We sat her in the back of the car to get the details of the suspect/s. She said she wasn't too worried about the theft except that her house keys were in the bag and that she was expecting her daughter home from school. Having obtained her details we offered to take her home to see if we could help to get her in the house – ever chivalrous. She lived in St Charles Square which, again, consisted of large Victorian buildings with pillars either side of the steps leading up to the outside door which could be opened by another resident by the pressing of an internal button.

Luckily, she lived on the ground floor with a large bay window overhanging the 20 foot drop to the basement. It was a short distance for me to jump from the side wall onto the roughly 18" wide concrete window sill. Then, with the ever-present penknife, I jiggled the retaining catch between the upper and lower sash windows. 'Twas easy really – I should have been a burglar'. Having lifted up the lower window and starting to climb in, I could hear a small dog barking. I asked the lady if there was a dog in her flat.

She said, "Yes, and he will go for you." She replied.

Luckily I am not afraid of dogs so I climbed into what was a bedroom. The door to the hall was closed. My colleague started to climb in and as he got his leg over the sill, hiding behind the door, I opened it. The dog, a small Pekinese, immediately ran towards him and I slipped out, laughing as he scrambled back to safety.

The internal hallway led to her front door which led into the communal hallway. There was a lock which I could open from the inside. However, I saw an orange space-hopper so, to try to cheer the lady up, I jumped on it. I was dressed in full uniform including my flat cap. I opened her flat door and bounced into the communal hallway where she and the other officer were waiting. They began to laugh as I manoeuvred into the hall. I then heard the door behind me, which was on a spring, slam shut. No laughing matter now. Guess who had to climb back into the house via the bedroom and a yapping, snarling Pekinese? Pride comes before a fall, they say.

Beware of the Other Dog

Each new recruit, especially if one was a bit cocky, was usually 'initiated' and many are the tricks the old sweats used to get up to. As a probationer one was seldom ever allowed in the Area car. One night duty, however, Bravo 3 drove alongside me as I walked my beat and I was told to jump in as there were "suspects on premises". The dog-handler (deceased October 2020 – RIP) was in the back with his German Shepherd. We arrived at the scene in Elgin Crescent with blue lights on, sirens sounding. (It was later that I was given a lesson from a prolific burglar about going to the scene of a burglary with all guns blazing) The derelict house was under renovation.

We searched the house with no success but, as we left, the dog handler suggested that the dog had to find someone at a search to keep his 'paw' (my word) in. There was a small cupboard on the way out so the dog handler suggested that I hide in there and the dog would 'find' me. I did so. Suddenly the doors opened and I was confronted by a snarling Alsatian on his hind legs being held on his leash. As I mentioned earlier I am not afraid of dogs so the incident unfazed me, much to the chagrin of the other officers who were laughing at my supposed plight.

Dog-Gone It

Innocence reigns again. I was not long in the Force when, as I passed Henekeys pub in Portobello Road in the early hours, two men approached me. I recognised one as a Detective Sergeant (DS) from the station. He introduced the other man as the landlord of the pub who said that his dog was trapped in the cellar. I followed them into the pub and the landlord invited me to have a drink. I said, "What about the dog?"

"What dog?"

He then proceeded to pour us a pint, or two, or three. It was nearly booking off time so I staggered back to the station and hid in the toilets. I heard the Duty Inspector shouting out my number but I ignored it. He continued shouting and I eventually replied because the rest of the relief could not be dismissed until all officers were accounted for. Drinking on duty, of course, was taboo. They were having a laugh at my expense.

Incidentally, from old photos, you may have noticed that the police in those days wore a broad dark blue and white band on their lower left arm and you may have wondered why. Officers sometimes used to travel to and from work in their uniform. It was to show licensed premises landlords if you were on duty or not. He should not serve you if you were wearing one. They were not difficult to remove.....!

Incidentally that DS, who, as a DCI, wrote in an official report under 'Other Matters' :-

Xxxx is the subject of many previous complaints against police and also the subject of a collator's card at Notting Hill (BH). The record there is both comprehensive and accurate and I was able to gain valuable background material from the records and the collator prior to dealing with Xxxx. You may consider referring these papers to Chief Superintendent BH who can cause to be included what details from the papers as might be properly recorded on Xxxx's card. The diligence of the BH collator was much appreciated.

I oft-times wonder if he remembers me from the canine encounter.

CHAPTER 18

CAR ACTORS AND HIGH JINX

Shaw Taylor MBE

It was with sadness that I read in the June 2015 edition of the London Police Pensioner (LPP) magazine that the intrepid television presenter, Shaw Taylor had passed away. I relate an incident in which I was involved with his production team of 'Police 5' which highlighted individual crime scenes, hoping that members of the public could assist in identifying the miscreants.

A van containing two men was being chased by police, at speed, from the Shepherds Bush area. As it came around the roundabout at the end of Holland Park Avenue and headed east, it mounted the narrow central reservation narrowly missing the 'keep left' bollards. It came back to the correct side and then suddenly turned left into the eastern arm of Royal Crescent. Unfortunately this was against the one-way system and the van hit a car coming in the opposite direction. It continued into Norland Road where it knocked down a girl, crashed and the suspects decamped and, at that stage, had not been caught.

I volunteered to drive the police van, replicating the incident, and I was briefed by Shaw and his team. I followed the route exactly, crossing the central reservation and turning contra-flow into Royal

Crescent. It needed only one take of which I was proud. As a result of the reconstruction several witnesses were found in the (then) Income Tax offices at the corner of Holland Park Avenue and Addison Road. The suspects were subsequently arrested after important information from members of the public.

I never saw that episode on TV.

Two for the Price of One

Another incident that happened nearby occurred on a very dark and wet night. The traffic lights were defective, stuck on green for Holland Park Avenue (HPA) and red for Royal Crescent, and a policeman was posted to direct traffic. He was dressed in his dark uniform. He had not been issued with white reflective forearm over-sleeves. HPA is a major arterial road with two lanes of heavy traffic in each direction.

As mentioned, Royal Crescent was one way into HPA. As there was no apparent traffic coming out of Royal Crescent the officer raised his arm in the 'STOP' position and waved on the HPA traffic. Unfortunately a vehicle came out of Royal Crescent at speed and knocked down the officer, breaking his arm. The driver said that he had not noticed that the traffic lights were on red and had not seen the PC.

A telegram was sent to the officer's parents and his in-laws. It read along these lines:

"We are sorry to inform you that your son/son-in law is in St Charles Hospital with a broken arm but we are happy to inform you that your daughter/daughter in-law is in (Can't remember) hospital having just given birth to a child."

Look Both Ways

Another incident at the Royal Crescent junction was when I was riding the Noddy bike. A French girl was trying to cross HPA but looked left instead of right and was knocked down by a passing car. Her good fortune was that I was able to call an ambulance immediately. Thankfully she was not seriously injured.

Banged Up

One Christmas morning, just after midnight, there was a call to the Chelsea Embankment: "six men allegedly fighting with knives." There was no answer from any of the nearer stationed Area cars from B, F or A divisions and we were a long way away. I should have been driving Bravo 3 but it had a flat battery so I had taken out the spare car, Bravo 5 – both Triumphs. It also had a dodgy battery but it had started. My operator was a young woman police officer.

As the call came in I had just driven into the back-yard at Notting Hill police station and behind me, to my surprise, was the Bravo 3 car being driven by the Duty Officer (Inspector). He flashed the blue light indicating that he was going to answer the call and he drove out. A young policeman standing in the yard asked if he could come as he hadn't been in an Area car before. The more the merrier, so far as I was concerned. I followed 'Bravo 3' and managed to overtake it along Kensington High Street and turned down Earls Court Road. There was a slight drizzle.

As we left Earls Court Road at about 70 MPH and continued into Redcliffe Gardens there was a loud bang from the engine and thick smoke emanated from the bonnet. I immediately attempted to brake but the servo (vacuum-controlled, it assists in the hydraulic braking system) had been disabled. I had visions of being unable to stop and landing in the Thames. I put the automatic car into neutral and braked very hard, unassisted by the servo. I told the crew to get out as soon as the car stopped and to run backwards fearing there might be an explosion. I managed to steer to the kerb and, before I had stopped, the PC in the back had exited and had run as suggested. Smoke was still streaming from the front of the car. As soon as I had stopped I got out and started to run but looked to see where the woman police officer was. She was still sitting in the car. I ran back, jerked the door open and, in no uncertain terms, told her to get out.

She said, "I have to get my handbag and radio."

Words failed me.

The smoke slowly dissipated. Lifting the bonnet we saw that it had been caused by engine oil splattering over the hot engine. What engine? It was smashed with the pistons scattered around the car and in the roadway. We picked up the debris and put the metal into the front well of the car. We retired to Chelsea Police Station and informed our recovery service.

Having written up our report we were given a lift back to Notting Hill. On the way we passed and then stopped the recovery vehicle the job of which was to take the car back to the police garage for repairs. We asked the driver what was wrong with the Triumph.

"It has only got a flat battery," was his reply.

I suggested he jump up and look inside the car and he was absolutely astonished to find the remnants of the engine. Strange to say, no questions were ever asked by the engineers and we never discovered what went wrong. I suspect that there had been a blockage of the oil system but one wonders what would have happened if we had crashed, we could have been killed or seriously injured.

Up and Over?

I was the operator, in full uniform, one Sunday morning on Bravo 3 which was a new Jaguar. There was no observer. My newly qualified Class 1 driver, (the highest category one could attain at the renowned Hendon driving school) wanted to go to open land behind Wormwood Scrubs prison (The Scrubs) for some reason, so we drove down the narrow road between the prison and Hammersmith Hospital. When we got to the end the barrier was down. We had to reverse.

"I wonder how fast this will go in reverse?" my driver pondered. He started off.

Any driver will tell you that just a small tweak of the front wheels when in reverse exaggerates the manoeuvre. We began to swerve violently from side to side and as we approached the T junction with Du Cane Road the front bumper of the car scraped all along the whole side of a parked car.

There was a man sitting in it. I got out to speak to him. He was reading a newspaper. I knocked on his window. He looked up then continued reading the paper. He must have known that his car had been hit because there had been a loud grating noise and the car would have rocked. I knocked on the window again.

He wound down his window and said, "What?"

I said, "We have just hit your car and there is a lot of damage."

"So what?" He then wound his window up again.

I went back to the police car where the driver was examining the bumper. There was a very small, insignificant scratch on the bumper. What to do? The other driver was obviously not interested. A bit of spit and polish and there was no discernible mark on the Jaguar. Was he waiting for someone to come over the wall of the Scrubs or was he a Special Branch or other surveillance officer? We were in a quandary.

It so happens that in October 1966 George Blake had escaped from The Scrubs and the two-way radio equipment that had been used was found in a flat in, I think, Kelfield Gardens on Notting Hill section. However, I do not think this was the incident because I would only have been 10 months in the Force at that time and I doubt if, with that short a service, I would have been in the Area car: but I can't be sure......

The Great Escape – for him or us?

Or was It UP and Away?

Well-Heeled

Early one bright Sunday morning two very young youths in a Ford Cortina were travelling at speed along Westbourne Grove. It was 'worth a stop'. I was driving, Bravo 3, a Triumph 2000 PI. We tucked in behind them. The car accelerated and would not stop despite the flashing blue lights and horns. A chase ensued along Westbourne Grove towards and onto Harrow Road section at speeds of over 80MPH, ignoring red traffic lights. Luckily it was very quiet with few cars or pedestrians in the vicinity. Having been chased for some distance through the back streets of Harrow Road section, followed by several other police cars, it drove west, at high speed along the Harrow Road towards Shepherds Bush/Willesden/Kilburn. Just past the junction with Wellesley Road there is a fairly sharp left hand bend. The driver lost control of the car and instead of taking the bend the car went straight on and the front offside (driver's) side smashed into a large unyielding tree.

The young male front seat passenger was unhurt, apart from shock. It turned out that he was the son of a police officer. There was great concern about the driver as the whole of the front wing and wheels had been pushed right into the central transmission shaft which ran through the centre of the car between the driver's seat and the passenger's seat. It meant that both of his lower legs and feet would be completely crushed. However, when we managed to open the driver's door the driver did not seem to be in pain and was speaking lucidly. A miracle had occurred. He was wearing the fashionable wooden high heeled boots worn by pop stars and they had taken the impact. To free him we just had to cut the leather from the soles of the boots and he was released, unharmed. The luckiest 15 year old that I have ever met!

We were lucky too. My operator, as he gave a running commentary, kept his finger on the 'send' button thus being unable to hear the warnings from the chasing pack. Further along the Harrow Road was a humped back railway bridge. A builder's lorry had been strategically placed just over the brow and if the bandit car had carried on that road he would have been unable to proceed. We, too, would have been scrambling to stop in time.

Rolling Along

Kensington sub-division bordered Notting Hill to the South and we sometimes assisted them with calls. Riding the Noddy bike one evening I followed a Rolls Royce along Notting Hill Gate, Palace Gardens Terrace and then into Kensington Church Street. The car was swerving all over the road, even mounting the kerb, and was on the pavement when I flagged it down. The driver, dressed in a dinner suit, was very drunk, hardly able to stand. He was a very well-known Irish builder who had a multi-million pound business. He was no bother and I ignored the proffered wallet. Having been arrested he was taken to Kensington Police station. He was too drunk to be charged so he was placed in a cell awaiting sobriety. I never heard another word about him and I was never called to court. I wonder what happened to him!

He Fell for It

This reminds me of one of my first arrests. I noticed a car driving erratically up Holland Park Avenue. I stepped out to stop it, which it did, and opened the door to speak to the driver. He fell into the roadway because he was so drunk he could not stand. I was dumbfounded. I hadn't a clue what to do. Luckily a member of the public must have rung the police (remember we had no radios or breathalysers in those days) because Bravo 3 arrived, called the van and helped me with the arrest. Boyo, was I glad? (Bravo 3's operator was an uncompromising Welshman who didn't take kindly to sprogs who were trainees/probationers.)

CHAPTER 19
THE COCAINE CURSE

Drugs

Not all cocaine, of course. Illegal drugs were, and still are, the scourge of society. I hesitate to use the expression 'civilised society' as many of the users/abusers are or were members of the alleged 'enlightened' establishment. I believe that they have a heavy burden to bear. They regularly use substances which are banned yet hypocritically rail against those whom they perceive to be the lower classes whose only hope or escape from the drudgery of everyday life is to resort to substance abuse to alleviate their despair. There are many well-intentioned and laudable agencies who are involved in the treatment and/or rehabilitation of regular misusers. Unfortunately the bulk of the after effects lands in the lap of the very hard working and overstretched NHS and probation services. The police, of course, are heavily involved: not only dealing daily with the immediate consequences but also the related effects of crime be it burglary, shoplifting, theft or robbery etc. The purchase has to be financed. I find it interesting and disturbing that in my early service – late 60's/early 70's - women seldom came into the radar of crime but since the dependence on drugs increased so the incidents, (especially shoplifting), by the female sex became more prevalent.

. . .

Watching Question Time on the BBC on 13th February 2020 it was disclosed that Scotland had the highest number of drug-related deaths in Europe. Dundee, in particular, had the unenviable reputation as being the 'capital' centre of this insidious malignancy. The seemingly easy and undetectable importation by unscrupulous criminals is an anathema to hard-pressed detection agencies who have limited resources and staff shortages. Cutting off the importation and supply must be the priority.

Sit Tight and Don't Move

Various drugs were omnipresent throughout the 60s and 70s and no more so than in Notting Hill which became the honey pot for the hippies and 'flower power' community. Many of the punters were squatters in the old terraced Victorian houses which were decaying and virtually uninhabitable. It would seem that many landlords could not afford the maintenance of these crumbling edifices and left them to stagnate and deteriorate.

Several had 'M U S T A R D' daubed on them. This acronym stood for 'Multi-racial Union of Squatters to Alleviate Racial Discrimination'.

I was involved in the eviction of squatters from an expensive three-storey house in Chepstow Villas (which had belonged to an Arab Princess) and a man called Michael Stewart aka Michael Archangel or Michael X, was arrested. He claimed to be connected with the above named organisation. We had to use shields to cover ourselves as we tried to gain entry to the front door as bricks and missiles were being thrown down on top of us. Michael assaulted me on the way in. The warrant of possession had been issued by the High Court Sherriff of Greater London and executed by him and his employees. Therefore the defendant had to appear at the Old Bailey where he was fined and given a jail sentence of three months and one month consecutive, suspended for two years for resisting the Sheriff and for the assault.

. . .

Tenants of other houses were hounded and oppressed by ruthless landlords. It was the era of the Rachman-type landlord who either forced the poorer tenants out by strong-arm methods or charged them extortionate rents.

That Inkling Again

Having been to Crown Court in plain clothes (one usually appeared in Court dressed as one was at the time of arrest) my colleague and I were finished early as the villain had pleaded guilty. Being at a loose end we commandeered the GP (General Purpose) unmarked car so that we could patrol in the areas of Pembridge and Chepstow where there had been a spate of high class burglaries. It was a very hot summer's day.

A young man ran out of Chepstow Crescent into Pembridge Villas wearing a jacket.

I commented, "Why is he running on a hot day like this?"

"Maybe he is going for a bus."

"No", I said, "he has passed the bus stop."

"Maybe a taxi then?"

"No, an empty taxi has just passed him."

"Going for the tube?" (Notting Hill Gate Underground was close by.)

"I don't think so. Let's follow him."

He kept running and eventually entered a car which was parked on the North side of the south arm of Pembridge Square. A very narrow pavement separated it from the railings around the gardens. There was another youth sitting in the passenger's seat. I parked the car parallel to his so that he could not drive off. and went to speak to the driver.

"Why were you running?"

"I am in a hurry."

I noticed he had a Scottish accent. I asked him to step out of the car. As he did so I saw a plastic bag behind his seat.

"What's in here?" I asked.

I reached in, opened it and saw that it contained a slab of what appeared to be cannabis. He suddenly pushed me and ran in the middle of the road east along Pembridge Square. I gave chase and, by pure luck, another officer who had been to court, was driving his car back to the station when he saw me chasing the youth. He put his car across the road and got out and started grappling with him. I then heard the footsteps of my colleague coming behind me.

"Where is the other man?" I asked.

"He is still sitting in the car. I thought I would help you."

I had the feeling that the other youth wouldn't still be waiting for us and I was right. Our man was arrested for possessing a large quantity of cannabis resin. When I contacted the Scottish police in Edinburgh they were delighted. They had been trying to track the man, a major drug-dealer there, but didn't know from where he was getting his supply.

Planting Evidence

Whilst driving a Panda car with a colleague as passenger in Stanley Gardens on a busy Saturday afternoon, we spotted two youths apparently engaged in a drug deal. They spotted the police car. One of them jumped over a low metal railing into a small communal garden area. I followed and saw him pushing something into the ground at the base of a tree. I recovered a small plastic bag containing a quantity of herbal substance which he admitted was cannabis and said that he had just bought it.

He was arrested and subsequently appeared at Marylebone Magistrates Court in front of a stipendiary Magistrate and pleaded guilty to possession. I gave the brief facts of the case. The Magistrates head jerked up and he looked at me quizzically when I said that the drugs had been 'planted'. He smiled when I explained the circumstances. Magistrates did have a sense of humour after all.

On Prescription? I Don't Think So

The theft of prescription pads from doctors' surgeries was a favourite ploy in the late 60 and early 70s. Some doctors were lackadaisical in their security and would leave the pads (often pre-stamped with the surgeries' details) on their desks. Their theft was an easy exercise by unscrupulous drug addicts who would then sell them on or use them themselves to obtain prescription drugs. One or two doctors turned a blind eye, becoming Nelson-like or subliminally conspiratorial. Perhaps they thought they were 'helping' society but their patients were dragged into the depths of despair. That there was a lucrative profit to be made by these practitioners probably had nothing to do with it! Uppers and downers and Methadone – a heroin substitute - were the favourite tipples.

These unfortunates were often beyond help. Their heroin addiction took them into a previously unforeseen world where their bodies could not cope with the excess of foreign, and often lethal, substances. They became thin, malnourished and thence emaciated, incoherent, anti-social, anti-authoritarian, devious and unscrupulous. They had to beg, borrow or, more often, steal to maintain their habit. Shop-lifting and burglary became their daily routine. They wandered around in a dazed condition in their scruffy unclean clothes and often long dirty hair. They gathered scraps of vegetables that had been left over or dropped when the stalls were packed up for the evening in the Portobello Road or Golbourne Road. Searching their squats or flats was a challenge: the stench from rotten vegetables was often over-powering and it was difficult not to retch when searching their waste-bins. What better place to hide the smell of drugs and also to deter an officer or dog from searching too far?

How Much?

The other extreme was when we were informed by a Judge that his daughter had involved herself with an undesirable (at least to the Judge) and that they were using drugs which he abhorred. A warrant was issued for their top floor flat in Elgin Crescent and, believe it or not, both the Superintendent and the Chief Inspector decided to come on the raid. It was about 11pm. I think the Ladbroke Arms pub had been their previous stop! These two officers searched the bedroom which fronted on to the street with no good result. I then went in and, on searching a pair of the young man's trousers which were on the bed, I found a wrap of cannabis. The man readily admitted it was his and, in his rather posh voice, asked if I could dispose of it as the window was open. Out aloud I calculated my present salary, and my future salary prospects, took an average and then multiplied that by the years I had left to serve and informed him that £1 million to £1 ½ million would be the minimum I would accept. He got the message. We didn't charge him with attempting to bribe a police officer.

Just Another Inkling

On a very cold December day we received information from a highly reliable informant that any type of illegally obtained prescription drugs would be found in the top floor of a multi-flatted terraced house in Tavistock Road. Having secured a search warrant we quietly entered the front door and crept up the stairs. However, as we subsequently found out, we had been spotted. The occupants, two male and two female, were obviously not surprised by our clandestine entry and, unusually, were unfazed by our presence. We searched diligently, including the waste bins. There was a nasty smell which turned out to be a large amount of rotting Brussels sprouts in their net container. The 'principal' spokesman was too assured of himself and I questioned him closely but no admissions were forthcoming.

I then had one of those instinctive moments. I remembered that I had noticed the window on the mezzanine landing below the flat had been open. Why, on a very cold day? I went downstairs and there, hanging outside the window, was a plastic bag containing many types of drugs. When I showed them to the occupant he smiled.

"I knew you would find them," he said.

Another job done!

Scripts

Then there was the time when I saw a hippy-dressed man putting something behind a green telephone junction box. When he disappeared into All Saints Road I checked and found a large pad of prescriptions with the doctor's surgery stamp on each of them. There was also a small quantity of 'legal' prescription drugs. I awaited his return and when he had retrieved the items I stopped and arrested him. He was very surprised that I knew where he had hidden his contraband. Job done.

White Coats

Staying with the medical theme, I relate a story about Boots, the chemist. There was a fairly large store in Portobello Road. As we drove slowly past in Bravo 3 in the early hours of the morning, we noticed three men in white coats in the shop which was all lit up. They waved to us and we initially thought that they might be stock-taking. However, my wise old driver, drove on and called for assistance which arrived very quickly just in time to see the three men attempting to escape from the back. After short chases and diligent searches all three were captured. Their haul would have been huge.

Too Good to be True

Whilst in plain clothes with another officer patrolling in the area of Pembridge Square which had a high burglary rate, we stopped two youths who happened to be French. They were smoking a reefer which they discarded when we introduced ourselves. One of them was compliant and stood very quietly. The other, however, was aggressive and started struggling violently. When he and I were on the ground an elderly lady approached swinging her handbag. I told her that I was a police officer and asked her to find a phone, dial 999 and ask for assistance.

She kept saying,"Let him go, let him go," hitting me with the bag. Unexpected unhelpfulness came from the most surprising people.

The sequel: after positive analysis the 'stroppy' youth appeared at Chelsea Juvenile Court and was sentenced to a conditional discharge. The other youth, who had voluntarily returned from France, appeared at Marylebone Magistrates Court before a stipendiary magistrate. The defendant pleaded guilty. I gave the brief facts and mentioned that the other youth had been very volatile and told him the sentence that he had received. The magistrate, who was known to be against illegal drugs, sentenced the defendant to 3 months imprisonment. The clerk of the court whispered to the magistrate that he could not issue that sentence for a first offence for possession of a small quantity of cannabis. The magistrate then issued the sentence of a £50 fine. The defendant indicated to the gaoler police officer that he did not have enough money to pay the fine. The magistrate then sentenced him to 3 months in prison in default of payment.

Justice? I despair.

Can They Have It Both Ways?

A short time after this, a directive was sent out that if there was a quantified minimal amount of cannabis then the arrested person would not be charged. I had previously arrested someone with a small amount but by the time it was analysed and he appeared in court in front of three lay magistrates, the directive was in force. They dismissed the case and I was not too pleased so, tongue in cheek, I asked the magistrates if I could, therefore, return the small amount to the defendant as he had not committed any offence. Both they and the court Police Inspector were dumbfounded. The magistrates issued an order that the drugs be destroyed.

The court Inspector gave me a b ....g. Was I right or was I wrong?

We'ed Missed It

The scrap-yard mentioned elsewhere featured in another interesting incident. Our very tight handpicked drugs team had information that a boatload of cannabis was on its way to the UK from Morocco via Spain and those in the yard were the main importers. With the necessary authority and paperwork completed, a listening bug was placed in the operative caravan on site during the night. The technical men, aided by others including a dog handler with his long catching pole, scaled the corrugated iron fence. The three snarling Alsatians, who were growlingly pacing the yard, slinked and hid under the caravan: so much for guard dogs. A listening device was installed in a nearby tower block overlooking the site and was monitored and tape recorded each day.

Unfortunately there was a breakdown in communications whereby one Saturday night/Sunday morning it was not being monitored but, on listening to the tapes on Sunday morning, it was evident that the boat had arrived in a port on the South coast adjacent to the Isle of Wight. Through liaison with a county's Regional Crime Squad their motorcyclist was immediately dispatched to make enquiries. Customs knew nothing about it and nor did the locals. He came back with a negative reply. What a disappointment. Apparently it had been a wild night with a choppy sea.

One of the scoundrels, on return to the yard, was recorded to say, "I fell in and my balls were like walnuts." (I've missed out the universal expletives.)

The boat or cannabis was never found. The following year that motorcyclist was back at BH on another job and during conversation about the above he admitted that on that night "an old tub had come in and gone up the Hamble River" but he had discounted it.

Popularity is often transitory......

If at First You Don't Succeed

There were many small quantities of drugs, mainly cannabis, found on persons by patrolling uniformed officers. Most large seizures are by specialised plain clothes squads, primarily from Scotland Yard who had the equipment and expertise. Importers were hard to identify and even harder to bring to justice. However I shall relate two significant finds. A small dedicated team of uniformed officers led by a detective sergeant had been set up at Notting Hill to try to deter the flow of drugs into the area prior to the annual Notting Hill Carnival.

An experienced officer had cultivated (appropriate word?) the trust of a very reliable informant who, although not 'clean', was in a position to pass on fantastic information. He indicated a number of large Victorian terraced buildings which were due for demolition. These were in the Maida Vale area. Members of the squad went to reconnoitre the area and when they looked over a garden wall of one of the houses they saw, through the kitchen window, a set of weighing scales with about a half slab of cannabis resin thereon. They ducked down quickly and a search warrant was obtained for the following morning.

As I was an 'honorary' member of the squad (I was the collator at the time) I went with them. My initial job was to open the front door as quickly as possible. It, ostensibly, had three locks on it – one Yale type and two deadlocks. When the building had been surrounded and secured and, at the appointed synchronised time, I hit the door with a sledge hammer. The door immediately flew open and smashed against the inside lobby wall. The Yale had been the only lock that was is in use. I ran in followed by other officers and a drugs' dog. I began trying to smash down the door at the end of the corridor which was proving very difficult. The officers behind me were going into the main area of the house through a side door in the hallway. I heard laughter from the other side of my door and when I eventually smashed through a panel I found that this was the back door and I had been trying to smash my way out. A thorough search of the building, which consisted of two houses that had been knocked into one, revealed some wraps of cocaine and small traces of cannabis on the scales but there was no sign of the large quantity that we were expecting. The occupants, a gang from Dublin, obviously denied having any more than was found and we were perplexed.

After some time the dog-handler decided that he had finished his search and made his way out. As the dog padded down the lobby he suddenly stopped and started sniffing the wall panel lining indicating that he had found something. When the panels were removed there were many wrapped bundles of cannabis resin on shelving constructed in the cavity. When the dog had run in he obviously had not had time to smell it. When they appeared at the Old Bailey the suspects cheekily tried to ask for compensation for the door that I had smashed down, in a squat that didn't belong to them!

Flower Power

The same informant indicted another address in the Kilburn (I think) area where there was allegedly a large quantity of cocaine. It was another three-storey building, the ground floor being occupied by an elderly couple. There were several men on the upper floors and, as we had insufficient officers, we had to handcuff one of the suspects to the stairs where he sat quietly throughout the search. They were all foreign but I cannot remember from where. Two fist-sized wraps of cocaine were found but, again, not the larger haul that we were expecting.

During the search the informant arrived to check what was happening and he was 'arrested' to allay suspicion. He could not help us as to the whereabouts of the main stack and, despite a thorough search, we did not find it. The suspects were arrested. A few days later our informant found out that the drugs had been hidden under a large plant in the front garden. More 'planted' drugs.

What's in a Name?

There was an even more significant operation. Again, as the result of information, an address in Ealing was searched and the occupant arrested for a quantity of heroin or cocaine. (I cannot remember which). This was on a Thursday. I would describe him as an 'old hippie' – aged in middle 50s, greying pony tail and open-toed sandals. Buddha-like, he later sat cross-legged in his cell. He was detained overnight and further information was received in the morning that there might be a domestic garage connected to him. This was searched and, on entry, the smell of cannabis was overwhelming. There was a rivalry between the drugs' dog and a young officer as to who would find it first. The garage was full of old furniture and other household goods as the man's associates were involved in house clearances. The young officer won. He found a cricket bag containing what turned out to be old cannabis resin. The suspect admitted that it was worth about £65,000. The squad were obviously delighted and ecstatic having never found so much cannabis before.

On their return to the station they rang me at home and asked me to come in to celebrate. I was a bit reluctant as I was watching the 'A' Team but they persuaded me. (We called ourselves the 'A' Team from then on.) The idea was to have a couple of pints before going for a curry.

When charged with, and cautioned for possession, the suspect – and I quote his exact words – said, "You found them in my garage and I am saying no more."

This suited us as it was nearly closing time in the Ladbroke Arms pub which is opposite the police station. When he was being put into the cells he turned to one of the officers (a very silver-tongued and persuasive man) and said, "I may as well tell you about the liquid cannabis as well."

When questioned where it was, he intimated that there were two sachets of it in an adjacent garage to the other one. All thoughts of a festive night were abandoned. Some of the squad had already left for home. The Superintendent happened to come in to the station for his routine nightly visit and 'silver tongue' asked him if I could go with the others to execute the raid. I must explain that I had been barred by the Chief Superintendent on the Monday from incurring any more overtime as I was averaging about a 100 hours a month. The guvn'r refused but, after much persuasion, he relented to granting me 2 hours.

We headed off to Ealing. It would have been courteous, if not manda-tory, to inform the local station that we would be coming on to their ground to execute a search but, for some reason, this was overlooked. When the doors of the other garage were opened, again, it was stacked with furniture. The man pretended to make a cursory search at the front of the furniture and declared that the sachets were missing so must have been recovered by his associates, whom, of course, he would not name. However there were two cool boxes, approximately 20" X 16" X 12" each over half full of a dark brown liquid – liquid cannabis - which had the consistency of, and resembled, treacle.

Asked how much there was and how much it had cost he said, A million pounds and if you don't get the guns here soon, you are dead'.

Frantic communications were made to obtain assistance. Apparently the substance was used in the following method. Something like a toothpick was dipped in the liquid and then smeared along the edge of a cigarette before smoking it. Each drop was charged at £5. This cache, however, was to be used to impregnate the old cannabis resin thus making it more potent.

Our suspect then pointed to an adjacent derelict three storey house with basement and said that if we searched it we would find other interesting items. We were all in plain clothes and three of us climbed into the adjacent garden. The other two went around the side of the building as he had indicated that there was a broken window there and that a key to the house was inside. In the meantime I noticed a light through the French (again appropriate as it happens) windows on the ground floor. The garden was at a much lower level and an iron stair-case led up to the windows. As I climbed up, the windows suddenly opened and two males appeared. They were silhouetted against the light. They saw me and, brazenly, I produced my warrant card and said I was a police officer. They turned and ran inside. I suddenly had the gut-wrenching feeling that we had been set up and that this house held the villains and possibly the gunmen. I ran up the remaining steps to see one of the men running towards a package on the table.

Suspecting that it might be a gun I started shouting, "Armed police, armed police," suspecting that it might be a gun. I then grabbed the nearest of the two and pushed him up against the wall.

Luckily uniformed officers from Ealing had just arrived and we discovered that the two youths were French and were squatting. The package was half of a slab of cannabis which they had purchased in Brixton. Little did they know that there was a more lucrative source nearby. The Ealing officers were surprised and delighted that we handed these two over to them. They hadn't seen so much cannabis.

We searched the otherwise human-empty property and, amongst other drug-related paraphernalia, we found a large metal printing press which was being used to impregnate the liquid cannabis into the resin. The 'old hippie' had over 80 keys on him. He was involved with others in house clearances and I believe many of the keys were to gain entry into empty houses. As you can imagine it is very difficult with so many types of keys to identify where they fitted. A dedicated officer managed to identify all of them bar one. Another unoccupied house nearby was subsequently searched and another large haul of cannabis was found. That weekend we spent many hours building up evidence on what was a large scale operation and making other searches. The owner of the many houses that were identified was investigated by Her Majesty's Revenue and Customs (HMRC) and was fined about eight million pounds – an unexpected spin-off.

As a collator my normal hours would be 8 hours a day, Monday to Friday. At that time, if you did not have 8 days' notice, you were paid overtime at double the rate. Suffice to say that as I worked extra time on the Friday, then Saturday and Sunday I clocked up 42 hours overtime. I did not hear a word from the Chief Superintendent.

Who were the other members of the gang? From then on our suspect would only say 'It is staring you in the face' and would not elaborate.

This was frustrating to say the least. However his wife was a little bit more forthcoming and mentioned the name of another man who was using a passport with a false name. She supplied us with both names, enquiries were made and it was discovered that he was wanted. Apparently, four years previously (as a mule/courier) he had left two suitcases full of cannabis at Paris Orly airport suspecting that he might have been rumbled by the Douane (French customs). He had been. British Customs traced him to a flat in Maida Vale where he was living with his girlfriend and their daughter. Customs officers raided the flat on a Sunday morning. Fortunately for the suspect, he had gone out to buy the morning papers and when he returned he saw that the flat door had been broken down so he had just walked away. He had then obtained a false passport using the name of a deceased Irish child, the name of whom he had found on a gravestone. What was amazing was that, despite being a prolific and worldwide drug courier, he had never been arrested anywhere either in his own name or that of the alias.

Investigations were made and it was discovered that his girlfriend was still living at the address which had been raided 4 years previously so our team, in their own authorised cars, went to cover the address until a specialised surveillance team from Scotland Yard could be conjured up. Their luck was in. They saw the suspect leave the flat with his young daughter and get into his car. They tried to follow him with limited vehicle resources and they suspected that he had spotted them (true) so they withdrew.

A nondescript black van was available so I was asked to drive it. The suspect returned to the flat, dropped off his daughter, and drove off, loosely followed by the team and the van. He drove to Hammersmith Grove, parked the car and went into a basement flat. Most of the team had not eaten all day so it was decided that they would go to nearby Shepherds Bush police station for light refreshments. It meant that only two cars and the van remained at the scene to keep observation. It was our intention to follow the man to see if he would lead us to any other gang members.

Unfortunately the suspect decided to leave and drove off towards Stamford Brook where he stopped beside a communal grass area with a telephone kiosk. He got out of his car to make a phone call. We decided that, as we had insufficient vehicles to justify a successful 'follow' we had better arrest him. There was a suggestion that he was a black belt at judo so care had to be taken. I drove the van onto the grass and stopped it in front of the door of the telephone kiosk preventing him from leaving. A very talented policeman, an amateur cartoonist, captured the moment:

P25. Telephone box cartoon

He asked me why we had stopped him. I said that I had been told that there would be a man in the kiosk at quarter to eight with some cannabis on him. I looked, and it was exactly 7.45pm. He looked sceptically at 'innocent' me.

A search revealed he had a very small piece of cannabis resin in his sock — enough to arrest him for that alone. He was very suave and sophisticated, with dark sunglasses on his head and open-toed sandals. He looked a typical rich playboy. It was a very hot evening. He asked what would happen now as he had never been arrested before. I tried to allay his fears and said that he would be taken to the police station, processed, the cannabis would be sent for analysis and he would prob-ably be bailed pending the result.

Whilst waiting for a marked police van I asked him for his name. He gave me the false name, Xxxxxx Xxxxx. It was a typical Irish name. I asked him if he had a middle name. He said he didn't. I asked him if he was Catholic and had he been confirmed. He said he was and that he had. I said that he would have been given a confirmation name and asked him what it was. He was very cool and said he never used it as he did not like it. I knew what it was. I said that as a police officer nothing fazed me. He said the name was "Mary" and I said that name was often used for a confirmation name for boys. He was arrested and taken to Notting Hill police station. Whilst awaiting processing his car was searched and, amongst other things, was a map of South and Southwest England on which were marked various place names. We suspected that these were either drop-off or pick-up points for the drugs operation but we never had the time or resources to investigate them. He was then confronted with his real name, at which point his demeanour of sophisticated self-assurance collapsed and he became compliant.

The basement flat in Hammersmith, which is where he said he stayed with a friend, was searched with a drugs dog. One small cannabis plant was found in the yard at the rear. Down the side of a very heavy old sofa bed a WPS (Woman Police Sergeant) from the TSG (Territorial Support Group) found a plastic bag containing, about £2,000 cash, I think, and three passports (his own, his girlfriend's and his daughter's) and three air tickets to Kenya for the following day. He had been caught just in time. He gave valuable information about how drugs were smuggled into the country by boat either on the Welsh or Scottish west coast and named members of the aristocracy who were involved.

Apparently, whilst in prison awaiting trial regarding the cannabis at Orly Airport, having a false passport and other minor offences, he twice attempted to commit suicide. The court verdict, however, surprised us. The Judge said that there was no evidence that the drugs in France were destined for London so there was no offence in the UK.

He was given a minimal sentence for the passport offence and other minor offences and was released. It had not been possible to prove that he had been involved in the liquid cannabis although he knew and we knew.......

About a year later 'Mary' was arrested at Dover attempting to bring in another large quantity of cannabis and he served a prison sentence. After release he was seen in the Notting Hill area by 'silver tongue' and admitted that he was "s......g" himself when we searched the Hammersmith address as there was a large quantity of cannabis in the sofa. No wonder it was so heavy to move. The drugs dog hadn't detected it either. Some you win and some you lose.

Incidentally, our cross-legged hippy friend at beginning of the tale vowed that if he was sentenced to more than 7 years in prison (why that arbitrary number, I have no idea) he would commit suicide.

Funnily, he was sentenced to 7 years imprisonment.

P26. Carnival drugs newspaper cutting

CHAPTER 20

BELLS, WHISTLES, CHIN STRAPS AND TIES.

Whistle Down the Wind

I used the whistle twice in my career both times with excellent results. Again, not long in 'The Job' (as the Police Force was called and the Police Service still is), I had occasion to speak to the driver of a van that was double-parked in Westbourne Grove near the junction with the traffic lights at Kensington Park Road (KPR) on a very busy Saturday morning.

The response by the driver was the usual, "I'm just moving guvn'r."

However, I had noticed that the RFL had a different number to the registration of the van. When questioned, the driver stated it was his van but when I pointed out the discrepancy on the RFL he suddenly took off and ran down KPR. I chased after him and, as usual, my helmet was discarded and I took out my whistle. We did not have radios in those days. As I ran after him blowing my whistle I was losing ground. However a member of the public sized up the situation very quickly and, spreading his arms out, he succeeded in slowing the offender down sufficiently for me to catch him. A search of the vehicle found that it was full of stolen property from a shop burglary the night before, on Harrow Road section which is adjacent to Notting Hill.

Unusually, the Detective Sergeant asked if I wished to sit in on the interview but to remain silent. The DS was very fair and immediately struck up a rapport with the alleged thief. He questioned him very closely about his movements on the previous Thursday evening, suspecting that he may have been involved in the burglary as opposed to just handling stolen property. The suspect was very frank. He was able to state that he had been working on the Thursday, had returned home for dinner which his wife could verify. He had then gone to his local pub where he played darts until after closing time which could be verified by any number of his mates. He had then returned home, watched television with his wife and they had then gone to bed and had not risen until the following morning. He said his wife could verify his alibi which seemed to be fool-proof. The DS questioned him very carefully but could not shake his story. The suspect was very smug.

"You seem to remember everything that happened on Thursday night and you have a cast iron alibi. Now this burglary happened on Friday night so you should be able to tell me exactly what you did then," commented the DS.

The poor man was deflated as he realised that he had been conned. He immediately admitted the offence of breaking and entering.

I have never forgotten that lesson nor the words of my first Chief Superintendent (yes, that one) who happened to come into the charge room. I had only been in 'The Job' for 7 months. He said, "Well done, Scott." That, of course, boosted my ego and I was determined that I would always try my best.

As a result, I received a commendation, dated 19th July 1966 from the Divisional Superintendent on 'B' Division: -

"Dear Scott,
Superintendent XXXX has brought to my notice the excellent arrest you made
of a man for workshop breaking and larceny on 16th July. My congratulations
and thanks for the ability you displayed in effecting this useful arrest."

Who Cares? He Didn't.

This act of encouragement was in stark contrast to the reply by a Chief Superintendent some 20 years later when I was the collator. I had noticed that one of the reliefs (D Relief, I think) had had an outstanding night shift (this was a three-week tour) with many good arrests so, remembering the boost I had received, I suggested to the Chief Superintendent that he speak to that relief when they came on to late turn (2pm after finishing night duty at 6am). He refused and told me that was their Inspector's job. I was astounded and said that the Inspector saw them every day and an acknowledgement for work well done would be more beneficial from a person of his rank. The phrases 'Man Management' and 'Ivory Towers' spring to mind! I guess I was 'whistling in the wind'.

Whistle Again

The second incident was in Notting Hill Gate when I was chasing someone. I was blowing my whistle when another passer-by helped to stop the man. I cannot remember the exact circumstances but we were always appreciative of the help given by members of the public.

Don't Ring Me, I'll Ring You

In Ladbroke Grove just north of the junction with Lancaster Road, there were multi-flats above the shops. The entrances were set back and they were a convenient recess to keep out of the weather and out of sight for observations purposes. My colleague and I, in full uniform, were hiding in a doorway one night when we heard shouting,

"Hello, who is it?"

We peeked out but saw no one. A short time later there was more shouting and we again looked out but saw no-one.

On the third occasion the voice said, angrily, "Who is ringing the bell?"

I suddenly realised that I had been leaning against a row of bell pushes for the flats above. We awaited a short time and then sheepishly crept away.

Chin Straps and Ties

Helmets were fitted with chin straps which were helpful in a strong wind. These had to be worn down although, in summer time, this regu-lation was relaxed because if one wore it down for any length of time a white, un-sunburnt, stripe might be seen down the side of the cheeks thus marking one as a police officer. With the strap down there was a potential of being strangled if someone pulled the helmet backwards.

In later years, a normal tie was replaced by one with a pre-made knot and the tie just clipped under the shirt collar to prevent choking. In my early days we wore blue long-sleeved shirts with detachable collars which were fastened by studs front and rear. A dark mark was often seen on the throat where the front stud pressed. They were replaced by white shirts with attached collar, either long-sleeved or (later) short-sleeved for summer wear. One could not fold up the sleeves of the former, neatly folded 1" above the elbow, in hot weather unless autho-rised by the Inspector, and all officers on the sub-division had to comply at the same time. Rules are rules.

Other pieces of equipment carried were a whistle and a truncheon made of Lignum Vitae – a very hard wood. When I joined the Force in 1965 handcuffs were not carried until, I think, the early 1980s.

CHAPTER 21

COURTING CONTROVERSY

(Embarristing?)

Another Unlucky Barrister

Whilst on Bravo 3 we received a call to two men acting suspiciously in Pembridge Road and Notting Hill Gate. We found the men and, as I was in plain clothes, I was dropped off to watch them. They kept going into different shops, staying a few minutes and then leaving not having purchased anything. By their manner they had obviously been drinking. They were reasonably dressed in suits, shirts and ties.

Eventually they walked down Ladbroke Road and got into a parked Ford Consul motor car. They sat there for some time. I was joined by a young passing uniformed officer and we kept observation. The round rear light cluster was made up of three segments. One was the red reflector, one was for the brake light and the other was for the amber indicator light. As we watched, one of the red segments kept coming on and off at sporadic intervals.

The car was in between two other cars and there was not much manoeuvrable space. I was hoping that Bravo 3 would reappear (we had no radio) but suddenly the car started reversing. Fearing that he was going to drive whilst under the influence of drink I rushed up to the driver's door just in time to see him take the keys out of the ignition and drop them between his knees. We did not have a breathalyser kit which had to be administered by a police officer in full uniform. Luckily Bravo 3 came back and the man gave a positive sample of breath and he was arrested and charged.

Don't ask me why, perhaps it was ordained, but I went out and checked which segment was which and discovered that the flashing segment was indeed the brake light and it would not come on and off unless the keys were in the ignition. I satisfied myself that I had not been mistaken.

There was a plea of 'Not Guilty' at Magistrates Court so the case was referred to the Crown Court. In my evidence I explained that the car had only reversed about six inches before we stopped it. This was to be in my favour when our Queen's Counsel pointed out to the jury that 'I could have exaggerated but I had told the truth'.

The Queen's Counsel for the defence commented, "I put it to you officer that it was not the brake lights you saw coming on and off but the reflection of headlights of other passing motor vehicles."

"No M'Lud."

The Barrister continued in the same vein repeatedly suggesting that this was in fact the case.

I eventually said, "Other passing vehicles did not have their headlights at that time of day."

"Come officer, are you trying to tell the members of the jury that at 8pm on the 21st May (or whatever date and time it was – I cannot remember) other vehicles did not have their headlights on? How could you possibly remember that?"

I nonchalantly flicked to the back of my incident report book and said, "Because lighting up time that day wasn't until 9pm."

Lighting-up times (between half an hour after sunset and half an hour before sunrise) are published in Police Orders (was it two or three times a week?) but why did I think about checking them on the day? I have never done it before or since. The world is a weird place.

Our Barrister looked at me quizzically and in astonishment. I gave him a quick nod. He took out his diary, looked up the relevant lighting up times, smiled and showed it to the defence counsel. A short silence prevailed before the Judge interrupted and said, "Any further questions Mr...?"

Down hearted, the defence counsel said, "No further questions, M'Lud," and sat down.

Another victory.

And Another Embarrassed Barrister

Taking over from the crew of Bravo 3 one morning at 6.45am, my colleague and I were informed that there had been an accident whereby a large lorry had ploughed into the railings of a terraced house in Tavistock Crescent and was overhanging the basement area.

We decided to take a gander and we then received a call from MP (Scotland Yard radio room) that the two suspects were near Ladbroke Grove Underground station. We raced there where we were met by a black man who said the two white men who had been in the lorry, had just gone down Lancaster Road towards Nottingdale – both with suits and the younger one, about 25 years old, with dyed blonde hair. He dashed for his train before we could get his details. We drove into Lancaster Road and, sure enough, the only people there were two men walking unsteadily on the pavement. One had dyed blonde hair. They were obviously very drunk so we arrested them for that.

When searched at the station broken glass was found in the left-hand side pocket of the older man, aged about 45. We went to the scene of the incident and noticed that the side quarter light of the lorry was broken and the glass was similar to that found on the man. It would have been too expensive to send the samples to the Police laboratory for comparison.

Despite their denials we felt that there was sufficient evidence for a charge which was all that was required to bring the men before a court. We gave our evidence to the custody sergeant. However our Inspector said that the men should not be charged. I was not happy with this decision but I went up to the CID office to enter the details of the accident and the taking and driving away of the lorry. (It only became the theft of a vehicle if it hadn't been recovered within a month). I was relating the story to some CID officers who agreed with me, when the Inspector came in and ordered me, in no uncertain terms, to go back out to the streets. We went to our satellite station, Nottingdale, for a cup of tea and were discussing the incident with the officers there when the Inspector came in again and ordered us back to the streets.

By 9am a SOCO (Scenes of Crimes Officer) came to examine the vehicle and he pointed out to me a clothing button which was in the well of the cab of the lorry on the passenger side. (No, there was no thread attached.....). I took it and compared it with the ones on the suit of the older man and, sure enough, it had a button missing and it was identical. I held the button in my hand and went to the Inspector.

"I've got them Guvn'r," and opened my hand.

He looked at me disdainfully. He obviously thought that I had taken umbrage and had conveniently 'found' the button. He said that all I was interested in was helping to claim insurance compensation for the owners of the damaged property. Something like that would never have entered my head. He still refused to have them charged so I said that I would take the matter up with the Chief Superintendent as I felt there was sufficient evidence to prefer the charge. He then relented and said, "I hope they plead guilty for your sake."

Naturally they pleaded not guilty and appeared at Knightsbridge Crown Court.

I was in charge of the case which is unusual as a CID officer would normally be dealing with it. The Prosecution Barrister who is, after all, only one's spokesman, should be guided by the officer in the case. Our Barrister was dismissive of my suggestions and interventions which, again, annoyed me as this was now a matter of pride. Our evidence was impeccable. The defendants, who were of the Irish travelling community and were living on an authorised site in Nottingdale, went in the witness box and gave spurious evidence. When I pointed this out to our Barrister he ignored me. I was not happy because I desperately wanted to prove the Inspector wrong. The jury was sent out and as we stood outside the court room I heard the defence Barrister say something to our Barrister,

"If they are found guilty I intend to appeal."

"Are you now?" I thought and went up to them.

"Did I hear right that you intend to appeal if they are found guilty?" I queried the defence counsel.

"Of course" he replied, haughtily looking down at me.

"Then I intend reporting you to the Bar Council."

Now this is a very, very serious matter for a Barrister.

"You can't do that PC Scott: on what grounds?" our Counsel asked.

"Did you get a copy of the previous convictions (Form 609) of.... ?" (the younger man), I inquired of the defence Counsel. I knew he had because I had served them on him as was the condition at the time.

"Of course I have."

"How come then that you put it to the jury that your client didn't have a driving licence (probably true) and couldn't drive and he confirmed it from the witness box, yet he has seven previous convictions for taking and driving away motor vehicles?"

(Do you know any traveller that couldn't drive, - probably from the age of about 12 years?) There was a bit of harrumphing and mumbling between the two legal eagles - or should it be squawking? The jury returned verdicts of guilty within 20 minutes. Oh, the joy! Returning to the station I couldn't wait to see the Inspector.

"They were found guilty, sir," I told him.

He shouted at me and said, "That just shows me then!" He then muttered sotto voce, "I was wrong."

Well said – he went back up in my estimation for being so humble. He believed my evidence from then on.

They did not appeal.

You Can Run but You Cannot Hide

Portobello Road was a one-way system running north until it reached the junction with Cambridge Gardens. One afternoon, probably a Saturday as the road was busy, I was driving Bravo 3 at a crawling pace with a uniformed operator (RIP). We saw a black youth carrying a carrier bag, which seemed to be heavy, walking south on the east footpath. I stopped and looked at him. He looked back, turned around and started walking back towards Cambridge Gardens, glancing occasionally behind him. I drove parallel to him and he turned round again so I put the car in reverse. He did this twice and then he suddenly dropped the bag and ran toward and then up Tavistock Road. My colleague got out and began to chase him as I began to reverse through several pedestrians, but I deemed this to be unsafe so I also got out of the car. The suspect ran to an open door in which was standing an elderly black man who seemed to weigh up the situation and slammed the door in the face of the suspect, thus allowing him to be caught.

My initial thoughts were that the bag and contents would have disappeared but it was still lying in the roadway. I had the young man in an arm-lock and bent down to pick up the bag. I was suddenly surrounded by a gang of people both male and female, who tried to release the prisoner and pull the bag from my grasp. It was a tussle and he was getting the worst of it: every time I tried to deflect blows and hang on to the bag his arm was being twisted. My colleague called for assistance on the radio and luckily the station van, with the driver only, came hurtling along Cambridge Gardens and into Portobello Road. Incongruously I thought, 'He is driving the wrong way down a one way street'. Were we pleased to see him! Normally the van would have at

least two officers on board and when they saw the van the crowd scattered, allowing us to upload the detainee.

A quirk occurred which I cannot remember why or explain. The
following morning the youth was interviewed in a holding cell at
Marylebone Magistrates court before his appearance. It was conducted
by a Detective Constable (DC) who took contemporaneous notes.
Also present was a legal representative who happened to be a barrister.
Had he already been at Court and taken advantage of the situation or
had he been hired to advise the man? I don't know. Fast forward to the
defendant's appearance at Knightsbridge Crown Court, having pleaded
'not guilty' to burglary and/or handling stolen goods. Enquiries had
revealed that the contents of the bag were 78 RPM records which were
the part proceeds of a house burglary the night before. Strangely, the
defence barrister was the same one who had been in the cell some
months beforehand. He wore brown shoes which I thought were 'out
of step'.

During cross examination of the DC the 'legal eagle' kept trying to
correct the verbal evidence. For example when the DC said that the
defendant had said "No'" to a question, the barrister, looking at some
notes said, "Officer, I have recorded that he said, "No, No."

He continued to challenge the officer about the alleged discrepancy
between each other's version. The Judge intervened and established
that the barrister had been present during the Magistrates Court interview and asked him if he wished to continue as the legal representative
or become a material witness. He still wished to represent his client
but did not change his tactics whereby the Judge told him that if he
continued he would report him to the Bar Council. He was oblivious
to the warning, persisting in the same vein. He was so bad that I
wondered if he were an actual barrister.

The burglary victim was a young woman. The barrister kept asking her
about her love life, how many boyfriends had she had and how often
did she have sex. No-one knew where this was heading and the Judge
advised the girl that she did not have to answer such personal ques-

tions. She was unmoved and brilliantly answered all the impertinent queries. The inquisitor eventually came to the point.

"I put it to you that it was your boyfriend who committed the burglary because he was annoyed at you."

"No", rectified the girl, "my boyfriend was in Dublin that night."

"He could have flown over without your knowledge, committed the burglary and flown back," was the riposte.

Such absurdity. No explanation of how his client was in possession of the goods unless, of course, he was in cahoots with the suitor. He then queried her as to how she knew the records were hers.

"Because my initials are on the record sleeves," she replied.

That nearly deflated him but he continued with more inane questions. He was a disgrace to the profession. His client was found guilty and the upshot was that, as he was an illegal immigrant, he would be deported back to his Caribbean island - the client, I mean.

Oops! I forgot to mention two other gems.

"Have you ever seen my client before?" queried our persistent inter-rogator.

"I cannot see him now," replied the exasperated damsel.

Our learned friend whipped back his gown, spun around (as did everyone else) to see only the two prison warders on either ends of the dock. The alleged defendant had ducked down with his head in his hands, probably because he was bored with proceedings or he was disillusioned with the antics of his brief.

"Oi!" shouted the counsel loudly in an otherwise silent room.

As per the 'Carry On' series, a titter ran through the court. That is when the Judge reported him to the Bar Council.

Under examination I was faced with the habitual accusation, "You only stopped my client because he was black."

Again, for some uncanny and inexplicable premonition, I had come prepared and was able to prove that, on that day, we had stopped three white people. Had I anticipated the allegation?

The whimsy of a Crown Court...

Judge for Yourself

There were unoccupied flats above a row of shops in Notting Hill Gate. The shops were one storey high with flat roofs and the two storey flats were set back. The latter had sliding panelled windows. Squatters had occupied the flats and as we tried to evict them, standing on the flat roof, one of the squatters slammed the window shut on my arm and broke my watch. He was eventually dragged out and arrested. For some reason, which I cannot now remember, he appeared at a recently refurbished, quite magnificent, Knightsbridge Crown Court.

I was in charge of the case. There was concern about the young man's mental condition and before he was granted bail the Judge requested that I come to Judges' Chambers to discuss the matter. I had no idea what this would entail suspecting that I was about to be given a lecture about my conduct in Court. With trepidation I walked through the court and followed him through a side door.

Much to my surprise he went into a small narrow room which was lined with the old green tiles prevalent in Lipton's tea shops at the time. The contrast between that and the opulent court room was staggering. He took off his wig and proceeded to make the two of us a pot of tea – with biscuits as an addition. I don't know if he went up in my estimation for being so humble or down in my estimation for bursting the bubble of esteem. I think the former. We had a cosy chat with no sign of any airs or graces and he wanted to know the circumstances of the case before he granted bail as he was concerned about the man's mental condition. It was felt that he would receive better treatment in prison before his trial rather than be let loose in society. We returned to court and the formal proceedings were continued. I was never in awe of Judges again having witnessed their humanitarian and practical side.

There was an article and photograph in The Sun newspaper of 12th January 1974 regarding this incident.

Here Come the Moroccans

The north-east corner of the Notting Hill area, known as North Kensington around the Golborne Road area, was less salubrious. There was an influx of migrants from many airts and, increasingly, from North Africa. One would have to be a polyglot to understand the diversity of foreign languages and regional accents. Accommodation was just above slum level with those ruthless landlords preying on the poor, and sometimes illiterate, incomers. Some of their income was sustained and augmented by petty thieving, which brings me to another encounter.

The theft of pedal cycles was on the increase. Despite the advice and the publicity regarding marking their cycles or even writing down the serial number, most people were either sceptical, too lazy or had other reasons not to take advantage of the advice. Subsequently it was very difficult to prove the lawful possession of bikes especially when they were cannibalised and morphed into completely different structures. There was a spate of these thefts. On one occasion, with another officer, I stopped several youths who were riding around and it was obvious that most of the bikes had been 'altered'. They also had stolen property on them. I decided that more in-depth questioning was required so I brought them to the station. What a hornets' nest.

There were three Moroccans and one Portuguese boy. They lied and lied and lied despite overwhelming evidence of their guilt. Not only had they been stealing pedal cycles but had been involved in burglaries and theft (shoplifting). I questioned them all carefully in the presence of their respective parent/s and interpreters. It took me about three weeks to dissect the various offences and accumulate sufficient evidence to charge each of them with individual or collective charges.

They eventually appeared at Chelsea Juvenile Court. Between them they pleaded guilty to 18 charges but not guilty to many others to which I offered no evidence. Because some of the charges were committed by a mixture of the miscreants, to calculate the amount of compensation for each was like a Gordian knot. The Magistrate was a tetchy character. I had registered all the separate offences for each youth and calculated their individual penance. They were very complicated but, because I had been meticulous, I was confident that I would be able to explain my evidence succinctly. Copies had been handed to the magistrate and their counsel for their benefit. The magistrate perused my documents and said that he did not want it presented that way: he wanted, each offence dissected giving the details of which culprit was responsible. This would have been a mammoth task to try to unravel the intricacies.

I gulped. I gave my due respects to the Magistrate and invited him to listen to my evidence "which, I am sure, Your Worship, you will understand".

He said, "You can start, PC Scott, but when I tell you to stop you will do it my way."

I then gave the brief facts which took over 20 minutes. The magistrate remained quiet throughout. All defendants were made subject of Supervision Orders for a year and ordered to pay their respective dues. After the case I was commended by the Magistrate. To receive one at Juvenile Court was an accolade indeed. I was more proud of that than the ones I had received for alleged bravery.

The Magistrate, Mr Silverman, said:

"I would like to congratulate you on the way you have presented the case. This was an extremely difficult case to present, and it must have involved you in a lot of work."

I also received a Deputy Assistant Commissioner's (DACs) commendation

"for diligence and ability in a case of
Burglary, theft and other offences."

Stop or Else (you will appear in Court)

An irate driver came into Notting Hill Police station to report that he had been involved in a traffic accident (called 'collision' now) on Hammersmith section. I recorded the details and examined his vehicle noting the height of the damage, the length of the scratches and the colour of the residue paint on the car etc. Enquiries were made and the culprit identified.

The upshot was that the alleged offender, a pleasant young man, appeared before West London Magistrates court for the offences of 'Failing to stop and Failing to Report an accident'. He pleaded 'Not Guilty' and represented himself. The prosecution was conducted by a Hammersmith Sergeant. I gave my evidence as did the 'injured' party. The accused gave his evidence. He was found 'Guilty'.

After the case the cantankerous Magistrate, made the following comments:

"I have never heard a case where two witnesses, both the private witness and the police officer have given better evidence, or where a case of this nature has been so well prepared."

Admirable words, one might say. However, he had missed someone out. The young man conducted himself so well, being confident and respectful and lucid, that the Sergeant and I tried to persuade him to join the police force where he would have made an excellent officer. Whether he did or not, is beyond my knowledge.

. . .

A story goes that a defendant was accused of dangerous driving around Hammersmith Broadway. The same cantankerous magistrate dismissed the case before any evidence was given by pronouncing,

"It is impossible to drive around Hammersmith Broadway without driving dangerously."

Living Like a Lord (with his 'lady')

Another case comes to mind at Marylebone Magistrates Court. A droll Scottish policeman from Harrow Road station, with a strong Glaswegian accent, had given the brief facts regarding the arrest of a prostitute who had been running a brothel. She was white, in her middle 20s, had peroxide blonde hair, was well overweight, wore no make-up and, frankly, looked a mess. Having been fined she went up to the spectators gallery to await the verdict on her black pimp who had pleaded guilty of 'living off the earnings of a prostitute'.

The officer addressed the stipendiary magistrate, who was a very fair but pernickety man and would have known the officer after many court appearances, and began to give the man's antecedents.

"Your Worship, XXXXX XXXXX, lives with his common-law wife at...."

"Officer," he interrupted, "there may be such a thing in the laws of Scotland as a 'common-law wife' but there is no such a thing in England. Could you rephrase it please?"

Using another Scottish expression the officer said, "Certainly Your Worship. He lives with his 'good lady'......"

Well, the Court fell about laughing as did the magistrate and the 'good lady' who sniggered in the gallery. It livened up the usual humdrum of the court.

Thou Shalt Not Swear in Court

Another pithy story springs to mind. A traffic patrol officer, fully
regaled in his jodhpurs and boots, was giving evidence one morning
regarding a case of disorderly behaviour. He included the details that
the miscreant had used the word,'f.....g'. The magistrate dismissed the
case saying that the word was used so frequently that it was no longer
classed as an objectionable word. However he was mortified when the
same officer, that afternoon, in his evidence regarding a noisy motor
cycle, stated that "it had a 'f.....g' big hole in the exhaust."

Thou Shalt Swear in Court

I was accused by a barrister in court of calling his client "a black
b.....d." I objected to the Judge stating that I did not swear (true)
unless it was part of verbal evidence. He made the succinct and witty
observation that, "You swore when you took the oath, officer." The
allegation was withdrawn.

My children had never heard me swear until I related the first 'shaggy
dog' story. Golf, I am afraid, has changed my phraseology.

Marylebone Magistrates Court

This covered the jurisdiction of not only Notting Hill but also 'D' division stations – Harrow Road, Paddington, and Marylebone. If you had
an arrest on night duty or had a prisoner on remand, you had to be at
court by 10am or 10.30am at the latest. If you booked off at 6am (or
7am if you were on the RT car) you maybe had just enough time to get
home (I lived in Ealing), grab two hours sleep and a bit of breakfast,
before you had to be at the court in Paddington.

The timing of your appearance with your prisoner before the magistrate depended on the whim of the court gaoler. He had to juggle with
many diverse cases from straight remands to protracted applications
for bail or hearing cases. You did not want to upset the gaoler!
However, if the morning list had not finished your case could be put

off until 2pm or much later. You then had to return home and try to sleep for a few hours, during which time the children would be home from school so uninterrupted sleep was a novelty. After a late dinner you had to be back on duty by 9.45pm or 10.45pm. To compensate for these inconveniences, you were allocated four hours overtime plus two hours travelling time, no matter how long you stayed at court. With three weeks of night duty on the trot and with multiple court appearances during that time, it is little wonder that some officers succumbed to ill health.

Dickensian conditions were an appropriate description of the dark and dingy conditions at court. The small communal gaolers' office was usually crammed with policemen 'sleeping' standing up and mixing with those prisoners who were either on remand or had been arrested the day before and had not been granted bail. The majority were sobering-up drunks or vagrants with their associated swearing, snuffles, smells, snide remarks, shoe-shuffling and sympathetic pleadings. There was one direct telephone line to New Scotland Yard's fingerprint department. You had to check your prisoner's details as, surprisingly, some gave false details at time of arrest! There would be queues of officers waiting for their individual results, so any delay was, again, reliant on the speed of an NSY (New Scotland Yard) officer.

The main (No. 1) court was presided over by a stipendiary magistrate (Your Worship) who was a salaried professional lawyer who would have had vast experience of many diverse criminal activities. Some minor cases, which can only be heard at a magistrate's court, would be summary and would be dealt with a maximum of 6 months imprisonment for one offence to a maximum of 12 months. If this was deemed insufficient punishment usually the case would be referred to a Crown Court as would more serious indictable only offences. There are hybrid or 'either-way' offences which can be dealt with at either court depending on the severity of the case.

Lay magistrates (affectionately known as 'Muppets'), made up of, usually, three Justices of the Peace on the Bench, ran other courts guided and supervised by Justices clerks whose role was to ensure that the law is adhered to and the proceedings are accurately dealt with.

There were three courts within the building. The 'fourth' court was the Harcourt Arms pub just 2 minutes' walk away where one could meet the magistrates in an informal setting.

Hang It on the Coat Hanger

As previously mentioned, Portobello Road was a hive of activity on a Saturday afternoon when the fruit and veg. stalls were augmented by antique stalls and open antique shops. While standing with a colleague perusing the crowd, I noticed a young man and woman discard two wooden coat-hangers. I was curious. We eventually stopped them and they were carrying two pairs of new jeans with no price labels on them. They stated they had bought them from a clothes rack outside a jeans shop but couldn't remember where. However, they were an unusual style and I had noticed similar ones earlier outside a particular shop. They willingly returned to the shop where jeans of the same style were displayed on a rack outside. The shopkeeper identified the jeans as being his but said that he had not sold any that day. Well, that was a leg-up! Now it was a hands-up job.

At court on the Monday I gave the brief facts.

"What made you stop them when they threw two coat hangers away?" queried the puzzled magistrate.

I replied, "I am a Scotsman, Your Worship, and the coat hangers are worth one and sixpence (7 ½p) each and I wouldn't throw money like that away."

I think he was amused and impressed – well, maybe not impressed but certainly amused. That 'inkling' again.

CHAPTER 22
INTERNATIONAL TRAVEL

Escort 1 (England)

If a wanted person is arrested elsewhere it is usual, if possible, for one of the arresting officers or charging officer to escort them back to the original charging police station. This is because they can positively identify him/her.

One day my sergeant told me that he had sent an arrest request to the police at Folkestone that morning for a man who was wanted for a fairly trivial offence and asked, if he were arrested that day, whether I would accompany him. Of course I would. Having had a couple of pints in The Mitre after early turn (which was normal) I went back to the police flat where I was living in Ealing. I knew I was expected to lay a carpet in the front room and when I got home my wife had removed all the furniture and laid it out on the grass area outside. However, as I arrived she informed me that the sergeant had phoned and had arranged for us to travel to Folkestone. There was nothing for it but to dress in my suit and wend my way back to the station.

We took a train to the South coast and asked at the railway station the time of the last train. We were told 10.30pm. We identified the pris-

oner and, because we hadn't eaten, we were directed by the local police
to a Chinese restaurant nearby.

After the meal and quite a few drinks I suddenly looked at my watch
and it was 10.15 pm. We ran back to the police station, booked out the
prisoner, handcuffed him and began running to the railway station. As
we did so he asked us where the car was. We said we were going by
train.

He said, "Not tonight you're not. The last train has gone."

We could hear a train coming along the track and as we burst into the
station I asked the ticket collector if this was the train to London.

"It's the last train and it stops at Ashford," he replied.

What to do? Oh, I thought. "Well Ashford isn't far from Notting Hill"
– thinking of Ashford in Middlesex. Little did I realise it was Ashford,
Kent that he meant.

Onto the train we clambered but had to get out a short time later.
Again, what to do? There we were, in the middle of the night having
had a few drinks and with a handcuffed prisoner. We tried to cajole the
driver of a coal train to take us to London but he declined. It may have
been because the miners' strike was on at the time. As we wandered
over the railway bridge we saw a Panda car and waved it down. The
surliest Sergeant I had ever met was driving. We told our sorry tale
mentioning that the station had given us the wrong information.
Thankfully, he assumed that it was the police station, not the railway
station that we meant and we didn't enlighten him. He gave us a lift to
the police station and the prisoner was put in a cell.

There was now a dilemma as to how we could get back to 'The Smoke'.
It was suggested that their South Kent traffic car could take us to meet
up with the North Kent traffic car and take us far as the MPD
(Metropolitan Police District). Unfortunately both cars were unavail-
able so we had to ring Notting Hill who said they would dispatch a car.
As we sat in the station an Inspector appeared and asked who we were
and what we were doing there. Remember, we were in plain clothes.
When he found out that we were from the Met. he was overjoyed. He

related the fact that when he was escorting a prisoner in King Street, Hammersmith, the man had escaped and he said that before he knew where he was he was surrounded by numerous police cars and the man was captured and that he was forever grateful. He instructed a uniformed officer to take us upstairs for a cup of tea. That would be nice.

Even better, when we got there, it was the bar (they had these in some county stations) and the Detective Chief Superintendent was there waiting for an incident to occur. He assumed we were CID officers and proceeded to ply us with drink (despite our protestations.....). Our transport arrived (it is a long way from Notting Hill) and we eventually got back at about 5.30am. We were supposed to be back on duty at 5.45am but it was 11am before we were (reasonably) sober enough to come back. I would recommend that Chinese Restaurant.

Escort 2 (Wales)

Off to Haverford West for the next episode. Where is that we asked? West Wales they said. Never mind, it is a day out – starting at Paddington. With another officer, a pleasant trip with a buffet car on board ensued. Changing at Cardiff we wound away across southern Wales, full of the joys of life. As before, we had to identify the prisoner. Then it was off to the local for lunch and some liquid refreshment.

Discreetly handcuffed, we escorted the prisoner to Cardiff and changed for Paddington. We began to nod off so we decided to take it in turns to have forty winks. I was asleep when I suddenly jerked awake. There had been a sharp shout from my colleague and I immediately thought that the prisoner had tried to escape. Not so: he was laughing. My colleague had also nodded off whilst smoking and his cigarette had burnt the back of his hand. A singe in time...!

Escort 3 (Scotland)

Nothing can beat this one.

A man, who was wanted for failing to appear at Marylebone Magistrates Court for an attempted theft from a motor vehicle (another trivial offence), was arrested in Falkirk one morning on the request of a Notting Hill Officer who was off-duty at the time of the Scottish arrest. The officer lived in Ruislip (I think) and the local police went round with a message to inform him. However, he was out so they just put the message through the letter-box. Unfortunately he did not return until late at night. Knowing I was Scottish and because he was reluctant to travel, he rang me and asked if I would go on the escort with another officer. I readily agreed and very early the next morning my colleague and I set off by train from Kings Cross to Edinburgh armed with the arrest warrant – the only piece of paper in my briefcase. There were disruptions with planes at the time and, in the event, the prisoner was reluctant to fly anyway. Having climbed the 39 steps at Edinburgh Waverley Station, (Immortalised in the novel 'The Thirty Nine Steps' by John Buchan) we mooched along to Rose Street (reputedly, at the time, to have more licensed premises in one street than anywhere else in the world) and had the usual liquid lunch.

Having checked the train time I telephoned Falkirk Police Station, told them the circumstances and asked how we could get from Falkirk train station to the police station. The response was what I had hoped for: someone would pick us up. On arrival we were met by the station van driven by the shortest police woman that I had ever seen who could barely reach the pedals of the van. No matter. Merrily we entered the charge room of the police station, suited and with collar and tie. The really grumpy Senior Policeman (as they called them) asked us why we were there. I smugly said that we had come from London to pick up a prisoner whom I named.

"He's gan," he said.

"What do you mean he's gone?" I quizzed.

"He went to Glesga Airport this morning."

I was sobering up fast. I said, "How could he? I have the warrant."

I withdrew the only piece of paper from my impressive briefcase. He immediately rang the Detective Inspector (DI). Now, up there, a DI is all powerful.

I asked him, "How could he have been taken when I have the warrant?"

"Get me DC -----," demanded the DI.

The poor DC arrived.

"'Did you take the prisoner to Glasgow Airport this morning?"

"Yes, sir."

"Did you meet an officer from London?"

"Yes, sir."

"Did you see the arrest warrant?"

"No sir."

"Did you see the officer's warrant card?"

"No, sir."

"What was his name?"

"DC -----, sir."

I said, "We don't have a DC ----- at Notting Hill Police Station." I did, however, know that there was one on the crime squad based at Kensington.

I was feeling much happier. The blame had been passed from us to the poor DC. Up to the CID office we went where we met the DC who had originally arrested the suspect the previous morning. He told us that, on his way to court, he had seen the suspect whom he recognised and knew that he was wanted. He asked the man to come to the station with him as he had a message for him, without revealing the true reason. When he was told why he had being arrested on the 'failing to appear' warrant, the man hurled a tray of cups and saucers across the room. A message had been sent to London and that was that.

However, when he had come into the station the following morning the gaoler had asked him what he was going to do with the prisoner in the cell. The DC said that the London police had picked him up the day before but, of course, that wasn't the case. Much gnashing of teeth. The decision was made to take the prisoner before the local Sheriff Court and ask for an order to keep the man in custody awaiting the escort. The Sheriff said he had no jurisdiction over a warrant issued in England but, with a nod and a wink, suggested that the man should be detained.

A further message was sent to Notting Hill which landed on the DI's desk. He was very annoyed as he was short of manpower[1] so he sent a message to the crime squad at Kensington.

The DI there accosted the first Detective Constable (DC) to arrive for duty and ordered him to get on the next plane from Heathrow to Glasgow to pick up the prisoner.

The DC said, "I have just arrived at 7am by train from Scotland where I was visiting my mother-in law."

He was told in no uncertain terms that he would have to go.

"But I have only £2 in my pocket, sir."

"You won't need money. You only have to pick the prisoner up and come straight back. He will be waiting at the Airport."

The DC 'flew off the handle' and trudged off.

Now, unlike the Kent police station, all stations in Scotland are dry.

The DI said, "You will be staying overnight and we'll go for a drink this evening."

We rang Notting Hill to tell them but the Chief Superintendent (who was actually at his own leaving party) ordered us back that day. The DI spoke to him and convinced him that there were no connecting trains: our own party was on. We were ensconced in a beautiful bed and breakfast, courtesy of the local police, had a lovely evening meal and went onwards to the session. And what a session: again, courtesy of the Falkirk Constabulary. We rolled into bed in the early hours and rolled out again after a short sleep, still in the early hours, to be escorted to the train station. It was a long day and we slept most of the way to London arriving at Notting Hill at about 6pm.

The custody sergeant met us and asked us for the warrant so that he could attach it to the charge sheet.

I said, "You don't need the warrant. The prisoner was dealt with yesterday."

"No, he wasn't. He has just arrived."

Now, you are not going to credit this. When the DC arrived at Glasgow Airport and was handed the prisoner, he turned to board the plane for the return trip just in time to see it take off. As I mentioned, there was some sort of airline dispute and there were no other planes that day for London. The DC had to take the prisoner to the Bridewell in Glasgow for safe-keeping and then, with only £2 in his pocket, find his way to his mother-in law's house – which I think was in Stirling – stay overnight, pick up the prisoner the next day and fly back to Heathrow. He had arrived at the station only about half an hour before us.

You are right. You couldn't make it up. What it cost the tax-payer I dread to think. All in a day's (sorry, two days') work.

The One That Nearly Got Away

A drink driver had failed to turn up at the station on bail. A Sergeant (PS) called at his flat on several occasions but he was always 'out'. Messages were left but he ignored them. Trying again the PS was met by a flatmate who laughed and said he was too late as the man was

getting married that day and was going on his honeymoon in the
evening to South Africa. Did I see a glint in the eye of the PS and a
wee twitch of the mouth in a suppressed smile and did I hear the cogs
turning in his head?

"No, he wouldn't," I thought. Oh yes he would. A check on the flights
out of Heathrow verified the time and off we went in the unmarked
GP (general purpose) car. The plane was stopped on the runway and
the bride and groom, with their luggage, were escorted to their honeymoon carriage, a Hillman Hunter, which was an appropriate name
under the circumstances. Funnily enough the absconder thought it was
funny and was not too fazed. It was something to tell his grandchildren
(if his wife ever forgave him). This time, I wondered how much it cost
the airline to delay a flight. (Not another pun, surely!)

---

1. Manpower or Man Power? – A WPC could not escort a male prisoner.

CHAPTER 23

A FEW FUNNIES

Watch Your Step(s)

At about 7am one morning a police officer found a ladder propped up against the flat roof above some shops in Notting Hill Gate. Fearing that this was an invitation to any would-be burglar he took the ladder to the police station for safety. A short time later an irate window cleaner managed to attract the attention of a passer-by and he was reconciled with his equipment. The best intentions of.......

Or Look Before You Leap

Incidentally the same officer went to assist a Judge's wife who had locked herself out. To reach the sash window he jumped across a gap onto the concrete window sill. Unfortunately the sill collapsed and he plunged into the basement area breaking his arm.

The hapless officer wasn't nicknamed 'Danger Man' for nothing.

Got the Message?

On a Friday, he was called to a Suddeath (Sudden Death, remember) whereby a woman had collapsed and expired in her kitchen. The officer had recorded the fact in his Incident Report book, and handed it to the communications officer so that a message would be sent to the coroner's officer (an authorised police officer) whose job it was to arrange removal by an undertaker. On Monday morning the grieving (now aggrieved) husband attended the police station and enquired when the undertaker would be arriving as, over the weekend, he and his children had to step over the body of his wife to make their breakfast. He thought that police did not work at weekends...! It turned out that the communications officer had failed to send the 'Death' message.

Missed

Having been up the West End with a colleague, we were standing on the platform at Piccadilly Circus when a man came up behind us and tried to push us on to the tracks. He did not succeed and we arrested him. The custody sergeant downgraded our (tongue in cheek) allegation of attempted murder to one of drunk and disorderly. It would have been interesting if there had been cameras on the station.

Doing Time

Another incident on Kensington section occurred when I was driving, off duty, along Kensington High Street with my future wife and her friend. As we passed the Kensington Palace Hotel there was a disturbance outside a shop, opposite. I stopped, got out and arrested a man and a woman for shoplifting. They were all taken to Kensington Police Station and my two passengers had to wait for about three hours whilst I processed the prisoners.

A Fishy Tale

As a police-related story on a scale (not another pun, surely) of one to ten, this is probably three.

My best man, John, was (and still is) a keen fisherman and he invited me, along with his piscatorial police friends, to a day's angling in the

English Channel. I had never been sea -fishing before (not easy from atop a 300 foot cliff). I lived in police flats at Ealing with an off-street car park. John came early in the morning but we took my car, which was an estate.

Travelling south towards the coast John glanced round and said, "Where are the rods?"

"I thought you put them in the car," I replied.

It was too late to turn back so we carried on at a rate of knots so as not to miss the 'Good Ship Lollipop'. We had to hire rods and for a young impoverished (aah!) recently married copper with child, with little spare money in the pot, this was inopportune. Never mind. Off we sailed into the choppy waters on a beautiful sun-shiny day. Anchoring about 3 miles off shore, the hooks were baited and the bait, consisting of the multitude of mackerel (fishermen will know what I mean), was soon dangling from the feathered lures. We then headed for the favourite fishing grounds of our wizened skipper and the serious business began. Unfortunately the wily fish had decided to turn turtle and head off towards France. Very few fish were landed – none by me. However, as I gazed dreamily on the mesmerising swell I noticed a huge log slowly bobbing along. It was longer than our boat. In my assumed innocence I asked my fellow very knowledgeable shipmates:

"Is that what they call plank-ton?"

Swimming three miles back to shore was not easy.....

On returning to the police flats we were surprised and delighted that all of John's fishing equipment was intact with the rods leaning against his car where he had left them.

There was no fish for the pot either.

Building Bridges

Not funny, 'Ha! Ha!' but funny peculiar.

With others I had been invited to Aldershot Army Camp and one of the disciplines that we tried was shooting on the range. On the way we saw two elderly men were walking away and I heard a singularly distinctive accent. To confirm it I asked the man where he was from. He said 'Caithness', (the most northerly county on the mainland of Great Britain) as I had suspected. I told him that I had been brought up at Dunnet Head Lighthouse and he said, 'Do you remember the stone bridge between the two lochs below Burifa hill?'

"Of course" I replied.

To my disbelief he announced, "My father and I built that."

It was only 700 miles away

Dubbed Neil

Because of the shortage of drivers and the lack of capacity for the Driving School to keep up with demands, it was decided that anyone who had a driving licence would be taken out by a driving school instructor. They would be assessed over a period of a day and, if suitable, would be authorised to drive a Panda. An officer, Xxxxx, was fair chuffed that he had passed so when he drove out of Hayes station the following day he proudly announced – as Neil Armstrong said when he was the first person to land on the moon - 'That's one small step for man, one giant leap for mankind'.

Naturally he was dubbed 'Neil' from then on.

After two years' 'probationary' service one is elevated to the substantive permanent rank of PC. This is conveyed by the Chief Superintendent. Xxxxx was due. The C/S was in his office with the relief Inspector who had his back to the door. A knock on the door prompted the C/S to shout 'Come in'. As Xxxxx opened the door the C/S said to the Inspector, 'Oh, he is one of yours'.

The Inspector turned around, saw who it was and inadvertently exclaimed, 'Neil', whereupon Xxxxx got down on one knee expecting to be 'dubbed'.

. . .

'Neil' was the most willing of officers who volunteered for any task but, unfortunately he was one of those Frank Spencer[1] characters whereby many unwarranted disasters followed him around. Several other 'Neil' stories could be told. (STS)

Bus Stop

The route through Notting Hill Gate has three lanes of traffic travelling towards Marble Arch. The inside lane was usually blocked by a parked vehicle. The outside lane was a right-hand turn into Palace Gardens Terrace in to which the route 52 bus used to turn into. If there was more than one bus at the same time the second bus often used the middle lane thus preventing other traffic to continue. A certain officer (RIP) would stand near the junction and, if the above happened, he would signal the second bus to drive straight on for causing obstruction. The driver had to comply with the directions of a police officer. However, because he had left his route, he had to disgorge his passengers in Wellington Terrace, just passed the junction.

In consternation, the bus Inspector called Scotland Yard stating that "A mad policeman is directing traffic in Notting Hill Gate"

'Directing' Traffic

I often wonder if this was the same officer.

The un-metalled highway from Marble Arch to, and beyond, Shepherds Bush, heading west, was used in the 1880s by H.M. Queen Victoria in her horse-drawn carriage on her way to Windsor Castle. In those days, only about 170 years ago, the Notting Hill area was covered in forest and highwaymen were want to roam and pounce upon unwary travellers. H.M the Queen would have had an armed escort.

There was a toll both at the junction with Notting Hill Gate and Clanricarde Gardens. (apropos of nothing, really − just a wee bit of history).

In the 1960s and 1970s, and maybe still today, the current Majesty is escorted in her un-numbered official car (usually a Rolls Royce), accompanied by the Special Escort Group of highly trained motor cyclists. These individuals would speed ahead, in rotation, and stop vehicles at junctions, using whistles to attract drivers' attention.

At some junctions uniformed police officers would be in control. The Holland Park Avenue (HPA) T junction with Ladbroke Grove is one such and is controlled by traffic lights. HPA, which is on an incline, has two lanes in each direction with steady traffic which a policeman had to stop. On one occasion an officer, facing up towards Marble Arch, awaited the appearance of the Royal entourage. The first car in the queue in the inside lane of motors from the Shepherds Bush direction wished to turn left into Ladbroke Grove which would not have been a problem. The driver had his left-hand indicator flashing. He tooted his horn to attract the attention of 'the guardian of law' who turned his head around, analysed the situation, shook it and turned back to concentrate on the task in hand.

The driver again tooted. The policeman's actions were replicated. The driver tooted again as did several other waiting vehicles which produced a cacophony of 'Toot', 'Toot, toot', 'Toot, toot, toot'. The PC turned around, took out his truncheon, and walked deliberately and menacingly towards the first offending vehicle. The driver must have envisaged a smashed windscreen, if nothing else. As he neared the car the PC started waving his truncheon in the manner of a conductor's baton and started leading the 'orchestra', much to the amusement of the appreciative other travellers.

A 'Crash' Course?

As I am at this junction, I shall tell you about a seasonal escapade that happened in the early 1970s (I think). The Mitre public house is at this corner and an 'afters' pre-Christmas session was being held after Late Turn for 'C' relief, of which I was a member.

Just after 5am (yes, am), four of our 'slightly' inebriated worthies left the pub and went to the police station across the road - probably looking for a lift home.

Jolly Japes! There in the backyard was one of the brand new (about 500 miles on the clock), Rover SD1 area cars with the keys in the ignition. The crew had come in for a cup of tea and the unfortunate driver had, inadvertently, left the keys in the ignition.

One of the quartet said they he would drive them home. They drove out of the station yard, turned left into Ladbroke Road and then left into Ladbroke Grove. All was well until they got to the T junction at Holland Park Avenue (HPA) where the driver lost control and smashed into the traffic lights across HPA. The driver was trapped but the other three managed to extricate themselves.

The only known witness was a taxi driver who was driving down HPA towards Shepherds Bush. The remnants of the relief, who had heard the noise, decanted (good word) out of the pub and saw the trio trying to release their mate. Advice was given and the three disappeared into the shadows.

Senior officers, uniform and CID, were called out. They were not very pleased at 6 am just before Xmas. The taxi driver was questioned but, because of the aggressive method of interrogation, denied seeing anything. The three 'missing' PCs were summoned from their home addresses but admitted nothing, stating that they had heard the accident and were trying to help the driver. Not believed but unprovable.

It turned out that the driver only had a provisional driving licence and had never driven an automatic car before. After hospital treatment he was charged with various offences including taking and driving away (TDA), no insurance, unaccompanied by a qualified driver and other offences. He was convicted at court and dismissed from the Service. The three others, whose story was unbreakable, were transferred to separate stations.

The Hub of the Matter

Many years later, one of the three (RIP) had his Police Service leaving party in the Devonshire Arms pub at the corner of Pembridge Road and Notting Hill Gate (NHG). With a colleague of mine, who also lived in Twickenham beside me, we wound our way towards the venue. We saw a hub cap on the side of the road, and as we did not have a present for the retiree, I had a 'light-bulb' moment, and we picked it up. We stopped at 'Oddbins' off-licence in NHG and obtained a cardboard box, wrapping paper and string. We 'manufactured' a pseudo property label and attached to the hub cap purporting it to be residue found at the scene of the accident.

We presented this to the 'leaver' who opened it up in front of the many guests, most of whom would not have known about the 'accident'. Although we did not relate the circumstances, he was not happy. He was angry and when he got angry he could become violent. Thankfully, he eventually saw the joke. What a wheeze!

---

1. 'Frank Spencer' was the name of an accident prone individual depicted in a British sitcom series 'Some Mothers Do 'Ave 'Em, by Michael Crawford as the hapless character.

CHAPTER 24
THE INTELLIGENCE CORPS

Home Beat Officer

In the mid-1970s there was a Force-wide initiative to introduce what became known as Home Beat Officers (HBO). Each was allocated to a particular beat (small area) and their function was to be a conduit between the police and the people in their area by promoting a friendly and visible presence of 'their own officer'.

Intelligence gathering was a primary function and, I believe, the system was fairly successful, relations between them and the public benefitting the populace as a whole. The HBO could pass on vital information gleaned from interested law-abiding citizens, via the collator, so that any necessary pro-active action could be implemented. They could regulate their working hours to maximise their potential.

You may note that I became the collator after my two year stint as an HBO.

Collator

As mentioned in an earlier Chapter, I was selected to be a collator in 1978 a post I held at Notting Hill for nearly 10 years.

The role of a collator was to record accurate, up-to-date and relevant facts of persons who were of an interest to the police and identify crime trends. Computers have now become the medium by which such information is gathered, analysed and distributed to investigating and patrolling officers. The method prior to this was to type/write the details on purpose-printed cards which were stored in metal containers in alphabetical order. Notting Hill was possibly one of the busiest in the MPD. Apart from the local criminals who travelled far and wide to commit crimes, it was a magnet for those who were active elsewhere and who traded their stolen wares in the turmoil of Portobello Market. Stolen antiques from country houses could be found mingling within the legitimate trade with some unscrupulous dealers turning not just one blind eye, but both blind eyes, to the nefarious activity: after all, profit was profit.

The area was a hotbed of revolutionary activity (below stairs and behind curtains). Members of the Irish Republican Army (IRA), The Angry Brigade, The Red Brigade, The Campaign for Nuclear Disarmament (CND), the Animal Liberation Front (ALF) and other underground organisations were virtually hidden within the rabbit warren of the central band between the very rich and the very poor to the east of Ladbroke Grove. Their influence, however, was felt all over Europe and perhaps beyond.

As previously mentioned, the increasing quantity and diversity of illegal drugs was a constant reminder of the insidious nature of these narcotics. The drug addicts' needs were enhanced by the profit from burglary, theft from motor vehicles, shoplifting, drugs, theft from person (dipping). Robbery, murder and the whole gambit of crime, was encompassed within the undefined, (to the perpetrator), boundaries of Notting Hill and Notting Dale.

Arrests were prevalent and the welcome, and often crucial information from a multitude of sources, kept me and my two members of the civil staff (non-qualified typists) fully occupied with an overload which became impossible to manage. This eventually resulted in a lack of information being disseminated to the local officers. Despite repeated requests for extra staff – a full time typist would have been a boon (I still only type with two fingers), none was forthcoming. The irony was that there were over 30 members of the administration staff, including five full time typists, deployed to deal with traffic offences and other non-criminal management projects.

Movement Afoot

Telephone enquiries came from the breadth of the United Kingdom and beyond (I had one from New Zealand). Visiting burglary, robbery, drugs etc. squads arrived, usually unexpected, from, not only Scotland Yard but most counties surrounding Greater London. A Detective Inspector (DI) from Essex came in one afternoon asking for assistance to find an OP (Observation Point). I was extremely busy with incessant telephone calls and each time he tried to speak to me the phone would ring. One call required a PNC (Police National Computer) check. It was an open office and I ran, jumped onto and ran across a desk, made the check and came back the same way. After about a quarter of an hour the DI just sat back and watched me.

"When I go back to Essex I am going to tell them that I actually saw a collator move," he said eventually.

What a compliment! I found that most squads were very appreciative of our assistance and some of the 'Letters of Appreciation' recorded will verify this.

On Top of the Job

I was proud of the fact that my staff and I could reach all the boxes whilst holding the (not a hands free) telephone. When I answered it and the caller gave me the name of his enquiry I would immediately be in front of the appropriate box, retrieve the nominal card and be able to read all the details within 2 seconds – faster than a computer. This obviously impressed the enquirer who thought my memory was so impressive that I had no need of a card system. I sometimes told them that I was psychic and knew that they were going to ring.

What is Good for the Goose......

A certain Commissioner, with a long and distinguished career exemplified by his honesty and integrity, visited, unannounced, our (by then) very pokey office in the basement (it was only crime after all). The swinging of the proverbial cat springs to mind. In fact, when the dinginess had been pointed out by a Chief Inspector on her first visit, I reassured her by saying that a sunbeam had managed to come through the 3 feet by 2 feet window, had spread around the office but managed to escape before the darkness swallowed it up, We worked in a mushroom world of strip lighting. I digress.

There happened to be two county burglary squads (8 officers in all) perusing the collator's records. I had a male and female assistant. The Commissioner arrived with his entourage – a high ranking officer 'bagman' and several of Notting Hill's finest Senior Officers: there was standing room only. When asked what I did (as if he didn't know as he introduced the 4 x 4 system of Intelligence - but that's another story) I proudly expounded my 9 years' experience. I said that these officers did not necessarily want to know that the suspect they were interested in had been arrested as that was recorded elsewhere. They wished to know his habits, where he lived, who were his family, where his kids went to school, what was the number of his car and mobile, which pub he used, which bank he used, who were his associates, where did he frequent etc. That was the intelligence that they sought.

The Commissioner, with a classic 'put down', stated "That isn't intelligence, that is information. It is what you do with it that makes it intelligence."

I was seething having been belittled in front of my staff and County CID officers. Later on he inadvertently made the mistake of saying "the intelligence you have on your cards..."

"With all due respect, sir, that is not Intelligence, that is information."

A 'squeeze' or 'mirth' of Senior Officers may be apt collective nouns as they tried to exit through the only door.

                          .   .   .

Irrelevant Information? – No Such Thing. It is the minutiae that captures the worm.

Little but Effective

Strangely many officers, CID officers in particular, shunned the system which should have been their life-blood. The smallest and seemingly innocuous pieces of information could be the key to solving many crimes. The Notting Hill rapist enquiry was a case in point as all the relevant details were on the collator's card. I know it is easy to put two and two together after the event. Any information, however insignificant at the time, was often the trigger or jigsaw piece that solved many a misdemeanour. Collators, or, as they became known, Local Intelligence Officer (LIO), were usually above average in thinking outside the box, especially as most had years of experience of their own locality and its inhabitants. Their collective knowledge throughout the MPD was incalculable. Their memories were honed by the repetition of dealing with many of the same faces who were persistent offenders. The villains' known methods were stored, sometimes unwittingly, in those dark recesses of the brain and manifested themselves when the spark was lit.

Fancy a Cup of tea?

The local collators were invited for a tour of Wormwood Scrubs prison – 'The Scrubs'. We were advised to wear plain clothes so that the inmates would be unaware of our status. We were taken to 'A' wing which housed the most notorious of prisoners. As we entered the enclosed area there was one trustee prisoner who was sweeping the central communal floor outside the cells. The prison warder shouted to him and asked if we could look in his cell. The inmate agreed. When asked why it was necessary to ask the man's permission, the warden said that this was the man's home for, probably, the rest of his life, so he was entitled to his own privacy. We asked why the man was allowed out and the warden said that he was a 'trustee' and that he made the tea for the whole block, including the wardens. The cell was immaculate with personal belongings and photographs neatly arranged. We then asked what crime the prisoner had committed to receive such a long sentence.

"He poisoned his workmates cups of tea but, not to worry as now he is made to drink the first cup before serving others," came the response.

I'm glad that I drink coffee.

UP and Away

Another wee perk that the collators had was to have a trip in the Force helicopter, call sign, India 99 – an invaluable addition to the Force's mechanical fleet. The Metropolitan Police Air Support (now National Police Air Service) airbase is at Lippit's Hill, Epping Forest, Essex, which is also where one of the training shooting ranges is located. The thinking was that we would have a general idea of the capabilities and usefulness of these machines. What an eye-opener! The panoramic view of Greater London was amazing. The aerial view of such land-marks as the Thames Barrier, Buckingham Palace, St Pauls' Cathedral, et al, was most memorable. We flew above the meandering Thames as far as the police sportsground at Imbercourt, landed and enjoyed 'afternoon' tea. On the way we assisted in following a suspect vehicle and whilst returning to base we lowered down in the Shepherds Bush area and could practically see into the living rooms of high rise flats and, with the zoom camera and/or binoculars, remarkable close-ups were eminently achievable.

It was a most interesting and informative day.

Collators' Reunions

In February 2018, on the day of a heavy snowstorm in Central London, the first Collators' reunion was held at the Lamb & Flag Public House in Covent Gardens. It was organised by Chris 'Fozzy' Foster and many of West London's 'most intelligent' officers gathered to exchange 'Stories from the Files'. It would be hard to evaluate the significance of each one's contribution to the collective crime fighting capabilities of the police family but there is no doubt that it was considerable.

However, a collator was only as good as the information gathered from many personnel and written sources. Without the co-operation and dedication of the many ranks of officers and the other agencies and informants who passed on valuable information, their task would be impossible. The art of the collator was to harness, evaluate, record and then disseminate relevant intelligence so that reliable material could be acted upon.

P27. L – R Standing: Syd Scott (BH XY/XE), Steve Mead (WA), Bernice Wandall (WD), Ray Fowles (WF,TR), Alan King (WF,WD), Dave Almond (QA), Chris Foster (EO,QA), Julian Payne (CB,CX), George Wilde (SB Liaison), Martyn Davies (XA), Eric Blackman (TF,TD) Seated L-R: John Boag (DR), Mike Berry (CV) and Dave Allen (CB). The initials in brackets indicate abbreviated identification of the designated stations to which they were attached.

CHAPTER 25
INSIDE JOBS

Trust No One. Keep Your Wits About You

When I was the collator I took it upon myself to show new recruits several search methods, either of a person or a vehicle. At one of the sessions were six probationers one of whom 'knew it all' so he was my target. If he reads this I hope he forgives me. Their task was to 'stop a person in the street whom they thought was acting suspiciously and search that person'. They had enacted similar scenarios at training school. I ostensibly placed their six shoulder identification numbers in a helmet and asked one of them to draw out the first 'patsy'. It was my target. He made a reasonable initial stop but when the 'suspect' became more agitated a struggle ensued whereby one of them broke a small glass panel in a door. Having finished his task I asked him to draw out the next number. It was his again.

"Oh, I said, I must have made a mistake. Draw another one."

It was his number again. They all had his number on them. The lesson was, 'Don't trust anyone.'

I took them out to the yard to give them some advice about prisoners and vehicles. The inside of the vehicle should be checked before putting a prisoner in and they should be asked to sit behind the passenger's side, sitting on their hands (already searched) or with them placed on the seat in front so that they were always visible. This was to reduce the risk that the driver might be assaulted whilst driving. Remember, we didn't have handcuffs. I asked one of them to search the car and, lo and behold, down the back of the rear seat he found a wrap of cannabis. I pointed out that this was the reason to search the vehicle before putting the prisoner in. I also pointed out that I had not planted it there. In other words, some prisoner had put it there. An unexpected valuable lesson was learnt.

Disappearing Act

Nominal Collators' Cards for each individual who were of interest to police were kept, updated as necessary. A long row of three-tiered metal boxes were placed on desks at about chest high for easy access. The top of the boxes were about 5 feet from the ground. A particular sergeant, who was always immaculately dressed as per training school, came into my office with a bottle of Tipp-Ex and a bottle of thinning liquid. Typewriters were the order of the day and if one made a mistake when typing one had to use the white correction fluid which often thickened and had to be thinned down. The best method was to tip the Tipp-Ex bottle, allowing a small air bubble area, pour in a small amount of thinner and then gently ease the application brush into the bottle.

The sergeant placed the bottle on top of the boxes, poured in the liquid and then pushed the brush down quickly. This caused the liquid to squirt out and it splattered the officer with spots of Tipp-Ex which are notoriously difficult to remove. Thinking he had not been spotted (pun intended) the officer went to clean his jacket. He returned later and nonchalantly resumed the operation.

I said, "That Tipp-Ex is good stuff, isn't it Sarge."

"What do you mean?"

"It made you disappear quickly."

A red-faced sergeant slunk out the door.

That Ink ling

On a similar theme, one of my assistants was not the sharpest pencil in the case. His typewriter ribbon was very faded and he asked what he could do about it. (For those who do not know what a typewriter is, a replacement ribbon was the solution). However, I suggested that he go to the administration store and get a bottle of writing ink. He did so and was about to pour it into the typewriter over the ribbon when my other assistant stopped him. She always quotes that episode when we meet.

Ali Ass

When a person was stopped by police and their details taken, the 'stop slip', as it was called, was forwarded to the collator of the person's home address. A young black lad and his mates were continually being stopped in Central London by various officers. He always gave the pseudonym – Stephen de Fartaze – which, if you were used to West Indian accents, was a whimsical alias. It did not seem to have been noticed by those officers working the West End. Perhaps they were young and inexperienced. When I was the collator I identified him through his date of birth.

One to DI For

One day I met the DI (Detective Inspector) coming down the stairs with a number of encased light bulbs in his arms. I don't think he was too impressed when I quipped,

"Sir, many lights make hands work!"

Don't Grass on Him.

On another day, coming down the stairs, I met another DI (it may have been the same one).

He had a nasty gash on the side of his face and forehead. I had read the previous day's reports and had not noticed anything untoward. I asked him if he had been in a fight.

He replied, "No. I bought myself one of those sit-on mowers and never thought about low lying branches and drove straight into one."

He must have had an 'acher', sorry acre.

I pointed that that had never happened to my wife with the strimmer.

Self Trained

One of the communication systems to Scotland Yard was by teleprinter. A short course rendered one eligible to work in the Comms (Communications) or Reserve room (as it was called) where the telephone exchange was centred. An Inspector asked a policeman (not me) to send a message to Scotland Yard. The officer told the Inspector that he had applied for a course, but that he did not yet know how to send a message. The Inspector said that he was unlikely to get a course and the only way to learn was to try it. He ordered him to send it.

A short time later the Inspector at the Information Room at 'The Yard' rang the Station and demanded to know who had sent a load of gobbledygook. He was directed to the Inspector who received a dressing-down. A few hours later the said police officer went to the Inspector and asked if he could borrow the revolver and some bullets that were always kept in the safe. A worried Inspector asked him why, so he told him that it was unlikely that he would be sent on a firearms course so he wanted to practise in the back-yard.

A Steal

I arrived on night duty and was accosted by the relief Inspector. He told me he was arresting me for handling stolen property. Perplexed, I asked him to explain himself.

He said, "Have you been eating the biscuits that Xxxx (a lady tele-phonist) brings in?"

"Of course, everybody does."

"She has been arrested for stealing packets of biscuits from the super-market to feed us on night duty," he informed me.

Bravo Hotel

A telephone PBX switchboard was installed in the comms. room and was usually controlled by a civilian operator. It consisted of switches and cords so that different extensions could be connected to each other. Police officers had to learn the routine so that they could take over when civilian operators were unavailable or on refreshments. Great fun was had by connecting extensions neither of whom knew who was calling who. I occasionally answered an incoming call with the words 'Notting Hill, Bravo Hotel', out of habit.

Surprised callers would ask, "Which Hotel? I thought I was calling the police."

Measure Twice and Cut Once

That old adage! Wages were fairly meagre in the late 60s/early 70s. Single Police officers were usually accommodated in buildings with individual sleeping rooms, sometimes above police stations or in large multi-bedroomed buildings called Section Houses which would boast a canteen, snooker rooms, ironing rooms etc. There was a nominal charge mostly to pay for the daily newspapers. Married officers were in receipt of a rent allowance with which they could augment their monies for a mortgage – if they could afford the deposit for a house/flat.

A young officer recently married and living in a police flat, intimated that he was going to buy a house. We all tried to dissuade him suggesting that he would end up in debt and unable to pay off the mortgage. (Little did we realise the wisdom of his foresight). He was adamant and on late turn (2pm–10pm) one evening he asked me if I could lay linoleum as he was moving into the house at 12 noon the following day and wanted a covering on his kitchen floor. I admitted that I had tried it once before so he inveigled me into helping him. After a couple of pints in the Mitre pub (again) I drove him in my estate car, picked up the roll of linoleum from his police flat and went to the house. The kitchen floor was very small with many ins and outs to be cut out with a Stanley knife. Between cans of beer I made a reasonable job (or so I thought).

"Great," he said, "You can stay the night and lay the carpet in the bedroom tomorrow."

I protested. "I have no idea how to lay a carpet."

"You'll manage."

He went home leaving me to sleep in/on the only piece of furniture there – an armchair.

The following morning, the carpet, which was large and very new (having been bought for a room in the flat), was brought over and we carried it upstairs to what turned out to be a small bedroom which had an unusual shape and a bay window recess. I had no idea what I was doing but, clever me, noticed that the underlay was still there so I suggested to him that we throw that onto the lawn outside, lay the carpet on top and cut around it. This we did and carried the carpet upstairs. It fitted perfectly – upside down. In my perceived wisdom I had turned the carpet upside down to make it easier to cut with scissors (note – scissors). We started laughing and couldn't stop. Hearing the hilarity his wife came upstairs, but we were helpless with tears streaming down our faces. It must have been at least 10 minutes before we could point out the error of our ways. She was not pleased. We then had to jiggle about putting the cut out pieces under wardrobes or other furniture. Strangely, he never asked me to help him again.

The maxim, 'Don't bite off more than you can chew', springs to kind.

How the Mighty Fall!

One night duty I stopped two young men who, to my mind, were acting suspiciously and I decided to stop them. Having found no evidence of any offence but still sceptical, I recorded their details on to a 'stop slip'. This was given to the collator who recorded it on the subjects' collator's cards. Several years later I took over as the collator with the previous collator as my assistant. When a certain stop slip came in I scrutinised it and mentioned to my colleague that I believed that the details given were obviously false and wondered how the 'stopping' officer had not spotted it. He smiled and withdrew a card from the index and pointed to an entry with my name as the informant. I recognised it as the stop I had made. He then pointed out that the details that had been given were the names of a local estate agent. I then remembered that when I stopped the two men that there had been a 'For Sale' sign behind me.

Canteen

Dolly was one of our cooks known to hundreds of policemen at Notting Hill and Kensington as she flitted between the two. She was a large rotund West Indian lady who was loved by all. She could teach troopers how to swear but her cooking was impeccable. Her repartee was second to none and there were few who could outmatch her. Remembered with affection.

SQ23

I have mentioned this previously as being a section house where single police officers were billeted. Card games were omnipresent both here and during refreshment breaks at the station. Many a week's wages have been lost and the occasional car keys tossed into the 'pot'. Thankfully, over the years, I came out with a reasonable profit. After late turn many a night was spent until the very early hours interspersed with visits to the KFC takeaway or kebab house.

Tongue Tied

A certain officer, let's call him Paul, had a penchant for stray dogs and, to the chagrin of the Station Officer (SO), he would bring them to the station to be picked up the following morning for transfer to Battersea Dogs Home. This was not always welcome as some would bark all night upsetting the neighbours. Sometimes a dog handler had to be called to sedate an exceptionally raucous hound. One late turn our friend called on the radio that he was bringing in a dog which had bit him. This was the cue for the Station Officer to hatch a plan. The Divisional Surgeon happened to be at the station. He asked that Paul be stripped to his underpants and put in a cell. Then, in loud whispers, he discussed the possibility of rabies with the SO, and asked for an ambulance to be called. The crew were appraised with the situation and asked Paul to put on a Hazchem suit and get into to back of the ambulance by himself. At Hillingdon Hospital there was a reception committee organised by a matron who was a friend/relative(?) of the SO. They were all in full body protective suits and escorted Paul to an isolation room. Unknown to him there was a two way mirror and he was observed by a posse of police officers and hospital staff for about three hours. During this time he was still just in his underpants and was seen to face the mirror, stick his tongue and inspect it for spots. I think he was 'cured' of his obsession.

CHAPTER 26

DRIVING SKILLS

Before joining the police most people would have passed their Driving and Vehicle Standards Agency driving test and felt confident in their ability to drive safely and adhere (tenuously?) to the Highway Code. However, the instruction rendered at the police driving school at Hendon was renowned as being one, if not the best, in the world. There were different classes depending on the amount of tutorage one received. I believe all citizens should take lessons equivalent to the Class 5 criteria – as a minimum.

(My own advice when driving is that you should try adhering to the mnemonic:
K Y D (think of your kid/s) - **K**eep **Y**our **D**istance. (March 2020 – suitable for Covid?). I believe that if you do many accidents could be averted).

The following is a rough synopsis of the training required to become a Class 1 driver- classified from 5 – 1:

Class 5

Four weeks on the Standard Course used to be the criteria for officers to become competent in driving a police vehicle without any warning signal (bell /siren). One could drive Panda cars and J4 vans (no towing allowed).

Down Hill all the Way

The first Panda cars were Morris 1000s.

P28. Panda car

Pretty small for big men (especially when one was supposed to wear one's flat cap at all times when driving) but, again, it suited me. Imagine a bright sunny morning at about 7.30am driving along without a care in the world, waiting for the Metropolis to awaken and the fun to start. Kensal Road rises fairly steeply as it approaches Ladbroke Grove. Ah! There is an empty school bus at the top of the slope waiting to turn right into Ladbroke Grove. The driving school mantra pops into one's head. 'Don't get too close in case it rolls back'. It is rolling back! No problem. Just press the horn in the centre of the steering wheel. No joy. Keep pressing. No joy. Press frantically. No joy. Bang! The front of car was rearranged. It was then that I realised that I wasn't driving the Morris but the new Austin 1100 which had the horn on the indicator stalk. It turned out that the school bus driver only had a provisional licence and was uninsured.

Class 4

After a further week's course one was authorised to drive Morris LD vans (Black Marias) superseded by Ford Transit and J4 vans. They had a blue light and one was authorised to tow and drive stolen or prisoners' vehicles back to the station.

Class 3

This was called the Intermediate course and lasted 4 weeks. One could drive the fast area cars with blue lights and 2 tone horns. This was meant to be a transition period for up to a year to gain more experience in driving before attending Hendon for 2 weeks to train to be a Class 2 or 1 driver. (I spent several years driving as a Class 3)

Class 2 & 1.

This was a very intensive and highly advanced course and depending on your competence one was classed as a Class 2 or 1 – the highest accolade. One could then drive coaches, lorries, Q cars (plain cars with sirens and blue light attachments (used by the 'Sweeney') or any other vehicle. (AH)

"I remember when I was Traffic removing a left-hand drive French registered 30 ton HGV with a draw-bar trailer from a Pedestrian Crossing approach in Notting Hill Gate to the pound at Hammersmith, as I was a Class 1 and it was legal for me to do that at the time. (Happy days). The French lorry driver wasn't

best pleased shelling out pound notes to get his rig back from the pound though." (AH)

I eventually attended the latter course and, although I say it myself, I was very competent. However, after about 5 minutes on the final drive, which is supervised by a Senior Traffic patrol officer (Superintendent or Chief Superintendent) I unfortunately misinterpreted the directions by the officer (not entirely my fault) but it affected my subsequent drive and I failed miserably. I returned to the station as a Class 4 with the option of trying again. In the meantime I was selected as a Home Beat Officer (HBO) and when the driving school was unwittingly informed of this by another Notting Hill officer, they wrote me off – unknown to me until much later. However, 2 years as an HBO led me into collating and, as they say, the rest is history. I still drive to the diktats of my advanced driving lessons (although much slower).

A Stone's Throw Away

When I was on the advanced driving course our instructor was renowned for frugal buying and, apparently, took a calculator (remember them?) when he went supermarket shopping. He also liked buying potatoes and vegetables when in the Norfolk area. I was driving and he missed the turning into his favourite supplier so he suddenly said, "Turn round here."

I saw an in/out driveway to my right so immediately, at a reasonable speed, turned in front of this 'posh' house. Unfortunately it had a gravel driveway and a hail of small stones rattled the windows. We didn't hang around.

Having picked up his weekly shop including two bags of potatoes, I was still the driver. Every time you got into a police car you are supposed to speed up to 30mph and then test the brake and comment on the effect. I did so and commented that the breaking was affected by the extra weight in the boot. The instructor berated me, took off his cap and started hitting me with it. As they say, "If you can't take a joke....."

Fenced Out

One of the regular routes taken on the advanced course included a very sharp hairpin bend which was a 'trap' for the driver. The approach was up a fairly steep country hill with hedges either side so the road suddenly just disappeared. At the apex of the bend was a farmer's field and he used to leave the gate open because many an unwary student ended up in the field.

CHAPTER 27

THE CHASE IS ON
AND SOME HAIR-RAISING STORIES

Around and Around and Around We Go Again.

The West London Air Terminal used to be in Cromwell Road. There was a narrow, one vehicle only, concrete up-spiral, a level drop off zone across the front of the building and then a similar down-spiral. One night a London taxi, with a fare aboard, had stopped to get some cigarettes from a machine in Cromwell Road. The engine was still running. An opportunist thief jumped in and drove away. I don't know how but a police car started to chase the cab which went up the down-spiral. It was followed by two or three police cars, including ourselves.

The fare was terrified and screaming for the man to stop. The taxi went down the up-spiral, along Cromwell Road and back up the down-spiral. It did this several times before the driver of the night duty CID car decided to stop at the bottom of the up-spiral. The occupants had just time to decamp from the car before the taxi came down and smashed into the rear of the CID car. Unfortunately its handbrake wasn't on so it then smashed into the wall opposite. Needless to say most of the trailing police cars disappeared into the night never to be seen again.

NB. Taxis were very convenient places to have a wee kip at night for lonely, weary and bored officers, especially in cold weather, because the back doors did not lock.

Horse Power

Triumphs (or were they?)

The Triumph 2000 PI vehicles were sometimes used by the Metropolitan Police as Area cars. They suited me as I could see over (and not through) the steering wheel. They were fast and manoeuvrable in the tight confines of London streets. However, they had an idiosyncrasy. In very hot weather, when the inside of the boot heated up, it was occasionally very difficult to re-start the car. The petrol pump was in the boot and, for some reason, (don't ask me the scientific answer) the fuel would not flow until cooled down. We had learned to carry some packs of ice which were placed near the pump.

There was a call to the panic alarm at the wages office at Derry and Toms – a large department store in Kensington High Street. Three PIs attended and the crews ran into the store. The lifts were all occupied so it was a run up the stairs to the top floor. A long way for a false alarm. Returning to the cars, which had been abandoned (with the blue lights flashing) in the High Street, we were very embarrassed when all that could be heard was the screech of starting motors trying desperately to suck up the petrol to start the cars.

Horses for Courses

There was a series of steps which led from West Row up into Ladbroke Grove where the building was marked 330. I remember this very well because there was a school crossing at the pedestrian crossing there and one of our officers had the shoulder number, PC 330B Jim Blundell.

Anyway, whilst standing on the central reservation directing traffic I heard a commotion and saw a lady running out of a nearby shop where she had been shoplifting. The shop keeper was shouting at her so I gave chase. Much to my surprise I heard the sound of hoof beats behind me and I was overtaken by a mounted police officer who lent down and grabbed the alleged thief. The puffing policeman was grateful.

and the chase is on again

One Horse Power v Hundreds of Horse Power

A car was being chased around Hammersmith section. The reason escapes me. There were many fast cars pursuing it including the Daimler Dart from Barnes Traffic Garage. The vehicle went over Hammersmith flyover three times in the wrong direction. I was the observer, in plain clothes, in Bravo 3, a very old Wolseley which, according to the driver was lucky to reach 50 MPH as it had done over 100,000 miles. We decided to take a trundle to the vicinity and, much to our surprise, the suspect car came around a bend and crashed into a builder's skip right in front of us. The chasing gaggle of eclectic Metropolitan Police's finest horse powered vehicles was lost. The suspect immediately clambered out of the car and jumped a fence into a back garden. There were probably about 20 back gardens, between two rows of Victorian houses, divided by fencing, wooden or otherwise, and/or hedges of various heights and foliage. I jumped after him. By this time he was two or three gardens in front of me. Valiantly I scrambled over the fences after him.

There were resident spectators on the balconies watching this Keystone Kops scenario. I heard one of them shouting. "He is there. He is there," a woman cried, pointing at me. I looked around to find that a police dog was being helped over the fencing by its handler. Now, I know they are clever animals (the police dog I mean) but I doubt if it would know the difference between me (in plain clothes), or the suspect and I am sure his handler wouldn't have known either. It spurred me on but I was losing ground. The villain arrived at the end of the row and climbed up an outside metal fire escape to the top storey and went in through the back door. I wheezed after him and when I went through the open flat door there was an elderly woman, with two shopping bags, pressed against the corridor wall, obviously in shock. As I ran past I told her who I was and followed the man's path through the front door. Looking down onto the street I saw that the man had been apprehended – by a passing Mounted Branch officer on his way back to Hammersmith stables. One horse power was enough! Guess who was left holding the baby? Or was it just a bay?

Fenced In

Another chase on Hammersmith section involved a car which had been chased from the Golders Green area, North London. A known burglary suspect had gone out to buy cigarettes in the late evening. He was still wearing his slippers. He was recognised, requested to stop but he decided to 'outrun' the police. By the time he arrived in the Hammersmith area he was being chased by a multitude and assorted mix of the finest 'wheels' in the Metropolitan Police and their equally 'finest' drivers. I was the operator on Bravo 3 – a Jaguar - and we decided to join in the motorised crocodile. Somehow we found ourselves third in line behind two other Jaguars hurtling down Ravenscourt Road. Two foot patrol officers had the notion to push a hand-barrow into the middle of the road. This was before the era of 'stingers'.

Unfortunately the fugitive managed to get past - fortunately there was a gap in the pavement at the entrance to a builder's yard and the chasing pack managed to swerve through the chink. I can still see the two officers in fits of laughter watching the comic strip scenario. The bandit turned right into King Street and then right again into Hamlet Gardens. He obviously did not know the area and he drove into a dead end. He ended up hitting a high fence which led into a field - and I mean up. It looked as if the car were trying to climb over the fence. Naturally, those vehicles that weren't directly involved scurried away into the night.

There were the proceeds of a burglary in the car.

The Other One That Got Away

One early morning in the area car my operator and I had just arrested a young man in All Saints Road for possessing a small quantity of cannabis which he had just bought. As he sat in the back with my colleague, I saw a car flash past at speed down Tavistock Crescent. The instinct was there: a stolen car. We decided to follow and immediately a chase ensued. Having tried to lose us by driving down several side streets, it drove down Cambridge Gardens and the two male occupants decamped at the T junction with Bramley Road. The driver, on foot, turned left and I followed in the area car whereupon he leapt over a 6 foot wall. I jumped out and chased him leaving the blue lights on and the sirens blaring. (I doubt if the neighbours were pleased). As I tumbled over the wall I could see that he was trapped in the garden and he came quietly. I could open the gate in the wall from the inside and as we came out my colleague was there to meet us.

"Where's the prisoner?" I queried.

"He is in the back of the car," came the reply.

Oh no, he wasn't. This was the second time this had happened to me.

The passenger in the stolen car wasn't so lucky. As he scrambled to get away from the scene he was hit, as he stumbled in front of another police car which had been in the chase, and his leg was broken. At training school they set up similar scenarios where two or three things happen at once to test your reasoning ability under pressure. This could have been one of them.

A Tale of Two Syds (Actually One was Sid)

A car, containing four men, driving erratically, caught our attention in Ladbroke Grove and we decided to follow it. It ignored our attempts to stop it with blues and twos (Blue flashing light and two tone horn). It sped north, through the red traffic lights and right along the Harrow Road. It then turned left into 6th Avenue off the Harrow Road, down a side street and stopped. The occupants got out – the two at the front getting out of the nearside door. This was an attempt to confuse us as it was a left-hand drive vehicle. Not to be fooled, I stopped the driver who, of course denied that he was such. (He was that six foot plus man again – you know, the one who is always bigger than me) We waited for assistance before we could breathalyse him. My colleague was trying to pacify the other occupants who were boisterous and had notified the occupants of a nearby house where a party was being held. They came out with their beer cans in hand.

"Hit him, Syd, hit him," they shouted.

I couldn't understand this as I was on Harrow Road section and did not recognise anyone in the street. The taunting continued until help arrived. It wasn't until we arrived at the police station and discovered that the arrested man's first name was Sidney, (with an i) that we understood the significance of the name. To be fair, he gave us no bother despite his previous criminal record. He did, of course, plead "Not Guilty" and we ended up at Crown Court but the jury were not fooled by his defence that he had been the front seat passenger.

CHAPTER 28
PORTOBELLO ROAD
(AND ITS SURROUNDS)

The breadth of knowledge that one can glean from the internet continues to amaze and fascinate me. I often wonder who actually inputs the billions of items of data.

Sometimes the lack of awareness of our surroundings is criminal (no pun intended....). It is only since I started to do a bit of research for this book that I discovered the origin of the names, Portobello and Vernon as in Vernon's Yard which I have mentioned elsewhere. The WWW informed me that there was a Spanish port in Panama called Puerto Bello which was captured by Admiral Edward Vernon in 1739 during the lost War of Jenkins' Ear, thus the nomenclatures. Delve into its history if you wish.

It is allegedly the biggest antique market in the world and, as such, attracts not only the genuine dealers who trade from the breadth of the UK and beyond but also the curious tourists who flock here each Saturday. It is a microcosm of the world with a multifarious mix of cultures. To police it was not only challenging and exciting but also educational.

Two Twos and a Queen (Find the Lady)

This was a prolific con trick. Two or three East End spiv gangs would infiltrate the unwary punters in Portobello Road, set up a small stall, surround it by their 'heavies' whilst the dealer/trickster 'shuffled' three playing cards, one of which was a queen, and slapped them down onto the stall. At first he made it look easy for people to place their bets on the whereabouts of the Queen with his henchmen joining in and, naturally, winning. It seemed too easy. The gullible were conned to bet. They were allowed to win a small amount but when they put on a bigger bet, they lost by the slickness of the trickster. If they won they were hustled by the henchmen allowing the trickster to escape with the nicker (urban language for a pound or a quid). The teams had lookouts and they were very difficult to catch but watching them in the reflection of a shop window sometimes gained results. The fines at court were derisory and they could earn that within 10 minutes.

There She was – Gone (Find the other lady)

The officer sent me this story after I had sent him many strange and unexplainable 'ghostly' or psychic incidents that have happened to me.

A certain officer (PC 309B) relates that he was on patrol one night as the observer on

Bravo 3 when he and the crew spotted a young man crossing Portobello Road in front of them at the junction with Westbourne Grove.

"As we approached the junction a young guy crossed in front of us followed by an old woman, when we reached the junction we were all eyes about and all said together,

"Where's the old lady gone?" There was just the young guy walking on his own!

We all jumped out and stopped the guy, who almost freaked when he realised she had disappeared. There was nowhere for her to go! Just a very closed pub, impossible for her to have entered, and a few parked cars which we opened with

our jigglers (special adapted 'skeleton' keys). They were all empty. We nearly crapped ourselves and the young guy legged it".

Yep 100% a ghost. (RS)

Babylon

A popular song in the 1980s by Boney-M was 'Rivers of Babylon' and if a police officer was seen coming up Portobello Road or in the vicinity, the juke box in the Colville public house (frequented mostly by black clientele) would resound as a warning that the 'enemy' was in sight. If one stood diagonally opposite, as I frequently did as the local beat officer, it was played over and over again until I wandered off. The reggae song is about homesick slaves looking for revenge so, I guess, the West Indian community was making a statement.

The most frequent verbal reaction used by the black community when one stopped was, "You are only stopping me because I'm black."

I sometimes said, tongue in cheek, "You are right."

This took them by surprise and they usually smiled or laughed.

I would then say, "Now the reason I have stopped you is....." If I had replied, "No it isn't!" that would start an argument which could carry on for some time; however they couldn't argue after my 'confession'.

Not one of my most salubrious poems but I think it captures some of the atmosphere of

∾

A Day in the Life Of Hill and Dale

I wondered slowly, oh so proud
In overcoat, o'er Hill and Dale
When all at once I saw a crowd
Looking for an antique sale
Down the Road, beside the stalls
Seeking bargains of the dolls.

Continuous like a sinuous snake
That slithers in between the bays
They do not want to buy the fake
On each and every Saturdays
Twenty thousand I did count
Looking for a good discount.

The sights and sounds of Portobello
Outshone the appeal of any market
The costermongers, they did bellow
To those of them who fought a target
I watched and studied from afar
That bustling and unique bazaar.

For oft, when seeing as I did,
The dodgy deal or sleight of hand
When the Queen of Hearts was hid
By the furtive East End band
To find that elusive playing card
To catch them in the act was hard.

The day is coming to a close
Down come the shutters, one and all
Satisfactory it is for those
Who enjoyed the day and had a ball
Having seen the hues of every nation
I wander back to my wee station.

Sydney T. Scott – 7th December 2018
(With apologies, appreciation and acknowledgment to
William Wordsworth)

Shell Shocked

A certain police officer at Notting Hill (an ex- World War II veteran who was renowned for his 'F' word, his cigarette ash falling on his scruffy uniform, his unwillingness to get out of the driver's seat of the van and his meanness) was 'puppy' walking a new recruit. There was a stall selling prawns in Portobello Road and, as usual, he obtained a punnet and assured the stall holder that he would pay the £5 later as he had no money on him at the time.

"Don't worry" said the recruit," I'll pay for them and you can pay me back".

Our erstwhile friend was not too pleased - having lost out on his 'perk'.

The Mangrove

Much has been written about this controversial restaurant so I will not dwell on the many disputed incidents which occurred in or nearby. I shall reiterate just one personal one. A few black youths were stopped outside by two very tall police officers (PCs) who suspected that they might be carrying drugs. One refused to be searched. Although only 16 years of age he was very big – about 16 to 17 stone. It turned out that he was from the Harrow Road area and was not known to the officers who were on regular patrol in the area.

A crowd began to gather and the PCs called for assistance. I arrived with a colleague in Bravo 3. I approached the youth who was carrying an open can of Coca Cola. I explained that I was going to search him but as I reached out he swung my arm away spilling some drink over my uniform. We were now getting surrounded and he said his mates wouldn't let me search him. I explained to him that there are 26,000 police officers in London and, if necessary I would bring along as many as was needed. He then allowed me to give him a cursory search but nothing was found. I suggested that the two officers move away as the crowd were laughing and jeering. When I returned to the car I wound down the window and in an audible voice said to the youth, "Thank you for the information."

He began ranting and raving, chasing after the car shouting, "I told you nothing, man! I told you nothing!"

I thought that was a little bit of deserved pay back. Perhaps you disagree.

Gentrification

All Saints Road and its surrounds were beginning to get seedy and amelioration was required. Kensington and Chelsea council in consultation with the crime prevention officer from Notting Hill (the one who liked Guinness – see later) and many other stakeholders and interested parties introduced a comprehensive programme of refurbishment, one of which was to eliminate the doorway recesses to prevent hidden dealing. It has exponentially transformed the area into a chic and desirable location.

St Luke's Mews, which is attached to All Saints Road at right angles, is very narrow. The old terraced buildings originally had stables for the many horses that were required in the Victorian era. Notoriety attracts the wealthy. I recently Googled the Mews and was truly amused to note that the renovated properties are advertised for between £2,500,000 and £2,950,000.

If I knew then what I know now.................

Whatever Comes in Handy

We stopped our car in Westbourne Grove beside two youths who were attempting to steal a car. They decamped. I chased and caught one.

The WPC operator chased the other and threw her handbag at him. It forced him to stop. Good for her. You may have seen it in films but I saw it in real life.

Get On Your Bike

Well he hadn't, which made me suspicious. Inkle, inkle, inkle.

Ambling along with a colleague north in Portobello Road I saw a youth pushing a lady's bike on the pavement on the other side of the road. My instinct was raised especially when the youngster started crossing the road directly towards us. We stopped him and after questioning established that the bike was stolen. After a struggle we arrested him. My colleague was curious as to why I had stopped him. There was the fact that it was a lady's bike and he wasn't riding it, but more importantly, to my mind, he had brazenly and purposely headed towards us and, in my perverse thinking, it indicated that he was trying to bluff us.

Objective Adjective

Training school again. Advised to say, "A lady's black bike" not "A black lady's bike."

CHAPTER 29
NOTTING HILL CARNIVAL

This annual event captures the vibrant West Indian culture with most, if not all, of the Caribbean islands represented. There is a deep rivalry between them and the natives of each vied to out-class the others with their exuberance, music, steel bands and the magnificence of their stupendous dresses. Traditional West Indian fare is sold from roadside stalls. It started from very humble beginnings in the mid-1960s. A small number of floats, usually open-backed lorries or vans, slowly wound their way through the north end of Notting Hill. One or two local policemen and traffic patrol officers would be with each float and were on hand to assist when they broke down. Good humour was the order of the day with the participants laughing, joking and dancing with the Constabulary.

After the 1977 Carnival, the local Chief Superintendent. wrote:

"May I particularly mention the following who, despite all the pessimistic forecasts, volunteered to accompany the bands. They stuck to their task in the face of considerable personal danger and their bearing can only be described as magnificent and in the highest traditions of the Metropolitan Police."

He named me along with 14 other Constables.

Undignified?

Where did that recent directive/suggestion come from that said that officers should not fraternise with the revellers? I think it was a senior woman police officer. I would hazard a guess that she has never policed the Carnival as a foot police constable and has never experienced the welcoming and friendly atmosphere towards the officers from the banter and goodwill of the majority of the populace, especially from the black community. Undignified, she said; public relations, I say. Many officers would also disagree with me.

The photographed officer, Graham Hamilton, PC 723B, (who obviously loved clowning around and with whom I spoke in March 2020) said:

"The band element of the Carnival is something to be celebrated and co-operation was everything when you were on a Band Serial. Dropped off in the morning and finishing in a new day. Just a radio to update re location. No refs. No relieving. (Imagine asking!). I have a copy of that photograph which is one of my fondest memories of working at Notting Hill. It is also something that set aside Notting Hill officers from everyone else in the MPS". (Metropolitan Police Service)

Having sought Graham's permission to print his name he replied:-

"The first year I did it (1982) I asked my relief Inspector about my progress as a probationer. He smiled and said, "You don't need to worry about that, you just led a band through the carnival."

Graham served at BH from 1982 – 1988.

P29. Graham Hamilton

Having been involved in over 20 Carnivals in different roles, including
being on a Band Serial at the first and subsequent ones, I can concur
with the officer. On these serials, accompanying a band, refreshments
consisted of handouts from the various stalls and included (dare I
mention) the odd can of Red Stripe beer, comfort breaks were taken at

a convenient building or side alley, and blood coagulated in your legs having stood or walked, sometimes, for over 20 hours. Over two days your senses were bombarded with the sights of the magnificent costumes and the decorated floats, the smells of the various open-air food vendor stalls, the deafening incessant noise from the huge loud-speakers, and the vibrant motion and excitement of the rollicking masses. There was no escape, and the experience each year was exhilarating and indelibly etched in the memory.

All the World's a Stage

This brings me to the Carnival of August 1980. I was the 'runner' for Superintendent Xxxxx and was there to assist him. We had been on duty since 7am, walking or standing the whole time. I think we had about a total of an hour for refreshments. As usual there was a very large, deeply packed crowd under the flyover of Portobello Road and Cambridge Gardens/Acklam Road. There was a stage from which live West Indian bands played through very large speakers which were placed at the corners of the front of the stage. They were about 20 feet high, piled one of top of the other. If these had toppled onto the crowd below there would have been devastation and serious injury, especially as the young children were at the front. One can, actually one cannot, imagine the volume of ear- splitting noise that emanated from them. The crowds were very good-humoured dancing, swaying and singing along.

It had been decided that all sound systems were to be muted at 8pm and our job was to pull the plug. We went to the back of the stage. The array of weapons under the stage was formidable – baseball bats, iron bars, chains, snooker cues etc. Each band had been given a half hour slot but the one that was playing had not finished by 7.45pm. This greatly upset the next band which was 'Aswad'- who were THE band at the time and are still going strong. Their members climbed onto the stage to remonstrate with the other band and a scuffle ensued.

· · ·

An extract from Tony Moore's book,[1] describes the incident —"During the Carnival itself, one potential serious incident was averted by a quick thinking constable when a scuffle, involving reggae bandsmen, broke out on the stage at Portobello Green at a time when nearly 6,000 people were packed into the area. Police Constable Sid (sic) Scott, who had served at Notting Hill for a number of years and who was standing at the rear of the stage when the dispute arose, quickly grabbed the microphone and told the crowd that it was an argument between the entertainers and that the police were no way involved. This was accepted by the crowd and no trouble ensued."

It had been a very long day and night. After about 21 hours by 4 am in the morning I could barely stand with the amount of blood that had accumulated in my calves.

One newspaper (The Daily Telegraph, I think) the following morning described the scene and called me 'intrepid'. I had to look the word up in the dictionary. Sadly, I can find no photographs of the incident. Daily Star, Wednesday 27th August 1980 also refers.

Never Take a Backward Step

On another occasion I was again the guide to an 'out of town' Superintendent. We had just turned into St Luke's Road and all was quiet. Suddenly a large crowd came running out of All Saint's Road towards us and missiles were being thrown. The Superintendent turned to run away.

"Draw your truncheon and stand underneath the trees!" I shouted.

The front of the crowd saw us, turned round and, thankfully, ran in the opposite direction. Unbeknown to us at the time, a CID officer had just been stabbed in St Luke's Mews and the crowd were being dispersed by the police who had raced to the scene. We were lucky.

Law and Disorder

The Carnival steadily grew over the years to such an extent that the police were hard-pressed to control the burgeoning number of revellers and the insidious criminal elements who took advantage of anonymity in the huge crowds to commit very serious crimes. It reached its zenith in the scorching heat of 1976 when some of these elements rampaged through the streets attacking anyone in authority whether they were police officers, ambulance personnel or even firemen. Their rapacity was ferocious. Vehicles were overturned and set alight and the occupants, who managed to escape, were pelted with sticks and stones. Officers had to flee, literally, for their lives. Their only defensive weapons were their truncheon and any object they could use as a shield against the barrage of artillery that was thrown at them. There are iconic images of officers defending themselves and protecting their fellow comrades with dustbin lids. The heat of the night was a very apt phrase.

There are many images on the internet that capture these cowardly and destructive attacks where many officers and members of the public were injured and property damaged.

'Steaming' became a phenomenon. Gangs of mainly black youths would line up in crocodile lines and run through the packed crowds. They would snatch anything that was on show - be it watches, jewellery, handbags, wallets etc., and, if challenged, knives would be used either to threaten the victim or slash handbag straps. There was very little that the police could do to prevent this at first but subtle tactics were later deployed. Surveillance and snatch squads became the order of the day.

As a consequence police officers were trained in riot control. Shields were issued along with fire-proof protective clothing – a far cry from the image of the British Bobby who mainly served with the approval and co-operation of the general public. Today, of course, their descendants are shrouded in black with protective helmets and with more gadgetry than a medieval knight. Sadly, they are necessary now, to protect not only themselves from vicious attacks but to defend the public and their property.

With improved assistance from the organisers and stake-holders of the Carnival and an increased police presence and extra stewards, incidents decreased over the subsequent years. However there was, and still is, always an underlying atmosphere of tension.

To summarise, there was a period of a few years that extreme violence invaded the celebrations but this was only instigated by a small minority who were hell-bent in causing mayhem. Thankfully, with the co-operation and dialogue between many interested parties, the disorder at Carnivals has been drastically reduced although there will always be an element of criminality by disaffected members of society. However, I don't think rigid and uncompromising policing, without an element of fun and joie de vivre should be the de rigueur of the weekend. An air of professionalism has to be maintained but not to the detriment of amity.

Tell It As It Is or Self Inflicted Wounds

Inspector Frank Wilkinson recalls that in 1976 the Carnival deteriorated into violence. The police were blamed so he wrote a letter to the Times newspaper saying that the police had two choices – either to let it continue with the same level of crime or confront it.

The Commissioner considered that he should have sought permission from the Director of Publicity or Communications (or whatever it was called) before sending the letter. His response was that it would not have been approved in time to be effective. Apparently the 'Police Review' magazine thought it was a good letter.

As a result his name was briefly associated, from a community relations perspective, with the Carnival that went wrong. As a result he was transferred to Kensington and his happy three years at Notting Hill came to an end.

In hindsight we can see that there was a middle way, including getting involved more constructively with the Carnival organisers, improving intelligence and more thorough surveillance. (FW)

Some years later when he was a Chief Inspector he returned and bumped in to the Irish Crime Prevention Officer (CPO). They went across the road from the station to the Ladbroke Arms Public House – a favourite watering hole. The CPO had made the point that he very rarely went into the pub. It was with some amusement then that the landlord said 'The usual Xxxxxxx?' It was a Guinness, of course. (FW)

---

1. Policing Notting Hill – 50 Years of Turbulence ISBN 978-1-904380-61-0

CHAPTER 30
VIOLENT TALES

In and Out of the Eagle

Message to the van from Information Room (MP) at Scotland Yard.

"Bravo Hotel 2, Bravo Hotel 2 (call sign for the van) "Fight in the Eagle Public House," MP over."

I was driving the van with the first black officer at Notting Hill. In the pub, two Irish men were fighting and we separated them. With the help of the bar staff I cleared the counter of glasses (potential weapons). One of the men started making very racist remarks at my colleague, which was very unusual for an Irishman. He refused to come outside quietly and started fighting with the officer.

"Don't worry, just leave it to me", said the PC as I went to assist him.

I took his advice and stood by whilst he overpowered the man and frog-marched him to the van. I was impressed.

Why Bother?

A call came from Information Room (IR) at Scotland Yard to an alleged fight in premises in Colville Square. We were in a two-manned

Area car. We answered immediately and, because it came over as a fight, we expected other units to answer. No-one else did and we knew it would be unlikely when the dispatcher said that a pregnant woman was involved. Houses in the Square were the usual dilapidated old Victorian three storey buildings with basements. Stone columns were at the bottom of the wide, stone steps leading to the front door with black painted pig-iron railings on either side. As we mounted the steps the front door was open.

There was a man lying, with his head towards me, in the corridor. His top half was naked. The lighting was dim and I at first thought he was a black man but I then realised that he was a white man covered in blood. I did not know if he was dead or alive. The pregnant woman was standing at the bottom of the internal stairs, screaming. Another man, about 6'2", was jumping up and down on this man's chest supporting himself with his hands on either side of the corridor. He was wearing big working man's boots. I ran forward and managed to push the man off, put him in a full Nelson wrestling grip and propelled him into the first door that I came to. It was in darkness but, thankfully, it was a bedroom. I pushed the struggling man face down onto the bed and held him there. He was trying to get up to get back at his victim.

"I'll kill him. I'll kill him," he yelled.

I told him I was arresting him for assault and cautioned him.

Luckily the Duty Officer (Inspector) and the Section Sergeant arrived and called for an ambulance. The Inspector, with whom I had previous experience at Trellick Towers, came into the room and asked if he could help.

"Just switch on the light, guvn'r," I suggested.

He then began to caution the man, whereupon I told him that I had already arrested and cautioned him. He was obviously trying to garner 'brownie points' in case the victim died and he could show an arrest for murder. Oh yes, such devious methods happened.

The victim was taken to St Charles Hospital where his condition was perceived to be very, very serious with the prospect that he might die. As a result Senior CID officers were recalled to duty, including the Detective Inspector. We went back to the scene and to a room on the first floor to find out what had happened, and why. Both men had been drinking heavily and it appeared that the smaller man had made advances towards the pregnant woman and the other man had taken umbrage and had hit him over the head with a bottle. During the struggle the larger man pushed the victim down the stairs. He had then ripped out (that shews his strength) some of the pig-iron stairs railings which had been broken in the fight and started smashing the other man with them. They reached the corridor on the ground floor and then he went outside and broke some more railings and started hitting the man again. He then began jumping on him which is when we arrived.

A CID officer went into the cell at the station to tell the arrested man that it was likely that his victim might die.

"I hope he dies on the slab," he responded.

The man survived. As I was filling in the crime sheet the Detective Inspector asked who had arrested the assailant.

I said, "I did but the Inspector tried to say that he had arrested him."

"Who put his hands on him first?"

"I did."

"Then it will be your name as the arresting officer on the charge sheet."

I thought he was being very fair.

The assailant appeared at the Old Bailey for attempted murder and despite the overwhelming evidence, the jury found him 'Not Guilty' of that offence but convicted him of grievous bodily harm with intent to cause grievous bodily harm. What more one had to do to kill someone I do not know.

A sequel to the story was that a few years later I was in the cell passage at the station. I noticed the victim's name chalked on the information board outside a cell. He had been arrested for drunk and disorderly. I went in to speak to him.

"You don't remember me, do you?"

He said, "No."

"I saved your life once."

"I wish you hadn't bothered."

Now that is gratitude for you.

Am I Bovvered? (with acknowledgement to Catherine Tate)

Dressed to Thrill

Local pub. Local 'heavy' Nottingdale family. Argument. Window smashed. Police called. Bravo 3 sent to scene. Me? I was the plain clothes observer dressed in black trousers, a red corduroy jacket and a hand-knitted (by my mother) rolled neck white jumper. The alleged perpetrator, one of the notorious Xxxx family, was shouting and swearing in the street as were many locals, friends and enemies, which can be dangerous when the crowd do not know that you are a police officer. I managed to grab him and put him in a police hold with his arm up his back. I was aware that the crowd was gathering around me – the driver and operator were trying to quell the crowd and find out what had actually happened.

Many of the crowd were women, relatives of the man, and they kept shouting at me about the man's arm and tried to pull him away. I was fortunate that I was not directly assaulted. The man himself kept going on about the pain in his arm but that particular hold is painful, especially if the person is trying to escape. The crowd, however, were very persistent that I look at his arm. I slackened off my hold so I could determine what they were so excited about. To my astonishment

I found that the front of my white jumper was smeared with blood. The man had put his fist through the window of the pub and had severely cut his wrist. The main priority then was to get medical aid so an ambulance was called. The uniformed operator went in the ambulance to the hospital.

As we, the driver and I, were making our way there, another emergency call came out that youths were causing a disturbance in Linden Gardens off Notting Hill Gate. There were hostels there and a group of young Swedish girl students had been booked in and the youths, with their joint bravado, had gathered to harass them. As we entered a short dead end off Linden gardens the youths decamped running past the police car. I got out, targeted one, chased him along Notting Hill and caught him at the corner of Pembridge Road. Not knowing what, if any offences had been committed, I decided to just hold him there until my driver found me. In the meantime one of the other youths, a big guy, came up and challenged me and tried to pull his mate away. I was in a difficult and potentially dangerous situation.

Thinking quickly I showed the youth the blood on my jumper. "I was in a fight earlier tonight – and I won," I told him.

He let me go, thought about it for a few seconds and then ran off. I was very relieved. Apart from the high jinks of trying to chat up the girls, no other offences were disclosed and the youth was released with a verbal warning.

Bottled Out

As previously indicated Portobello Road has a world-renowned antique market on each and every Saturday. Of course, the daily fruit and vegetable market co-exists and the local shops are grateful for the increased revenue from visitors from all over the world. It has been estimated that thousands of tourists wander through Portobello Road and its environs on any one Saturday. So, imagine how packed the street can become. Crime is omnipresent. Shoplifting, theft from person (dipping), three card tricks, robbery and drug-dealing are prevalent but usually hidden.

Visualise a pleasant summer Saturday afternoon. Suddenly there is the sound of breaking glass. I was on uniform patrol with another officer (RIP) and, turning around, we saw a man with a milk bottle in each hand. He had just thrown two others through a shop window. He was poised to throw the other two when we shouted at him. As we walked towards him he raised the bottles in a threatening matter with, I think, the intention of using them as weapons. He hesitated, decided that escape was the better part of valour, turned round and ran towards Westbourne Park Road. As he did so he threw his arms upwards and sideways and flung the bottles into the crowd. This was the ideal position for me to run up behind him, put my arms under his arms and clasp both my hands behind his head in a full Nelson wrestling hold (again). I then ran with him towards a parked car and held him with his face sideways down on the roof to await assistance.

This incident, unknown to me, was captured by an amateur photographer who was later awarded two hundred pounds by his local paper for the image.

dog-gone! EXCLUSIVE

£200

AMATEUR PHOTOGRAPHER
OF THE YEAR AWARD '78

Sponsored by The Guardian
and Morden Photographic

THIS entry by amateur photographer Keith Butler showing an incident at the Notting Hill Carnival reminds us that there's more to police work than lost dogs! Two local policemen, not the ones in the picture, were injured by bricks thrown in the riots but came straight back on duty next day. They were Inspector John Bartram and PC Roger Harwood, stationed at New Malden.

Pick-axe mugging charge

TWO young women were walking along Arthur Road, Wimbledon, late at night when they were "mugged" by two men, one of whom was armed with a club, and the other was wielding a pick axe.

This was told to the Wimbledon magistrates last week, when Stephen Lake, (19), of Monmouth Close, Pollards Hill, Mitcham, alleged to have been the one with the club, appeared alone in the dock.

He was remanded accused of robbing Sheila Stupples of her handbag containing cash and other articles, worth together £60, and at the same time robbing Dawn Painter of her handbag, containing cash and other articles worth £6.

Handicap...

SEVENTY-five-year-old Morris Henry Kerbel has had his clubs stolen from a locker room at Coombe Wood Golf Club.

our outlook on life. . .   SOUTH LON

P30. Dog-gone

Backside to the Future

With the wise old owl (remember him?) I went on an escort to Banstead Mental hospital with a man who had been sectioned under the Mental Health Act. We were just about to leave when we were called back into the building where a patient had gone berserk in the snooker room. He was a very, very large black man who was holding a snooker cue, threateningly, in his hands. He was at the far side of the table. There were numerous snooker balls – potential weapons – on the table. Members of the Hospital security and medical staff were in the room with a doctor who had a large syringe behind his back. No amount of cajoling would pacify the man. My driver in his laconic fashion started to roll himself a cigarette and casually challenged the man to a game of snooker. He agreed. After lighting his cigarette my driver picked up a cue and began playing. The man joined in. After a short time he had to move around the table to play a shot and as he bent down the doctor administered the fatal 'coup de grace' in his backside. The sighs of relief were palpable.

A Baying Crowd

Sunday 17th March 1968 will never be forgotten. Not because it was St Patrick's Day but because of the Grosvenor Square anti-Vietnam Riots. I was on beat duty at Notting Hill when, late in the afternoon, all available men at the station were herded into station vans and driven at breakneck speed to Central London. We were sublimely ignorant of the seriousness of the events that had been happening in Grosvenor Square although rumours had started to infiltrate. When we, about a dozen of us, arrived we were immediately deployed in front of the cordon outside the American Embassy. Thankfully for us most of the crowd were being gradually dispersed although fierce fighting was continuing on the fringes. Our task was to clear the Square and, as a group, we ran across the grass and pushed into the crowd who were vociferous, violent and vicious. Missiles were being hurled and close encounter fisticuffs were the norm.

I picked on one particular male participant who was striking out at us with a pole and decided to try to arrest him. Remember, this was in the middle of a melee. I managed to put an arm lock around his neck and began to pull him into the sterile area between the lines of policemen. However, his compatriots grabbed hold of him and tried to free him. I held firm but "the strength of the others managed to pull him away with blood now coming from his face.

"Five, One, Nine! Five, One, Nine! Five, One, Nine!" was the chant. This was my shoulder number and the crowd, of course, targeted me. Luckily I escaped serious injury although the badge on top of my helmet was dented.

It came to our notice that a Mounted Branch Officer had been dragged off his horse in Oxford Street and one of his feet was caught in a stirrup. The crowd were trying to kick him as he was dragged along close to the plate glass windows. Our Inspector ordered us to draw our truncheons and we charged and dispersed the baying crowd. No, it wasn't a bay horse- it was a grey.

CHAPTER 31
MISCELLANEOUS

10 Rillington Place

This address is infamous in the annals of gruesome murders. The exploits of John R. H. Christie who murdered several people are well documented with books and films of his notorious life.

When the heat was on after his final murder, he wandered the streets of London. He was spotted one morning on the banks of the river Thames near Putney Bridge: by that time, he was very scruffy and dishevelled. He gave his name as 'Reginald Halliday' which, of course, were his middle names. The officer was not convinced and soon established his correct identity.

William (Geordie) Johnson (WJ) – aged 89 in 2021 (RIP) - recalls that Christie was escorted from Putney by van to Notting Hill. He entered the back yard via the small back gate in Ladbroke Walk accompanied by Station Sergeant Spink (RIP). This was to avoid any hassle at the normal main vehicle access. An officer, Bryan Eckley (BE)(RIP), was watching from the canteen window on the third floor. He told me (STS) that 10 Rillington Place was like a dungeon - a most 'depressing and horrible site and sight?'.[1]

. . .

The following are accounts from 'Geordie'. This was in 1953. The crime scene had to be protected from curious onlookers and, especially, the press. The burden, of course, fell to the local police who, in all weathers, either had to stand outside in the cold or take succour within the building in which several bodies were found within its walls. Not for the faint-hearted. They were also involved in digging up the garden.

Pictured is the stalwart 'Geordie' Johnson. A reporter had asked him if he could photograph the building. 'Geordie' moved aside and did not realise that his image had been taken. He has related some other 'Tales of the Unexpected'.

P31. Rillington Place

Another officer escorted two women reporters into the building. One was American. 'Geordie' often wonders what the incentive was that persuaded him to breach the protocol. (WJ)

. . .

Sitting in front of the fire studying his IB in anticipation of a forthcoming exam WJ heard a noise on the stairs. Tentatively he went to investigate and found a cat creeping around.

I was told of another story when a young probationer was left, as he thought, on his own. Being apprehensive, he just sat on the stairs. Unknown to him another officer, who had hidden upstairs, tied some string to his boots and 'clumped' them down the stairs. What the petrified trainee said has not been recorded. (STS)

Hang On There

With the lack of any other means of communications, (Dr Who) police boxes were strategically placed around the sub-division.

P32. Police box

They were equipped with a blue light on top which the station could operate to indicate to a passing officer that there was a message to be dealt with. They also had a telephone which could be accessed by the public by opening a small hatch on the outside. Fun was often had when members of the public opened the hatch, lifted the receiver and immediately the officer inside opened the inside hatch and answered them stating he/she had just come straight down the tunnel from the police station. What a wheeze!

Patrolling officers had to ring in from a particular box at regular intervals so that the station could ensure that all was well. With a one-way window one could watch the passing world without being noticed.

During my time, the Westway flyover was being built and there were many Irish workers employed there. Many used the Kensington Park Hotel (KPH) pub. While idling my time in the box one evening a large man came out of the pub and was staggering quite badly; he would have been a danger to himself if he had fallen into the roadway. I went up to him. He was a very big Irishman with big arm muscles. As I took hold of his arm and told him he was being arrested for being drunk and incapable, he lifted his arm up with me hanging on to it. My feet left the ground. I thought, "Now I'm in trouble."

However, he gently lowered me down and chuckled, "Now you can arrest me!"

That's what I call respect.

Got Any Change Guv'nor?

Adjacent to this police box were two telephone kiosks. One evening I was with another officer when we heard the sound of metal on metal. We nodded to each knowing what was happening. We crept out and, sure enough, the young harum-scarum was just scooping up the loose change from the, now broken, cash box. This was a prolific offence when the coin boxes could be easily jemmied.

Locked In

Whilst patrolling Golborne Road one evening with another officer who was about 6ft 6 inches (1.98 metres) tall, we were called to a fight in a nearby pub. The disturbance had spilled out into the street and two men were fighting each other. My colleague grabbed one and took him away. I tried to grab the other and we ended up grappling on the ground, surrounded by members of his family - mostly women - who were trying to free him. Again, I thought, 'I'm in trouble here'. Suddenly a large hand appeared and grabbed the man by his collar, lifted him up and frog-marched him to a police box and pushed him inside.

"Where is the other one?" I asked.

"They are both inside" came the reply.

This was confirmed when an altercation started again in the tight confines of the box. Happy days!

Stay a Wake

As I have mentioned previously I was a bit unworldly when I came to London and seldom went to Church (there are not many near light-houses) and knew nothing about Roman Catholicism and had never been to a funeral. It was suspected that pubs at the north end of the division were selling alcohol after hours and I was tasked, one night, with trying to find out which one it was. Whilst patrolling Raddington Road at about 3am I saw two men staggering towards me, obviously under the influence. I had my chance. I stopped and asked them where they had been drinking. I still had a fairly strong Scottish accent: they were Irish.

"We've been to a wake, sir," one of them mumbled, in his strong accent.

I found that Irish people were usually respectful.

"I know you're awake but which pub were you drinking in?"

In his slurred speech he replied, "We weren't in a pub. We have been to a wake".

I persisted but could not find out which pub they had been in so I let them go. It was only years later, from my future Irish wife, that I found out what a 'wake' is.

Get on Your Bike

There was a pecking order in the night duty van (Black Maria) which may have held 2 or 3 officers in the back. The longest serving was nearest the back doors and the shortest serving was the furthest inside. The reason? If one had an arrest which required court the next day (usual) off night duty, one would earn 4 hours overtime and 2 hours travelling time, so it was expedient to be the first out of the van if an arrest was imminent. Of course it depended on how fast you were when the doors opened.

On this occasion there were three in the back and I was furthest from the door where I could see out of the front window. A cyclist came wobbling towards us obviously the worse through drink. The van stopped and I was out of the van so fast before the other two moved. I chased and caught the miscreant and was at court next day where the magistrate was amused - never having dealt with a drunk in charge of a pedal cycle before.

Feet and Feat of Clay

But did they belong to Cassius or Brian?

On 6th August 1966 a heavyweight World Champion fight took place at Earls Court between Cassius Clay (Mohammed Ali) and the British contender, Brian London (nee - Brian Sidney Harper). I was amongst a contingent of officers who escorted the fighters from their dressing rooms and we were then seated about 10 rows from the ring so that we were in a position to surround it if there were any after-fight shenanigans. We had just settled down comfortably in our seats when the fight was over. Cassius had knocked Brian out in the third round. Up we got and surrounded the ring, disappointed that the fight hadn't lasted a wee bit longer. Still, I will always have the memories of seeing the great man in his prime.

---

1. He spent his full service, 32 years, at Notting Hill. One of the ambitions as a policeman is to live long enough to claim the pension for more years than the 30 or so that they had served. Both he and WJ certainly have.

CHAPTER 32
DEATH MESSAGES

To Keen or Not Too Keen

Hayden's Place was a small turning off Portobello Road. I had been sent there to deliver a death message which no officer is comfortable doing. This was my first one and I was a bit apprehensive. Metal steps led up to the upstairs flat and I rang the bell. A middle-aged woman opened the door. She was dressed, head to foot, in a burka, something I had seldom, if ever, seen. As I was reading her the message about the demise of a man, a younger woman came downstairs, similarly dressed. When she heard what I was saying she sat down and immediately started keening and wailing and she was joined by the older woman. I was taken aback, never having seen such a show of grief. I was dumb-founded and backed slowly away leaving them crying and keening loudly. It was some experience. Sympathy? Empathy? More like pusilla-nimity (go on – look it up) I'm afraid.

Do I Have To?

A few years later I had to deliver a similar message to an address in a basement flat in Lancaster Road. A small Irish woman answered the door and ushered me in. There was no one else in the flat. I suggested she sit down whilst I gave some bad news about a woman who had passed away in St Charles Hospital. She took the information stoically and, although I suggested that I made her a cup of tea, she insisted that she would make me one and brought some biscuits with her. I stayed and chatted to her for about 20 minutes - my wife is Irish so we had an affinity. As I got up to leave she asked me if she had to go to the funeral. I said she didn't have to - it really depended on how close she was to the deceased.

"She was my mother" she declared.

This wasn't apparent because of the different surnames. Again, I was dumbfounded but in a different way. "There's nowt so queer as folk" was an expression that my mother often used.

The Silent Nun

I had to deliver another message of demise to a nun at a Carmelite Monastery of the Most Holy Trinity in St Charles Square telling her that her mother had passed away. On ringing the bell a nun appeared at a grated opening in the door. I asked to speak to Sister Xxxxxx but was told that I could not do so as it was a silent order. I passed on the message and asked her when the nun would be told. She said it could be some time and not until she had finished her penitence. And speaking about nuns...

I'm First

There used to be a large Convent at Westbourne Park Road, junction with Ladbroke Grove which became derelict. One late evening Bravo 3 was called to 'Suspects on Premises'. Our new Inspector, immaculate (as always) was in the car. The likelihood was that thieves would be trying to steal the lead from the dilapidated roof. On arrival there was a ten-foot wall to negotiate so I suggested to the Inspector, who was wearing highly polished shoes, that he leave it for me to climb. He was so enthusiastic that he was over the wall before I was and I have had a great respect for him ever since. It is not often that an Inspector gets his hands, or feet, dirty. There was 'No Trace' of suspects.

CHAPTER 33
SEX IN THE CITY -
TRUE SMUT

Heads I Win

Two of us were wandering along St Quintin Avenue on a very quiet and cold winter's night (greatcoat weather). We heard some noises coming from an apparently empty car on the opposite of the road. Because of its location outside a nurses' home we suspected some licentious activity. We decided to bombard the car with our torchlights. As we did so a female sat up on the passenger's side her head having been down at the driver's side. She appeared to say something when a man sat up on the driver's side. He looked out, smiled, wound down his window and shouted out a series of numbers which we immediately recognised as his warrant number. (Every policeman has a unique warrant number). Our suspicions were ratified and we strolled jealously away.

Se Men or Not Se Men? That is the Question

A rapist had been plaguing the southern and affluent part of Notting Dale at night for several years. The CID decided to stake out the most likely spots and if they saw a suspicious person going into basements they would bring him in for questioning. This was an opportunity for a wheeze on one of the cocky (watch it, watch it) new recruits. A glass phial was obtained and filled with yogurt and then labelled as if it were a genuine exhibit. The unsuspecting patsy was called in and asked to go to St Charles Hospital, speak to the Matron, and verify if the contents were semen or not. He duly did so. The Matron, of course, was forewarned. She took him into a science room and proceeded to 'check' the liquid with litmus paper, pipettes etc. After a while she said she wasn't sure whereupon she dipped her finger into the phial and sucked it and said 'Yes, that's semen alright'.

Without being 'punny', the officer wasn't so cocky after that.

Incidentally, the rapist was caught after about 6 years (He had been in prison for a part of that time) and had escaped capture previously due to a mistake in scientific misquotation. When caught, however, his profile matched precisely the information that was recorded on his collator's card including the fact that he listened to local police radio channels. As a result he had been able to eliminate a shoe print which had been left overnight at a scene and covered with a box waiting for examination by the Scenes of Crime Officer (SOCO). I had been the first officer to stop him and his brother many years previously after they had moved, as teenagers, from Wales and it was recorded on the collator's card of the miscreant.

A Flash in the Pan

Near the end of 2 years' service one had to sit a final exam at Hendon College. One had to travel there in full uniform. I was on the Northern Underground Line the doors of which opened in the centre of the carriageway. I was sitting close to the doors avidly reading my IB (Instruction Book) trying to cram in as much information as possible. (Too late now, I thought). My helmet was on the seat beside me. A very attractive young girl came and sat beside me and asked me if I was a policeman and if I was on duty?

Puffing up my chest (now all of 36 inches) I said that I was.

"We are always on duty ma'am", I informed her proudly.

"That man over there has just exposed[1] himself to me," she indicated.

I looked over and saw a very respectably dressed man, masturbating. Never having dealt with such an incident I was glad to have the IB so that I could look up to see if this was a public place under the Act. Before I could do so the train started to slow down and the man, who had seen me, got up to get out. However he had to pass me so I arrested him hoping I wasn't making a false arrest. We got out at the next station and I asked the ticket collector if there was a telephone nearby and he directed me to a pay box which was about 200 yards up a main road. The man was compliant but just as I reached the box he broke away. Fortunately there was a group of firemen in their uniforms walking towards us and they grabbed him.

When the van arrived we were taken to a police station nearby. I related the facts to the custody sergeant, the CID were called and the man was charged with 'flashing'. I, of course, missed the final exam that day. The following day the man, who was married with children, pleaded guilty. The CID officers were relieved when I said I could not go to the pub with them (I was still in full uniform anyway) so they had this beautiful looking girl to themselves. I continued to Hendon where I, and another officer who had also missed the exam the previous day, sat a different set of questions. Was I glad? I doubt if I would have passed the first set of questions but I got a star for the paper that I did complete. Lucky Jim!

And his mate **Flash Harry** (Not his real name)

"Xxxx and I were called to an allegation of 'flashing' at Pembridge Crescent, I think. We saw the complainant who pointed out a man who was exposing himself to her from a flat on the opposite of the communal gardens. As I remember, Sec 4 of the Vagrancy Act, there was no legitimate 'Power of Entry' as the incident was not in a public place. No problem! We worked out the house number and the top flat was probably flat D. We rang the bell of flat A and a woman answered. Xxxx drew himself up to his not inconsiderable height, brushed her aside with his left arm and, in a deep, magisterial voice, announced: 'Stand aside, Madam. I am in instant pursuit of a felon'.
It was one of those 'You had to be there' moments. So funny". (PC)

One Lucky B-----d (or was he?)

Meandering slowly along Colville Square one bright and beautiful morning at about 10 am with my thumbs firmly hooked into the button on the breast pockets of my tunic, I noticed a group of four or five men huddled in the centre of Colville Terrace. I guessed they were aged between 25–40 years, dressed in short-sleeved shirts. There appeared to be a deal going on and I suspected drugs. They did not see me approach and I noticed one of them had a bunch of notes in his hand. My suspicious did not diminish.

"What's going on here then, lads?"

They broke off and sheepishly stood aside. I asked several times what was happening but they were all reluctant to tell me. When I suggested that I would search them for drugs the money holder pulled me aside. He said they were the local dustmen (vehicles around the corner) and, as they did not individually have enough money they had pooled their resources together so that one of them could be entertained by the local prostitute who lived at no. 14. They had been drawing lots to see who the 'lucky' man would be. This 'lady' was well known, probably nearly 60 years old, scruffy and lived in a dingy basement apartment. I would have been glad to have lost the 'toss'. **Clap** (at the end if you want).[2]

Ok. Ok. Just one more 'Shaggy dog'.

More Clap

The area of Clapham (an appropriate name under the circumstances) was on 'L' Division.

It so happened that two officers from there were in our canteen one day so they were ripe for a bit of salacious fantasy. I asked them if they had heard about the PC who had been arrested at Clapham in the early hours of that morning.

"No", they said, so I enlightened them. They were enthralled.

When a police vehicle is booked out you have to enter the mileage used and sign the log book so I told them that:-

An off duty police officer who, unknown to anybody, had been taking out the van during night duty if it was idle in the yard. It was eventually noticed that, although it had only travelled a short distance each time, there were no entries for the missing mileage or a signature, which was required.

Surveillance was kept and the said officer was seen to take the van out. It was followed and it drove to Clapham Common where it picked up a known prostitute. After driving into a dark area, both the driver and said 'lady of the night' were seen to climb into the back of the van. The watching officers contacted the uniform Duty Officer (an Inspector) and a watch was kept. After a short time a naked man was seen to get out of the van, climb on the roof and remove the aerial (which, in those days, was screwed on to the bodywork). After he climbed back in the sound of 'whiplashing' was heard. The time was right. The back doors of the van were swung open and there was the gratified PC lying on his stomach on the bench seat whilst a nude, red-rouged, scarlet woman was happily applying some welts and wheals across a bare backside.

After closing their gaping mouths, the Inspector and crew arrested both the miscreants. The PC, of course had committed numerous offences including TDA, No insurance, fraternising with a prostitute etc. etc. At the station the Divisional Surgeon (changed to FME – Force Medical Officer or should it be (SME) Service Medical Officer? I can't keep up) was called to examine the 'Blushing Bobby'. The Inspector was barred from the examination room. The doctor had to complete a report. When asked what the diagnosis was he said, Wait for it, Wait for it:

"That's the worst case of van aerial disease I have ever seen."

The 'L' Division officers were less than enthralled...... (STS)

---

1. Commonly known as 'flashing' the relevant Act states: 'every person wilfully openly, lewdly, and obscenely exposing his person in any street, road, or public highway, or in the view thereof, or in any place of public resort, with intent to insult any female'.

    Contrary to Sec. 4 Vagrancy Act, 1824

2. In April 2020, I was reading a book 'Crime in London' by Gilbert Kelland, former head of NSY CID, and he mentioned this address (P.66) where the same basement was being used as a brothel in 1960.

CHAPTER 34

COMMENDATIONS AND LETTERS OF APPRECIATION

A selection of the above, in chronological order, appeared in my personal files.

I would like to think that they were not exhaustive but they represent the diverse level of investigators who were appreciative of the assistance of collators who, I believe, are unsung heroes. Their expertise of recording, thinking out of the box, memory and dedication were often crucial in the investigation of offences resulting in the subsequent arrest of offender/s. Their efforts were seldom recognised as they never boasted of their exploits. All of them would have received similar accolades. I salute them.

You will note that many of the appreciations were from outside Forces who would suddenly appear in the office. One Chief Superintendent, who was intent in curbing my overtime, asked me if they came by appointment. When I said 'No' he told me they would have to give me 2 weeks' notice. How that would have helped I am at a loss to understand as they would still take up the same time: so unrealistic!

One of the functions was to send a copy of arrests sheets to the 'home' collator. This meant getting in early and, using the binder winder, (remember that?), remove the arrest sheets, copying them and then forwarding them, internally to the relative home station. This took up a considerable time as Notting Hill was a very busy station. He said I had to stop doing it. I then asked him if I could borrow a car. He looked quizzical. I explained that I would have to drive to all the stations which had arrested Notting Hill villains overnight because if I didn't send them information they would not reciprocate.

Despite repeated requests for assistance and inviting any Senior Officer to sit in the office for 4 hours just to gauge the amount of work that was involved, they were declined. When I was 'accused' of giving jobs to squads rather than local officers I pointed to the telephone wire and said it connected with the outside world and that jobs were distributed to those who were capable of dealing with them.

- - - - - o o o o o - - - - -

Memo from Commander 'D' Division to Commander 'B' Division, 7th June 1976

Good Arrest

Will you please convey my personal thanks to P.C. 296B Brown and P.C. 519B Scott both attached to Notting Hill Police Station for their good work in effecting the arrest of a youth for theft.

The officers were returning from a call towards BH Section when they saw the youth sitting in a motor vehicle. Upon seeing Police he ducked down out of sight. He was stopped and questioned and it was discovered that he had stolen tape cassettes from the vehicle.

Signed by X.X.Xxxxxx
Commander 'D' Division

----- o o o o o -----

Letter from Avon & Somerset Constabulary 14th April 1981

To Officer in Charge, Metropolitan Police, 101, Ladbroke Road, Notting Hill, London W.11 3PL

(It refers to the court appearance of alleged burglars at Bristol Crown Court)

With reference to the above-named and previous telephone communications and correspondence, you will no doubt be pleased to hear that XxXxxxxxxx was convicted of two counts of burglary and sentenced to nine months imprisonment. Xxxxx was found 'not guilty' on both counts........ Thank you for your assistance given to my officers in connection with these two men. My special thanks to P.C. Scott, your collator, who was most helpful, frequently up-dating the some-what fluid situation.

Signed – DS 647 Watts.

----- o o o o o -----

Memo dated 5th May 1983 from Chief Superintendent Xxxxx at Hammersmith Police Station (FD) to Chief Superintendent, Notting Hill.(BH)

Re Xxxxxxx Xxxxx and Xxxxx Xxxxx

Arrested at FD (Hammersmith) for Armed Robbery.

Officers from this Station conducted enquiries culminating with the arrest of the above named for Armed Robbery, during which a shotgun was discharged. The assistance afforded them by Police Constable 519 'B' Scott at 'BH' was of considerable benefit and went a good way in expediting the enquiry. May this officer be thanked for his help in this case.

Signed by Chief Superintendent FD.

(Rider from C/Supt. BH – Well done – it's nice to be appreciated).

- - - - - o o o o o - - - - -

How to Make a Fortune

If you made a suitable suggestion to improve the workings of the Force and it was accepted you could be eligible for a monetary reward. I received this citation, dated 18th February 1985 from the Commissioner of Police (yes, the one I mentioned above) in which he wrote:-

Letter from New Scotland Yard 18 February 1985

Addressed to PC 155... S. Scott,
'B' District.

Dear Mr. Scott,

Your suggestion that Form NIB XX be altered to include the station code where the arrested person resides and whether a photograph has been taken together with your second suggestion that the collator's stamp be altered to show where the details and photograph of the arrested person are held, which you submitted in 1983, was considered by the force Suggestion Scheme Adjudicating Committee on 5th February 1985.

I am pleased to inform you that the Committee recommended an award of £25. A cheque for this amount is enclosed and details will appear in Police Orders shortly.

I very much appreciate the interest and enthusiasm which you have displayed in putting forward your idea.

Yours sincerely,

Xxxxxxx Xxxxxx,
Commissioner.

(I nearly retired....)

- - - - - o o o o o - - - - -

Memo from 1 Area Intelligence and Surveillance Unit, Barnes June 1985

Syd Scott 'BH'

I wish to thank you for the valuable assistance that you have given to this unit during my period as Office Manager, especially of your understanding of the problems we had in the formation of the Unit and in particular the extra work load I gave you in sifting out records for our data base..... Once again thank you for your support.

Signed Xxxxxx XxXxxxxx Police Sergeant CID

- - - - - o o o o o - - - - -

Extract from Letter from No. 5 Regional Crime Squad, Hatfield 22nd July 1985

Addressed to Commander X.X. Xxxxxxxx Q.P.M.at Area HQ, Notting Dale Police Station (BN).

Dear Sir,

Re: Operation Xxxxxxxx, - Arrest of Xxxxx Xxxx Xxxxxxxx on 9th July 1985

.....He has since been charged with the offence at Xxxxxxxx Xxxx, a result that would have not been possible without the professionalism of your officers. I would also like to bring to your notice the considerable help and assistance given to my officers by Police Constable S. Scott, the Collator at Notting Hill Police Station.

X.X.Xxxxx,
Regional Co-ordinator.

Reply from No 1 Area Headquarters from X.X.Xxxxxxxx, Commander 1 Area.

.... 'Rest assured that I will have the officers, including PC Scott, the Collator at Notting Hill Police Station, informed of your comment'.

- - - - - o o o o o - - - - -

Letter from Metroplitan Police, 'V' Division 22nd August 1985

To Commander 'B', Kensington Police Station.

Dear Sir,
I would like to bring to you attention to the work of your Collator, Police
Constable 519'B' Scott who was of great assistance in the Incident Roam at
Kingston in a recent case of double attempted rape and robbery whereby two
men received long prison sentences at the Old Bailey and others were sentenced
for lesser offences of handling etc. PC Scott devoted a great deal of time and
energy to assist the C.I.D. officers from this Division in their enquiries and his
help was directly attributable to the final outcome.

Yours faithfully,
Xxxx X.X. Xxxxx
Detective Chief Inspector 'V'

- - - - - o o o o o - - - - -

Letter from Bedfordshire Police 27th March 1990
Addressed to The Collator, Metropolitan Police, Hayes Police Station.

Dear Sid (Sic),

Please receive Bedford R.U.F.C. tie as a small token of our thanks for your help
and hospitality received on Friday 23rd March 1990, when we were conducting
enquiries with your police station.

Signed Xxxxx Xxxxxxxxxx and Xxxxxx Xxxxxx.

CHAPTER 35
MIXTURE O' MERCIES
(ANOTHER PHRASE THAT MY MOTHER OFT-TIMES QUOTED)

The Good, The Bad and The Ugly.

Before leaving Notting Hill for pastures new (they have fields in Hayes) I would like to add an eclectic mix of wee stories – not in any particular order.

Boot Leg

I had arrived at work, having forgotten my shoes so I was still wearing my big motorcycle boots, the outlines of which were clearly visible through my trousers - as were the big feet.

"What on earth are you wearing?" asked a WPC.

"They are my motorcycle boots. I have had them for ...er... 22 years."

"They are older than me."

There was no riposte to that!

A Whisker Away

Each year one had an AQR (Annual Qualification Record). On my first one, which was after 2 years when I had to be confirmed, The Chief Superintendent wrote:

"An intelligent young man. Not of good appearance but is keen and willing. Confirmed as above."

Prior to this, during a term of three weeks night duty, I had grown a beard which was allowed so long as it was grown on night duty. I was called into his office and he ordered me, yes ordered me, to shave it off as he disliked beards. Because of his attitude, (remember I had met him on my first day at the station) which to me was a type of bullying, I had the temerity to defy him and explained that, according to the G.O. (General Orders tome) I had every right to keep it.

I saluted with the customary, "All Correct, Sir" and walked out.

His punishment was to make sure that the Sergeants posted me to the furthest two beats on the patch until I complied with his order.

Sometime later I applied for a Noddy Course. It had to be signed by the Divisional Chief Superintendent based at Chelsea. When I got there, who was acting DCS but our CS? He asked me if I was going to shave it off and when I said, "No" he tore the application up and said that I would walk the beat until I did so.

I again saluted and said, "That's why I joined the Job, sir," did a smart about turn and walked out.

Some months later I shaved it off and he saw me in the corridor and ordered me into his office. He then handed me a fresh application form and if it wasn't that I was desperate to go on the course I would have told him to..........................off. It didn't do me any harm.

Interestingly, on page 18 of the London Police Pensioners (LPP) magazine of March 2018, there was an article entitled 'I want you for

PEEL'S Police c. 1839' which listed some of the requirements for joining The Job:

"Your working hours will be eight, ten or twelve hour shifts, seven days a week. Every encouragement will be given to officers to grow beards as shaving is regarded as unhealthy. However, beards must not exceed two inches in length."

Foreign Language Speakers

The swarm of human busy bees attracted to the Portobello Road on a Saturday, lured the rumbling of Italian ice cream vans to the honey pot. Unfortunately they would park dangerously at junctions or, even worse, at the approach to pedestrian crossings. The genial servers would have a variety of excuses for not moving from their lucrative sites. "No speaky de English", "I no understand", "Battery flat", "Driver he not here", etc. Whilst learning beats with an experienced officer we came across a van parked right on the junction of Chepstow Villas and Portobello Road.

"Move," he said to the sweet smiling Italian lady.

"Flat battery," was her response in a strong accent.

"Where is the driver?"

"He gone off with battery."

Not to be fooled the officer said, "Tell him to stand up."

He had been hiding.

"Move."

"I no understand English."

"Do you understand F--- Off?"

"Si," was the response.

"Well F--- Off then."

The driver smiled and drove off. I was fairly shocked as I was not used to such language. (Not many to swear at in a lighthouse).

Thou Shalt Not Laugh

A very pretty German student had been wandering along Notting Hill Gate trying to find the hostel which is in Holland Park when her backpack was stolen from her. She was in a distressed state but she was seen by a taxi driver who took her to the police station. She could not speak English and, despite our feeble attempts to interpret and find out her name, we were unable to get any sense from her between the sobs. Several officers tried but to no avail.

A call went over the radio asking if any officer knew German and the driver of Bravo 3 said that his operator did. This was a surprise to all of us. However, he came and said – you won't believe this – "Vot is your name?" I am sorry to say that we became helpless, convulsed with laughter. A phone call to the German Embassy soon sorted out the dilemma.

Why Did They Call Me Dumbo?

As a teenager with an idle mind and idle hands I learnt to recite the alphabet backwards, mastered the letters of the sign language, learnt Morse code and semaphore for no particular reason. The first, of course, was completely useless but the second came in handy (sorry!). Police were called to a burglary where the male victim could only communicate (as I thought) by sign language so, knowing I had ability, they brought him to the station. Now, I had never practised 'reading' it, just self-practising it so I was having difficulty (its back to front remember) interpreting his gestures.

After about a quarter of an hour of my excruciating embarrassment the man signalled, "Can I write it down?"

Now who would have thought of that?

English as She Is Spoke

On another occasion an Iranian, who could only communicate in sign language, was robbed but had a friend with him. I was asked over the radio to come to the scene.

"Ask his friend if he (the victim) can understand English?" I said.

"Does it matter, it is sign language," was the reply.

Naturally when I got there he could only speak Persian. Abracadabra didn't work either.

Child Prodigy

In the mid-seventies my family and I lived in police flats in the Grove at Ealing. My wife was in hospital expecting a second child and I was in bed, reading, when I heard the clunk of a car door outside – the unmistakable noise of my Triumph Spitfire. I peered out and saw a man getting into my car. I struggled into my trousers, called my brother-in law who had been staying with me, told his wife to phone the police and ran down the stairs. The man was sitting in the driver's seat. When I asked him if it was his car he said it belonged to a mate around the corner. A Spitfire is very close to the ground. I grabbed him and hauled him out. Yes, he was that 6'3"man again. I managed to put him in a standard arm-lock, as did my brother-in law, and we held him against the wall until the police arrived in their van.

I thought I was small but the officer who arrived was smaller than me, had ginger hair and wore big glasses. Was it the 'Milky Bar Kid'? (Those of you of a certain vintage will know who I mean). He was his double and when I told the Custody Sergeant at the station and described the officer he said, "Oh, you mean the Milky Bar Kid?"

Life or Death

I was on my way to work on my motor-bike and had stopped at the traffic lights on Ealing Road at the junction with the North Circular. A car travelling south crossed the junction, veered across the nearside pavement and smashed into a grey traffic sign post, bending it.

I immediately drove across and noticed a man slumped over the steering wheel, apparently unconscious. I was able to open the rear passenger's door which was undamaged. The male must have weighed about 20 stone. He didn't appear to be breathing. I managed to pull his head back (I was in the back seat remember). I attempted to give him mouth to mouth resuscitation but it was difficult and there was a gurgling noise coming from his throat. I felt sick but carried on. Other passers-by managed to open the driver's door and we laid him down on the ground and I continued with the pumping and the blowing until an ambulance and a traffic police officer arrived. I went in the ambulance and held the oxygen mask but I later found out that he had passed away with a heart attack.

I got a dressing down from my Sergeant for being late for work and not even praise when I told him the circumstances. I think he thought I was making it up. Some gratitude.

Most police officers will have performed good deeds whilst off duty, especially to save lives. It is the nature of their character. They should be praised for their actions and not vilified by certain factions of society who would be the first to call for the police if they were in a situation that required their presence. Remember, police officers run towards trouble whilst some others run away. Rant over.

I should also mention the members of the public who often come to the assistance of the police even in dangerous situations. They should be commended. From my stories you will note that I have been forever grateful for their help.

Snow Go

As everyone knows even a sprinkling of snow in the capital causes havoc to the transport system. When it is 2 or 3 inches deep, (which is not very often), panic ensues. Except for essential emergency services, traffic 'freezes'. Occasionally police vehicles were grounded for safety reasons.

No Go

On one occasion two women police officers thought that they could defy the elements and took out a Panda car. They got no further than about 20 yards up Ladbroke Grove which is a fairly steep hill before being 'rescued' and escorted back to the station.

A Bit Nippy

One late evening, with heavy snow on the ground, my colleague and I were stopped by a woman in Lansdowne Road stating she could not get into her house as she had lost her keys. She had a small child with her. A very expensive area and the building was three storeys high with attic rooms above, probably 80 – 100 feet above ground level. The property was protected by many security features. No duplicate keys were available.

"Why is there a light in the attic?" I pointed out.

"That is the au pair's room but she won't hear the bell."

What to do? We began to throw snowballs at the attic window. Eventually one hit the window and the au pair stuck her head out of it to find out what was happening. When she opened the door the lady of the house instructed her to pour us two glasses of whisky whilst she went off to put the child to bed. The servant, whom I think was Brazilian, obviously did not know too much about 'nips' as she poured two very big 'shots', much to the surprise of the occupant. Unfortunately (fortunately) my colleague did not drink whisky so it was left for me to take advantage. It would have been rude not to.

Crunch Time

These incidents remind me of the time I was staying at my mother's house in Scotland. She was elderly and the local youths would throw snowballs at her side window. This happened one night and I ran out just to see two teenage girls disappearing down a side street where they hid. They were surprised when I found them. Sleuth, of course, just followed their footprints.

As Ernest Agyemang Yeboah quoted, "Every day we leave a footprint."

Pho Netics Sake

There was an officer who put 'S 6' on a crime report instead of Essex and another who put 'Fish Hole Saler' instead of 'Fish Wholesaler'. No, the informant wasn't an Eskimo.

The Tower Beckoned

In the early 1970s the IRA were prevalent with many terrorism acts in London.

David Ormsby-Gore aka Lord Harlech, the film censor, held a party at premises in Ladbroke Road junction with Horbury Crescent. The Lords and Ladies of the land, film stars and their ilk were the privileged guests. In 1968 he proposed to Jacqueline Kennedy who spurned his advances and married a richer man – Aristotle Onassis. It was incumbent upon the police to protect the aristocracy and the famous. A small contingent of uniformed officers, of whom I was one, was delegated to ensure the safe arrival of the visitors. A plain clothes armed officer, whom I shall call Mr. 'B', was ensconced in the house as he knew Lord Harlech quite well.

At midnight the outer cordon was dismissed but the Inspector allowed me to slip away and join Mr. 'B'. There was a large room on the left as one entered the building where long tables were laid out and from where the 'breakfast' meals were being served by elderly, presumably vetted, ladies who were scurrying around. Alcoholic drink was in abundance and, being off-duty, I indulged in that and the proffered fare. Mr. 'B'. was not to be seen. However, when he appeared he invited me to join him in the hallway as some of the guests were leaving and Lord Lichfield was taking photographs. A renowned actress, Lee Remick, who was more beautiful in the flesh than on the screen, was about to leave when she kissed Mr. B. on the lips. Was I jealous? (of Mr 'B'.)

Mr. B. then urged, persuaded, and cajoled me to join him in the main body of the building. The whole garden had been covered over and artificial palm trees and other paraphernalia lavishly adorned the whole scene. There was also a free bar. Mr 'B'. and I sat down and I had a second meal served by an Irish lady who supplied us with the large tipple of our preferred request and surreptitiously placed a full bottle of each respective spirit under the table despite our vociferous protestations. Jacqueline Kennedy was sitting at a table within 10 feet of us. Dancing had started and having loosened my tie and with great bravado I asked a lady to dance. She turned out to be H.M. The Queen Mother's dresser and I asked her to pass on my regards to her as I had met Her Majesty at Dunnet Head lighthouse when I was a wee boy.

Fast forward to the time when many of the guests were leaving and we joined them in the large communal hall. Mr 'B'. had his revolver in a shoulder holster and when his jacket flapped open a woman, details not known, saw and grabbed it and started waving it about. I sobered up (Hic!) immediately, gulped and grabbed the woman's arm and took the weapon from her.

"Who do you think you are?" she said angrily.

"That is a loaded gun, madam."

"Do you not think I know how to use a gun?"

I'll never forget the words. Can you imagine what would have happened if it had accidentally discharged and killed Jackie Kennedy or another famous person?

Returning to the comfort of the rapidly evacuating marquee we headed for the bar where, nursing her drink, sat Lord Harlech's daughter, Alice. Her boyfriend (Eric Clapton?) was dressed as a Harlequin but she ignored him and started talking to us. She said that they had a small holding in Wales which I assumed would have cattle and sheep and I asked her how many head of animals she had. She eventually admitted that it was more like a commune and they only kept a few hens, ducks and pigs. She was very pleasant and interesting to talk to and we were the only people in the room. At about 5 o'clock, when daylight had been abroad for a few hours, Lord Harlech came down the stairs and demanded to know who we were. We explained that we were 'security'.

"Don't you think it is time you went home, officers?" he politely asked.

How we got there is another story.

Mr. 'B' adds:-

Two days after the party I received a letter from Lady Harlech thanking me for my professional help at the party ensuring the safety and security of all the guests. Later that day I was summoned to see the Chief Inspector who was responsible for operational duties.

"I believe you were all pissed," were his opening words.

I produced the letter of thanks from Lady Harlech and that was a happy ending. The majority of the Labour Cabinet was at the party.[1]

---

1. According to Wikipedia, (11th June 2020) tragically,
    - Lord Harlech died in a car crash on 26th January 1985.
    - His first wife, Lady Sylvia Harlech, died in a car crash on 30th May 1967
    - His son, Julian, died of gunshot wounds in 1974 in an apparent suicide.
    - Alice died of an overdose in poverty in 1995.
    - Lee Remick died 2nd July 1991 from cancer.
    - Lady Pamela, Lord Harlech's second wife, is still alive. (2020)

CHAPTER 36
MONEY FOR NOTHING

All That Glitters...

I have been reluctant to relate some stories as they are detrimental to the Service and I would not wish to sully or tarnish the reputation of the Force. However, I have recently read two books. One writer was a PC and then a DC and the other was an ACC (Assistant Commissioner, Crime). Was he the same one I mention in another place? I cannot remember. However, both were scathing about the corruption which had incrementally pervaded the Job over many years. The vast majority of officers are and were hard-working, dedicated and honest but one or two festered at the bottom of the barrel. You couldn't see them but you could smell them. NO names mentioned.

Take It When You Can

The lure of lucre is insidious. We humans have many traits: some good, some bad and some pure evil. Peer pressure, coercion, bribery, jealousy, greed, living above one's status, poverty and promotion prospects are just a few of the weaknesses that can persuade someone to derogate their morals. They may have been remorseful or attended confessional but, like smoking or drugs, withdrawal can be painful. Several, of course, would assuage their consciences and donate a small proportion of monies to selected charities and there is no doubt much was raised from these individuals.

Keep Your Head Down

Whilst I was a Home Beat Officer (HBO) I and another HBO, Roger Pierce (RIP), who was attached to Nottingdale Police Station, decided unilaterally to investigate some of the major criminals on the sub-division using information from the collators' cards and elsewhere. We were meticulous in recording and inter-linking their associates and activities. However, this hobby became bigger than we imagined and eventually encompassed the surrounding stations. We called our dossier 'West London Major Criminals'. It was also evident that Senior Officers, both uniform and CID (mainly) were being paid on a regular basis especially where a licence (liquor or otherwise) was involved including the 'speilers'. These were unlicensed gaming houses where Kalooki was played. This is a Jamaican card game. Of course an early-warning before illegal clubs were raided was a lucrative income. Illegal late night drinking dens (shebeens) were obvious targets where the commodity had to be seized. I say no more. The three card trick merchants in Portobello Road were a regular source of monies but we 'oiks' allegedly knew nothing about this...

Years later I did point out to a very honest Senior Officer that 'green backs' were acceptable currency after a 'speiler' raid that he organised was compromised. He was astonished. Our little close-knit team had been keeping observation on the premises as we knew from an informant that the proceeds of crime, mainly stolen credit cards, were being pedalled there each Wednesday - the day of the aborted raid.

Undercover

One late evening a 'hero' Detective Sergeant was seen by Roger outside Nottingdale Police Station lifting up the rear seat of his car and putting in, what appeared to be, a slab of cannabis. What to do? We did not trust anyone. We did not report it. Were we cowards or just circumspect? We approached a trusted uniform Sergeant, explained our fears but did not tell him specifically about the drugs. He advised us not to tell anyone, not even the Yard, even though Sir Robert Mark, a renowned honest man, was the Commissioner, because some of his lieutenants who were not so trustworthy might be informed inadvertently.

Some years later the DS was charged with the murder of his Colombian girlfriend and was sentenced to 12 months imprisonment for manslaughter. I speculate that she knew too much of his nefarious activities and that, what I perceive to be a light sentence, was negotiated because he knew too much. Or am I being too sceptical?

Scrap Information

There was a metal scrap-yard in Freston Road (Mentioned in Chapter 16 - Drugs section) on the Shepherds Bush side of the dividing line between it and Nottingdale. Technically, I suppose, it was in the 'Independent State of Frestonia' - an enclave created by disaffected and homeless people who occupied, as squatters, the derelict and seemingly uninhabitable houses. According to Wikipedia, they had their own ministers, flag and postage stamps and visitors' visas.

The occupants of the yard had connections with some major criminals – well they were villains themselves - and we began to keep observations from the gasometer at the top of Ladbroke Grove. It was suspected that there was a gold-smelting machine available to the team.

On 16th November 1976 there was a raid on the Bank of America in Mayfair. It was believed to have been the biggest robbery ever carried out anywhere. The following morning we saw the occupants of the yard (small 'y') gloating over the morning papers although there did not appear to be any direct connection. This information was relayed to an operation being run by the renowned untarnished thief-taker Commander Bert Wickstead (The Grey Fox) at Leighton Police Station. Having contacted him we were immediately seconded to his office without, so far as I know, the knowledge of our own Chief

Superintendent. (or were we naïve?). We drove to Leighton each day, in Roger's authorised car, taking different routes, in case we were being followed (by the CID).

We spent about 2 months collating information mainly on C11 (major crime investigations branch). Mr. Wickstead's name gave us unprecedented access to Criminal Records Office where we searched the misdeeds of these men and, as importantly, found out who had arrested them in the past. We were nicknamed the SSS (Secret Squirrel Squad) at BH and no-one knew what we were doing. We named no officers - just intimated that there was corruption. After completing the report, to our dismay, Commander Wickstead put it in a large brown envelope and labelled it A10 which was the department which dealt with investigating police officers. He walked into the CID office there, called over a DC and told him, out loud for the benefit of all and sundry, to take it to A10. Bear in mind we were uniform PCs, albeit in plain clothes:- everyone else was a CID officer. After three pints of Young's Winter Warmer, I told him what I thought of his action. His knuckles went white as he grasped his desk. Unknown to us he had previously been in charge of A10.

He, of course, had the last laugh. It was our last day there and we were invited into the general office for the usual Friday soiree. I had a few drams of whisky (Roger was driving). The three man lift is where there is a bet that a man, usually the smallest in the group, could lift three men at once. I was the innocent patsy who lay down in the middle of the floor with a man on each side. They then linked their arms and legs with mine. I was now unable to move whilst they poured beer all over my suit. Roger had tried to warn me but I had not heeded him. Lesson learnt.

Having heard nothing for many months we asked to speak to the ACC (Assistant Commissioner, Crime) to find out if there had been any progress. He shewed us into his inner sanctum at the Yard with the comment, "I have never had uniform PCs in my office before." He then offered us the obligatory coffee and biscuits. He tried to interrogate us (not very successfully) asking who these alleged corrupt officers were. We had not mentioned corrupt officers by name just intimated that any surveillance should be carried out by an outside force as the local villains knew the incumbent CID personnel. He was not very happy, expecting us to name names. He did not enlighten us of any progressive activity. We had made three copies each with a different code on it so that we would know if it were leaked, whence the leak had originated.

On our return to duties Roger became very nervous suspecting that the local officers had been told of our exploits. He asked for and was granted a transfer. I remained and was appointed collator and the rest is history.

About 10 years later whilst at West Drayton, a detective sergeant for whom I had great respect, suddenly died. The uniform Inspector asked me if I would empty his locker and, lo and behold, there was a copy of our report. I will not tell you whose copy he had copied but what a coincidence. I often wondered if the Inspector had seen it in there and asked me in particular to search it.

CHAPTER 37

ALL SAINTS ROAD

I have saved this Notting Hill chapter to the end as it encapsulates the political mood of the time and the enormous pressure from government for the police to be seen to 'do the right thing'.

Five Out of Six Ain't Bad

You may surmise from my various spats with senior officers that I was bolshie and disrespectful. This was not true. I always respected all ranks but I would not be intimidated or humiliated as I had been at school. If the circumstances warranted it I said what I thought. I had great admiration for many senior officers and one Chief Superintendent in particular whose bravado and ingenuity uplifted the depressed mood of his troops.

In the eighties, politically, All Saints Road was virtually a no-go area for police (don't listen to people who deny it) for fear of upsetting the criminal elements of the mainly black frequenters who, of course, benefitted. Drug-dealing was rife. The runners included young children with no compunction shewn by the main dealers. The Mangrove (previously mentioned) was allegedly the hub of activity. It was a bolt hole and intelligence and observations, over many years, indicated that drugs were either held or dealt from the premises. Several other outlets, recessed doorways and look-outs made it very difficult for patrolling uniformed officers to catch the perpetrators in the act of dealing. The intrepid Chief Superintendent Tony Moore decided on a different tack. He relates (verbatim):-

"A Detective Inspector was running the surveillance and, together with his Chief Inspector (Operations) and Detective Chief Inspector, Moore decided to bring it to an end on Saturday 20 February at the end of three weeks. He was aware the District Commander was going to Scotland for a long-weekend and, before he went, on the Friday the Commander visited Notting Hill and sat in the Chief Superintendent's office. The two discussed various matters relating to policing the division but Moore said nothing about the fact that he was intending to mount an operation to arrest the main drug-dealers on the Saturday. Anyway, on the Saturday morning, the six teams, each of three officers, rehearsed the getting in and out of two hired vans, at Notting Dale police Station, before they were driven into place, one in St Luke's Mews and one in All Saints Road outside the Apollo Public House. Two private cars had been driven to the locations very early in the morning and left there until the vans were ready to be deployed to ensure that there were two spaces where they were wanted. They were then replaced by the two vans around mid-morning.

The raid took place as described by Moore in his book, Policing Notting Hill: Fifty Years of Turbulence'. Five of the six main dealers were swooped up by the plain clothes officers and bundled into waiting police vans. Even though I say it myself, the fact that from the start of the operation to the end of the operation it was timed at 1 minute 53 seconds showed how carefully it had been planned and, indeed, carried out. The upward chain of command took no time in sending an unequivocal message to the District Commander in Scotland thus giving him the whole weekend to fume.

When the Commander returned from Scotland, Moore was immediately summoned to his office – I think it was Thursday 23 February – and he left him in no doubt of what he thought of his actions on the Saturday. I have since spoken to Moore and asked him why he did not tell the Commander what he intended to do. Quite simply it was because he believed it needed to be done, partly for the law-abiding public that lived in the surrounding streets and partly because it was important to maintain the morale at the station. The Commander was ambitious and didn't want anything done on the District which might detract from his personal ambition. Moore therefore believes, had he told him, he would have ordered him not to do the raid on the street.

Fortunately, Moore had been selected to become the Director of the Junior Command Course at the Police Staff College that June, otherwise the Commander would almost certainly have made moves to get rid of him. I have no doubt that an adverse report appeared on Moore's records so he knew he would not go further in rank. He stayed at the College for four years and retired in April 1986 with 28 years' service."

Repute or Disrepute?

The closeness to the hub of Portobello Road (with its reputation of being the source of a readily available drug supply) attracted the good, the bad and the beautiful. Many people from the film and theatre world and other well-to-do people would visit, often 'just for the hell of it'. These are some of the 'civilised' people whom I mentioned previously. They had big cars, often open-topped and occupants bedecked with jewellery. This was an open invitation for robbery whereby car windows were smashed to gain access to the treasure trove or, to make it simpler, reaching into open-topped sports cars. Any obstruction was met with physical violence often leaving the victim severely injured and robbed of their possessions. Knife attacks were not uncommon. Lawlessness reigned.

Knock on Wood

Some years later whilst having a drink in the Ladbroke Arms pub I was discussing All Saints Road with the then Superintendent. I suggested that I could solve the problem of the drugs and the 'no go' zone within 6 weeks or even less.

"How?" he asked.

"You put two policemen in the first day and they get harassed and intimidated. The next day you double the number. If this didn't work you double the numbers each day, even up to 64 or beyond, until such a time as we, the police, ruled the street. If that works you reduce them by halving the numbers each day and if that didn't work you increase them again."

Politically, of course, that would never happen. He got so frustrated he got hold of a pillar and started banging his head on it. I believe that the populace would have got the message and acquiesced to a type of truce.

Another Chief Superintendent later tried a similar tactic with 24 officers.

And now the 'T'Others Snippets'

CHAPTER 38

SCALLYWAGS' TALES

I asked other Notting Hill officers with whom I served to write some anecdotes of their experiences. These are their own, unadulterated, words. The subtitles are mine.

Arise Sir...

Information was received that a man, wanted for robbery with a firearm, was living in a basement flat behind Notting Hill Gate. As armed officers were involved, Chief Inspector Xxxx Xeee, who was well known to be most concerned about his career, attended. He was in plain clothes. On entering the flat the man was asleep in bed with his girlfriend and was arrested without any bother. A loaded pistol was found under his pillow. Much to the puzzlement of the prisoner and his girlfriend, the C/I, who saw it as an opportunity for personal glory, got down on one knee. He then asked a PC to dub him on the shoulder

And say "Arise Sir Xxxxx."

A knighthood never came but he did manage to get a High Commendation but it is uncertain for what! (FW) (BB)

Re-Buffed

I was reminded of the early turn when I was teaching beats to Xxxx (blind leading the blind). We were walking up Ladbroke Road from BH, loosely accompanied by commuters making their way to the tube station. We were on the south pavement whilst, on the north pavement walking in our direction, was a young woman who, I could easily see, was reading a letter that she had recently opened. Xxxx immediately crossed the road and walked behind her and said something like, "Can I help you?"

I suppose he thought she was reading a map and was trying to find her way.

She swung round and said to him in words to the effect, "No, go away and mind your own business."

Xxxx looked most hurt and crossed back over to re-join me, wondering why I was smirking. Neither of us spoke! (AM)

- - - - - o o o o o - - - - -

The following anecdotes were forwarded to me by John Kenny who was a Sergeant at Notting Hill and has agreed to be identified.

Bomb Alert

In the 1970s when the IRA was active there was a specially tasked vehicle named Bravo Eight Zero (B80) manned by a sergeant and a PC which covered the whole of B Division and was tasked with handling all suspect bomb calls.

An Initials Reaction

One night B80 was ordered to attend Ladbroke Underground Station regarding a vehicle parked outside allegedly packed with dynamite. When we reached the scene there was indeed a large van parked outside the station emblazoned in capitals with the letters, 'TNT', which, in fact, was the logo for 'Thomas's National Transport'! The wag was never caught.

Ticking Off

On another occasion we were sent to Trellick Towers where a resident on the top floor had found, on his doormat, two alarm clocks elaborately tied together with wires linked to a tin box. I decided it was a hoax and dismantled it and asked the resident if he had any suspects in mind. He said his daughter had been found cheating on her boyfriend and it could have been the boyfriend's idea of revenge to which I instantly replied, 'It was obvious his way of telling her he knew he was 'two-timing' him'. (Boom, Boom! – my extra words - STS).

I don't think he was very happy with my response.

Dutch Courage?

Another time we were called, by a very distinguished looking man with a military tie and moustache, to a house in Chelsea. He was just about to drive off to his country estate when he found, stuck under the front number plate of his Rover car, a large heavy cardboard box. I decided this did look suspicious and was about to call out bomb disposal when a man, who turned out to be the man's gardener, came running up to us. He said he didn't want his boss to forget to take with him to the country house some tulip bulbs which were in fact contained in the cardboard box. Then the man introduced himself as retired Colonel Brian Montgomery and he was the brother of Field Marshall Bernard Montgomery of El Alamein fame.

A Double Act

Around the same time some retired actor, Meyrick Edward Clifton James, who had resembled the Field Marshall, had a book published called, 'I was Monty's Double', telling the story of how the Allies had dressed him up in Monty's uniform and sent him on trips around Europe to mislead the Germans about the next attack. The book was serialised in the Sunday Telegraph and later I saw a wizened old news seller standing outside Sloane Square Tube Station selling the Telegraph alongside a placard advertising the book with the words, 'I was Monty's Double' boldly written on it. A couple of tourists were walking past and one looked at the placard and then at the news vendor and said to his mate, "He's nothing like the guy."

All Saints Road

I remember being night duty custody sergeant when we had the owner of a well-known restaurant in the cells arrested by an infamous officer for some offence: can't remember what, but too serious to justify bail. At about 11.30pm a famous actress of a renowned family appeared at the front counter wanting to stand bail. She, apparently, used to socialise in the restaurant after her stage shows. When I refused bail she accused me of being drunk and made an official complaint to A10 or CIB (The Scotland Yard Branch that investigates Police officers' alleged misdemeanours) and I was issued with the formal complaint form called a 163. (The print number of the form). The complaint was swiftly resolved in my favour.

(As I have previously mentioned people try to muddy the waters). (STS).

Breath Tests

The original Breathalyser kit consisted of a glass tube, the ends of which had to be broken off. One end was inserted into an adapted plastic bag and the other end into a mouth piece into which motorist had to blow.

Blow Me Down

I was warned about some prisoners trying to evade prosecution by not blowing properly down the glass tube into the bag. One night in the charge room a middle-aged businessman seemed to be pretending he couldn't blow down the tube. I started shouting at him to stop messing me about. Then he went puce in the face and collapsed to the floor. It was then I realised that I had forgotten to break the ends of the glass tube. Fortunately he didn't die on me.

Bung Ho!

On several other occasions we had obviously flat-out drunk drivers in the charge room who had failed the second breath test and had given blood or urine samples which, amazingly, came back below the limit. When a number of sergeants started to ask questions there was an investigation by A10 and it transpired that there were no problems when one of the lab liaison sergeants was on holiday but when he was on duty the odd result occurred. It transpired that he was receiving £500 a time for switching the positive results with those which had been analysed as under the limit. He was charged and went to court and was sentenced to 12 months imprisonment for fiddling his over-time but nothing for the corruption aspect.

Try Me – They Didn't

By coincidence, when his lab job was advertised I applied and happened to get it and had four happy years at Scotland Yard. Just after I passed my Inspector's Board I had a phone call from Xxx Xxxxxx, a former Notting Hill PC whom I knew well.

He said, 'Is it safe to talk, John?'

Then he went on to offer me £500 to fix a blood sample. I presumed it was an integrity test I had been given after passing my Board and played it straight down the middle. The bottom line is that Xxx Xxxxxx received 12 months imprisonment for the corrupt approach and the Detective Sergeant who, it transpired had put him up to it, was also charged. The latter threatened to commit suicide, went sick for three years, had the charges dropped and retired on an ill-health pension.

At the time I couldn't understand what was going on but later realised that, had he been convicted, then anybody who had been convicted for drink/driving could appeal on the grounds that if a blood sample could be switched from over the limit to one under the limit it could easily be switched from under to over.

Facing the Music

In the early 1970's I was custody sergeant at Notting Hill Police Station one quiet Sunday afternoon when one of my more zealous constables entered the charge room accompanied by a very tall, blond young man whom he had arrested for providing a positive breath test after driving a Rolls Royce through an amber light. As the second breath test was under the limit I released the prisoner and I was going through the paperwork to be as quick as possible as he wanted to watch a programme about himself on BBC2 that evening. This prompted me to watch and caused me to follow the career of Sir John Tavener. (Sir John was a famous music composer, mostly of religious works, who passed away on the 12th November 2013).

Boxing Clever

One Sunday morning in late 1974 I came on duty as custody sergeant at Notting Hill police station to find Terry Downes in the cells. Apparently he had been arrested for being drunk and incapable after having become detached from a group of his old Paddington mates with whom he enjoyed regular carousing. As he gripped the cell grille, pleading "Give us bail, guv." he seemed to radiate the charisma of an actor. When he signed the charge sheet I commented on his untidy style saying, "Your writing's terrible, Terry."

He replied, "'I'm a f******g fighter, not a writer."[1]

Name That...

When I was a sergeant, working in Notting Hill in the 1970s I put a group of drunk young bankers in the van to take to the station to sober up.

"Me muther will go mad if she sees the family name in the paper," he heard an Irish lad tell the others in the back of the van.

"Just don't give them your real name."

Another chipped in. "Think of a shop name like WH Smiths, Timothy Whites, Sainsbury's etc."

When they were lined up in front of the custody sergeant the group started to reel of their false names. Burton, Sainsbury, Smith. Then the sergeant got to the Irish lad – "Dorothy Perkins, sir."

- - - - - o o o o o - - - - -

The Golden Eagle Shift – was the day before 'once a week' cash pay day. (Before pay cheques). (FB)

A Wheeze or a Squeeze?

(Shrouded in Mystery)

A coffin was found in Bramley Rd. containing only a shroud. An officer was dressed up, put in the coffin and left in the detention cell for early turn shift (another pun?) to find. The early morning 'Skipper' (Sergeant) survived the heart attack as the lid was opened. (RS)

Three Hail Marys

A full set of Bishop's regalia was found in the street. A sergeant dressed up, including the mitre, and went in to the cell of a drunken

Irishman and began to give him absolution and made him say three Hail Marys. I wonder if he said anything at court the next day? (RS)

Magistrate: "Mr O'Fairytale. The drink has obviously affected you. Guilty. Two pound fine and three more Hail Marys." (RS)

Cobbled Together, Ground to a Halt, Down to Earth, Not A mews-ed.

Take your pick of the sub-headings but wait until you have read the sorry tale.

In May 1976 a group of football supporters alighted at Notting Hill Gate Underground station. Why there, when the nearest football ground was at Loftus Road in Shepherds Bush? They were probably causing a disturbance on the Underground as they were followed by a posse of lawmen who often accompanied a large contingent. They were chasing three fans along Notting Hill Gate.

Roy Skinner was driving a Panda along Notting Hill Gate,, saw the commotion, spun the car around and joined the chase, following then into Ladbroke Terrace and then into the cobbled mews behind the police station – Ladbroke Walk. He got out of the car and rugby tackled the nearest alleged miscreant, both sliding along the cobbles with the officer on top. He was then a bit concerned when a very refined English voice emanated below him:

"I say, old chap that was a bit off."

Oh dear! The person who I tackled was a 35 year old ex- SAS and Ghurka officer, who, thinking that the police were chasing thieves, decided to join in. His jacket and trousers were ripped and his watch smashed. He was escorted into the Police station via the back gate and offered the peace offering of a cup of tea and a bucketful of apologies.

The incident was headlines in the local paper, the Kensington News and Post in which the man expressed the opinion that it was a genuine mistake and praised the officer for a 'damned good rugger tackle'.

He was fully compensated for the damaged goods. (RS)

Instant Justice

There was a fight at the top end of our ground (Notting Hill section) where police intervened. It was probably a family feud as the encircling crowd started shouting 'Bastard Coppers' and men and women said they were going the police station to complain. When asked if they had turned up to complain the custody sergeant (RIP) said that they had.

"Where are they then?"

"They are in the cells." (SC)

A Light Relief

During the miners' strike BH suffered power cuts as did everyone else but necessity is the mother of intervention and so it proved. On walking into the station which was in complete darkness a Sergeant saw a faint glow coming from the front office. Sitting behind the station officer's desk, in full uniform including his helmet, was the station officer, (RIP), typing. He had a candle stuck in the rose of his helmet. Who was the bright spark? (SC)

Doubling Up

The front counter at BH was very long, one of the longest in the Met. The necessary recording books were kept on a shelf under it. If speaking to a member of the public and a book was required (Dog book, property book, unattended premises book etc.) a particular sergeant (RIP) would ask the person to wait a moment as he had to go downstairs to get it. He would then proceed to walk beside the counter lowering himself as he went along until he disappeared and then he would reverse the procedure with the book in hand. Very funny if one was watching it. (SC)

PC? It Grates on You

On night duty there were different civilian operators to act as telephonist. One was an extremely pleasant and competent young blind man whose ability was amazing. Let's call him Alf. (I drove him home one night and was amazed to find that he was renovating his flat and had built an internal wall which was immaculate without the aid of a spirit level. I digress). (STS)

A PC was walking through the front office towards the comms. (Communications) room carrying a four-sided cheese grater from the canteen. He was questioned by the Station Sergeant as to what he was doing with it.

"I was going to give Alf something to read," he replied. (SC)

(P.S. Just for the fun of the story I have added - When it was handed to Alf he indicated:

"I've already read this!") (STS)

Grate Man

This reminds me of another story. A rather corpulent officer had the habit of standing on a pavement grate of an Indian restaurant in Pembridge Rod to benefit from the heat emanating from the kitchen. Unfortunately physics intervened and the cartoon-like red faced bobby was suddenly struggling to extricate himself from some relieved 'pig' iron. (STS)

Whose Who?

The switchboards in those days were extending wires which were plugged in to the relevant extension as required. A favourite idle night duty ploy was to look up the telephone directory, pick out two people with the same name, dial and then connect each of them. The fun was listening to them arguing about whom, with identical names, had rung who in the middle of the night. (SC)

'Promoted' In the Pub

A certain male officer (RS) was at Chelsea when a bomb went off outside NSY. The Clarence Pub was practically demolished. He went to the venue to check it out and there was a man still sitting at the bar, drinking. When told to leave he said, "Those bastards are not stopping me drinking."

Another man started climbing in and the officer challenged him. The man asked who he was. He said he was a PC from Chelsea. The man then introduced himself as the Commander from the bomb squad and said to the PC that he was no longer a PC at Chelsea but was now on the bomb squad. (RS)

Name That Tune

The story goes that Sid Vicious (not me) and Johnny Rotten and two other Sex Pistols were stopped by a police officer, Tony Greig, in Portobello Road on their way to sign a new record deal with Virgin Records at their HQ studios in Vernon's Yard. They had a photographer with them. When they gave their names the officer said,

"Never mind the bollocks. What's your real names?"

Hence the Sex Pistols only studio record was called, "Never Mind the Bollocks, Here's the Sex Pistols."

The record was being promoted in a record shop owned by Sir Richard Branson and the cover was prominently displayed in the window. Tony is now a barrister in New Zealand and I emailed him. Someone suggested that Tony had arrested the shop manager but Tony recalls:

"I didn't nick the manager of the shop in Notting Hill Gate, but because I was a

bit of a prat, I decided to try and prosecute Branson for displaying obscene words (or something like that) there being the large notice in the shop window "Never mind the Bollocks". I made an appointment to see Branson, ambled down to his office at Virgin on Portobello Road and interviewed him under caution. He couldn't have been nicer, we had a cup of tea together and I think he found it rather amusing. No lawyer present, just him and me. A similar prosecution somewhere up north failed and the solicitors at Scotland Yard, quite rightly, decided to leave it alone and not prosecute. A badge came out with the record, showing Sid, Johnny and me, with "Never Mind the Bollocks" splashed across the middle. I bought loads of badges to give to girls to impress. I got through them fairly quickly, I don't think they worked. I have tried to track down those badges on EBay over the years without success."

P33. Johnny Rotten

and a CATastrophic alle-gory
(No. It is not a 'shaggy dog' story)

The Ghost of Kitty Past.

During the 1970s the IRA had a habit of stashing caches of explosives in dustbins and burying them in woods. A hidey-hole was found so the anti-terrorist officers staked out the area. They had been there for many days and nights with no activity. Suddenly, one night, a car was seen coming down the nearby track which ended at a lake. Instant high alert, the adrenaline was pumping and the coiled springs were ready to pounce like an ounce (snow leopard) (Good word that!). The vehicle stopped, a man got out and threw a bag into the lake. One team followed the man home whilst another team retrieved the kitty(!) bag which contained – a dead moggy.

Who was the evil b------d who suggested taking it to the man's house, dumping it on the doorstep and ringing the bell? Guffaws all round. The purr-fect ending of a boring night. I wonder what the man said in the pub that night? Anon.

Tom, Whose Tom? – Any bodies.

Brothels and prostitution was the domain of the vice squad. Prostitutes were known as 'Toms'. Why? Don't ask me but there is a suggestion that is Cockney for Thomas More i.e. whore. Anyway, they advertised their services on cards in newspaper windows, telephone kiosks or other public places. Our sleuths (in their brothel creepers? STS} would scour these adverts and ring up the 'girl' and enquire as to what extra services were on offer. This might have led them to a brothel rather than a sole operator. (Not another pun for goodness sake). Additional favours would attract a higher price. One was asked if she had a rack (as in torture).

"No", she said, "but if you bring some wood along we can knock one up".

You see, as I said, "Necessity is the mother of invention." (SC)

Dummies (Guess Which Ones)

Hayes and West Drayton again. Harmless(?) fun and the victims accepted their 'initiation' with levity and good humour. I wonder what would happen nowadays with some 'delicate' souls? (Not more 'snowflakes', surely).

The top half of a tailor's dummy, on a stick, was found dressed as an Australian bushwhacker (without the corks). I took it to West Drayton where a WPC was the sole occupant during night duty. I crept in through the glass front door holding the dummy up. She was on the telephone with her back to me so I knocked on the counter.

"I'll be with you in a minute," she said.

I knocked a little harder.

She said, a bit louder, "I told you, I'll be with you in a minute."

I knocked again. She became really annoyed, swung around to remonstrate against the intruder and it took her a few seconds to recognise the ruse. At least she laughed.

Only Two Fingers?

Or there was the one when the arm of a tailor's dummy was 'buried' in the ground with the hand sticking out. A WPC, who had never seen a dead body, was sent to investigate. After the initial shock, she laughed too.

Drop In, Why Don't You?

Another fully dressed tailor's dummy was found and taken to the highest building in Uxbridge Road. The van (driver aware) was summonsed with an unsuspecting probationer on board. As the van arrived with clanging bells with the dummy silhouetted against the night sky, the probationer jumped out just as the dummy was dropped right in front of him.

Gulps of air possibly?

A Floater

One evening, a deceased man was found floating in the Western Union canal which separates Hayes from Southall. There is no truth in the rumour that it was found on the Hayes side and gently pushed to the Southall side. The body was recovered and a probationer was sent to preserve the scene. However, with the connivance of the Southall control room, a Hayes PC went home for his inflatable dinghy and, in full uniform, with a colleague, rowed to the scene.

"Where is the body?" they asked.

"What body?"

"The one you are supposed to be guarding. We have been sent from Wapping (Thames Division station on the Thames) to pick it up."

"I wasn't told there was a body."

"You'd better get on to your control room then."

Control room (CR): "What have you done with the body? You were supposed to be looking after it."

Perplexed, the young man stuttered and said he knew nothing about it.

CR –"You had better find it as we are sending the Duty Officer (Inspector) to investigate."

The victim's face turned wan in the light of the silvery moon before he realised the subterfuge. There were many similar hoaxes throughout the Met. but this is a true story, not a 'shaggy dog' one.

Had Over a.........

Then there was the one when a barrel was found conveniently covered with Hazchem stickers, 'Poison' and other 'Beware' signs'. An unsuspecting seasoned officer was sent this time dressed in the full white hazard suit complete with hood and mask, gloves and boots. Unaided, he lifted it into the back of the van which took him to the backyard at Hayes. As he opened the back doors he was met by a reception committee of raucous laughing colleagues.

Nomenclatures

What about the Sergeant who used to put 'Piano Tuner' or even 'Brain Surgeon' on the charge sheet of drunks?

He was 'Bubbled'

A surveillance unit was ensconced in several rooms in the Inn on the Park Hotel. The sergeant in charge visited a room to check the progress to find the DC (He'll know who he is) relaxing in the bath with a mini-bar bottle of champagne. The 'fine' was probably a decent meal and accompanying wine. (SC)

Taken Aback

A high ranking senior CID officer went to the scene of a murder and the uniformed PC with him said 'You can rule out suicide here'. The victim had a dagger stuck in his back. When they turned the body over the senior officer, seeing the blood, collapsed. He could not be resuscitated so an ambulance was called and he was taken to hospital and recovered. (BB)

Gone but nor Forgotten

Sadly, Notting Hill and Nottingdale police stations no longer exist, swallowed up in the (in my and many others opinion) 'criminal' culling of it and many famous other stations. Lack of funding from central government, the advent of computerised crime reporting, the lack of 'foot-fall' and the dearth of substantive officers have been cited as the rationale.

The perceived short-sightedness of previous administrations drastically reduced an already beleaguered work force and resulted in the disposal of buildings and resources which were integral to the efficient mechanisation of the service.

In 2020 it was announced that 20,000 officers would be recruited over the next three years in England and Wales. With retirements and resignations will that be enough? The effects of Covid and the rise of unruly climate change and associated demonstrations have highlighted the need of an increase in personnel.

The 'Powers That Be' were warned......

Jump to it

The 'canteen culture', decried by the 'woke' brigade, no longer exists. There are few canteens. Refreshments are taken in McDonalds, Nandos, burger vans, Pizza Hut or any local café where the exchange of views, black humour to release tension, card games or general chatter has not only been inhibited but exorcised almost completely. Camaraderie has been jeopardised to the detriment of social cohesion. 'Police require urgent assistance' was the clarion call for all canteen occupants to decamp, en masse, leaving overturned chairs and uneaten meals. After duty the pub was for winding down and putting the world to rights.

---

1. Terry Downes, BEM, nick named the Paddington Express, was a very successful middle-weight boxing champion having held the world championship in 1961-'62. He passed away on 6.10.17.

CHAPTER 39

WESTWARD HO!

When You Have To Go You Have To Go

I was brought up with the adage "If you are going to do a job, do it well, or don't do it at all".

This mentality, of course, brings its own problems – obsession being one of them. I felt that I was fully dedicated to my role as collator and, as such, I was very pernickety in ensuring every iota of information was recorded within the directions issued by the Collators' manual. I adhered to it assiduously. However, with the amount of data that was forthcoming, it meant that overtime was inevitable much to the detriment to my health. I was working 100 hours a month extra and taking work home much to the disservice of family life. As is often said, you, yourself, are usually the last person to notice or acknowledge that depression has set in. Although this was never mentioned as such by Senior Officers, it must have been apparent to them.

In hindsight I acknowledged that they were trying to help me but, being blinkered, I resented their inferences and interference. The result was that I got further and further behind with my work and therefore more depressed. If it hadn't been for my wife I think I would have ended up with the men in white coats. At one stage an officer had informed the Chief Superintendent that he was 'frightened' of me and the C/Supt. had, allegedly, made a survey of officers. Fancy! They were expected to patrol the dangerous streets of Notting Hill but were frightened of me. I ask you?

P34. Collator cartoon

P35. Doctor cartoon

A decision was made at high level that I should be transferred. Naturally, after 22 years of dedicated service to Notting Hill, I fought tooth and nail to stay but the move was inevitable. I was granted a move to Hayes which suited my circumstances at the time. I never regretted the forced move. In fact it was probably the best decision that those senior officers ever made. Ironically, within months, I was instructed, yes instructed, to become the collator (now called the Local Intelligence Officer – LIO) there.

Inter District Transfer (IDT)

Many Metropolitan Police Officers were happy to remain at the same location for their whole career, not being interested in promotion or relocating elsewhere. They were often the backbone of a station whilst others flitted in and out. Most of them were dedicated, experienced and very knowledgeable about the 'ground' as it was called and the local inhabitants, be they the good or bad citizens. Unfortunately this sometimes led the minority into a lackadaisical attitude and perceived corruption. IDT was introduced whereby there was a five year tenure when officers were transferred to other areas or divisions regardless of the disruption it caused to their family or travel arrangements. Another innovation was to move CID officers into uniform for a period of time. These methods caused much resentment and gnashing of teeth.

As I was the collator I escaped this purge for several years but IDT was the 'lever' by which the hierarchy agreed to relieve me of my duties. An attractive Woman Chief Inspector (the one who missed the sunbeam) was the patsy who was the harbinger of the good (?) news. When she told me, I did not give her an easy time and delivered my feelings forcefully.

I quote the memo dated 19th November 1987 from the Superintendent (Personnel):-

Career Development Transfers

In the interests of Career Development you will be transferred to 'XY' Division with effect from Monday 5th January 1988. You will report to the Chief Superintendent of the Division at 10am on the date of transfer.

Your Chief Superintendent has been informed.

(It is interesting that there is no mention of, or thanks for, my 22 years' service at BH. In fact no officer of senior rank ever thanked me. Mind you, because of the way they had treated me, I barred them from my 'leaving do' which was packed with 'other ranks', except for one male Chief Inspector).

A Whisky Away

One of my last days at Notting Hill coincided with the Christmas lunch which is traditionally served to the 'troops' by the Senior Management team. I declined the offer of liquid refreshments from the Chief Superintendent, (who now attends the annual reunions) preferring to share my own with the other staff and colleagues. The 'top brass' then retired for lunch in their own canteen. It was at a sunken level with steps leading down from the door.

Although I had been at odds with them I had the idea of giving them a parting present. I went to Notting Hill Gate bought a bottle of Bell's 'Afore Ye Go' whisky and a large bunch of flowers. I opened their 'restaurant' door and stood at the top of the steps for about a minute with my gifts hidden. It was like a film scene. All eyes turned towards me, knives and forks were frozen in mid-air, and there was a frisson of apprehension in the silent room. I then marched down the steps to the far end of the table where the Chief Superintendent was sitting. I presented him with the liquor, saluted and said:

"This is for you and your team, sir. Have a Merry Christmas."

I then presented the said Chief Inspector, who was seated at the far side of the table, with the bunch of flowers and told her, "These are for you, Ma'am. I do not apologise for what I said, but for the way I said it."

She got up, leaned across the table and gave me a big hug. I left with a smile and a feeling of satisfaction. They probably thought, 'He is mad' but I think I had the last laugh. It still tickles me when I think of the looks on their faces.

A few months later there was an advert to recruit a new LIO at BH. Tongue in check, I replied listing my qualifications. I received a humorous and courteous non-acceptance reply from the said Chief Inspector.

Watering Holes

I would be remiss if I did not mention the two main licensed establishments used for relaxation purposes, especially after Early Turn (2pm finish) and Late Turn (10 pm finish): the Ladbroke Arms, directly opposite the rear gates of the station and The Mitre (changed its name to The Raj but then reverted back) which is at the corner of Ladbroke Grove and Holland Park Avenue – at least a minute away.

Many a story could be told about these two drinking venues. If only walls could talk...

P36. The Ladbroke Arms

P37. The Mitre

Since 2015 I have organised a reunion for ex- Notting Hill Officers of whatever rank - uniform or CID - each year. An ex-Chief Constable is one of the attendees as are many senior officers who 'cut their teeth' at BH. The Cabbage Patch pub, London Road, Twickenham is our usual venue and I am very grateful to the licensee, Stuart Green, for the use of the premises and the arranging of the buffets.

Reunions are a thing of the past

They have been very successful but the majority of the uniform atten-dees came from an era where, for many, long service at one station was the norm before IDT was introduced. Thus the years between the late 60's and late 80's were the most representative. There are over 270 contactable officers on my data base but I have over 500 other named colleagues who are somewhere in the ether. I probably know over 98% of them. The photo is of a group from the third reunion.

P38. BH reunion L – R:- Chris Channer, John Birt, Russell Evans, Kevin Young, Graham Crush, John Burrell, Kian Hargreaves, Chris Durward-Akhurst and Chris Crowley

Chris Crowley wrote of this photo –

"*Great reunion at BH3. These were great lads I worked with at Notting Hill.*

Great reunion organised by a 'legend' Syd Scott and his lovely wife and their best friend.

Looking forward to the next reunion. Still in touch after 38 years."

Fallen Colleagues - April 2021

Sadly there have been a few untimely deaths recently and tributes have poured in for each of them from ex-colleagues. I reiterate the following sent in by Tim Redmond concerning a Sergeant called Michael (Mike) Frankton (RIP) because it is poignant and humorous.

"*When I first went to the Hill as a probationer in 1974, Mike was running the Collator's Office and Beat Crimes. We all know what a strong, lively and larger than life person he was but of course, with such a central role in the station, you could not avoid being influenced by him. He then came onto 'D' relief as PS 19 BH, and what an affect he had! Mike was a true leader, full of enthusiasm and get up and go – and loads of advice and rollickings! Without a doubt he was one of the most influential people in my police career. He was a great station sergeant but I also remember doing a couple of stints on the Area Car, B3, with him as the driver. He certainly knew how to nick people! One brilliant memory I have of Mike is when, somehow or another, we acquired an old model skeleton from St. Charles' Hospital. What fun we had with that! I remember on night duty one night Mike was the station sergeant and somebody had draped his sergeant's police jacket, with PS 19 BH on the shoulders, over the skeleton and then sat the skeleton behind the station officer's desk. You can imagine the laughs we had looking at the public coming into the Enquiry Desk and seeing that skeleton!!! Funnily enough, I think we all thought at the time Mike was quite old, but I remember him having his 40th. birthday when he was on our relief – how young 40 seems now!*

I was fortunate to work with Mike after we both left the Hill. He went on promotion as an Inspector to Wandsworth, I think it was, and I went on promotion as a Sergeant to Tooting, both stations on 'W' District. This was after the famous 1976 Notting Hill riots and us all having to defend ourselves with bin lids. Mike and I became part of the 'W' District Shield Serial so we worked a lot together, at demonstrations but in particular at the many Shield Training sessions we had at, in those days, the old Hounslow Army camp. They were brutal sessions with the instructors and others chucking all sorts of things at us. Mike was our leader and what a leader he was! He was always in the thick of the action, barking orders and looking after his men. They, and I, would all have gone 'over the top' with him. (TR)

CHAPTER 40

OUT IN THE 'STICKS'
(AS THE OUTER DIVISIONS WERE CALLED)

Hayes (XY) and West Drayton (XE)

So, on 5th January 1988 I joined 'X' Division. I forgot about Notting Hill within weeks and immersed myself into the more sedate surroundings of the 'sticks'. My first tour of duty was night duty at West Drayton – a satellite station to Hayes. The Inspector suggested that I take it easy and that I wasn't expected to overstretch myself. No doubt he was cognisant of my tribulations at BH. He also said that overtime had been curbed for everyone. Self-motivation has always been my mantra. I was posted as van driver with a probationer. That night we arrested a youth for the TDA (Taking and Driving Away) of a moped and we incurred 2 hours overtime, each. Habits die hard. I was back on the beat and enjoying the freedom with the pressure off.

During this time I was awarded the Police Services 'Long Service and Good Conduct Medal' (PLSGC Medal) which was issued to officers after 22 years whose conduct was deemed to be very good. The inscription on it said that it was, 'For Exemplary Police Service'. This award allowed the recipient to wear a ribbon on one's uniform jacket.

P39. Long service medal: notice I have a beard

Some years later, whilst attending Uxbridge Juvenile Court, I was approached by the defence barrister. She asked me for what brave act I had received the ribbon.

"It was for being a good boy for a long time," I explained.

She didn't believe me so I left her in a quandary.

I spent a short time on the beat and in the control room before being ensconced as collator. (I never did like the nomenclature of LIO: I suppose I was a dinosaur, as I was later described by a certain Detective Inspector). I started this posting at Hayes but moved to West Drayton where I was co-worked with the collator there.

More Citations

From Det. Supt. X.Xxxxx, TVP, Maidenhead on 21 February 1991
To C/Supt. Xxxxxxxxx, Nottingdale.

Arrest of Xxxxx XxXxx
Arrest of Xxxxxxxx Xxxxs-Xxxxxxx
Re murder of Xxxxx Xxxxxx

May I take this opportunity to extend my sincere thanks and appreciation on behalf of Thames Valley Police, for the assistance recently provided by a number of your officers in the arrest of the above named suspects, in connection with the murder of Xxxxx Xxxxxx which took place at ....
at.....................on............

The murder, etc...................................

The below named officers (11 named, one of which was me), in particular assisted in respect of providing help and local knowledge to my investigating teams and I would be grateful if you would pass on my thanks to those individuals.

The enquiry in question has now been brought to a successful conclusion and without doubt this could not have been achieved without the excellent co-operation of the officers within your Force.

Get Back (on the streets)

After several years I had a contretemps with the then current Chief Superintendent regarding dissemination of information and I was duly returned to the streets on relief duties. What a relief (no pun intended). I joined a great team and had some exciting times on the beat, vans, cars and surveillance again. Of course it meant that I was dealing with street crime e.g. burglaries.

P40. L – R: Mick Chase, Kim Braybrook, Peter Croft, Mark Jones, Sydney
Scott and Malcolm Broome

Incident Reports

I, (me again!), felt that I wrote pretty comprehensive reports on incidents, especially burglaries for the benefit of the investigating officer. "If a job is worth doing……". Much to my surprise this came to the notice of the Training Unit and, as a result, one of my reports was introduced to the curriculum as a constructive example.

Report from Uxbridge Police Station (XU) dated 20th November 1992 from PS Xxxxxxxx Xxxxxxx. (RIP) Training Unit XU addressed to the Chief Inspector (Personnel and Training).

"I have recently been holding discussions with the Crime Analysts at XU in the course of preparing a training package. In particular, our talks focussed on the quality of both crime reports and investigations at the scenes of burglaries. Whilst both the analysts were free in their criticism of the general standard of

crime reports submitted, both of them mentioned a handful of officers whose standards were consistently high. Of these, PC Scott's crime reports were cited as being of an exceptionally high standard.

Having looked over a number of this officer's crime reports (especially Burglary reports) I fully agree with the comments of the crime analysts. Not only does PC Scott produce legible, complete and well-presented reports, it is obvious that he carries out methodical investigations with great attention to detail.

Whilst I am sure that his line-supervisors are aware of PC Scott's good work and professionalism, I would like the above comments brought to his attention, and I hope he will forgive me if I take the liberty of using some of his reports as examples of good investigations during the next cycle of training days."

Addendum (1)

Chief Superintendent,

I am well aware of the skills of PC Scott and the high standards of all his reports not only Crime reports.

It is refreshing to note that this officer with over 25 years service still carrying out all duties to a very high standard and it is because of these standards I have made PC Scott the Sector representative on such committees as Cad users and working party.

However, I ask that this report be retained on the Officer's Personnel File.

X.Xxxxxxxxxx (Inspector)

Addendum (2)

Insp. Xxxxxxxxx,

Has PC Scott been informed of the contents of this report? Even if he has can you pass my congratulations to him. There would be no point repeating the words above, suffice it to say that I am very impressed.

Please report back to me by the 24th January so that I can note his records and inform the Chief Superintendent of his good work.

XH 18/12/92
Signature (unreadable) C/I P&T

- - - - - o o o o o - - - - -

Theatrical Antics

Our team dealt with a spate of theft from motor vehicles.

Memo from Supt. Xxxxxx, Hillingdon Division 7th January 1993

Good Work Report.

"My attention has been drawn to a report concerning the arrest of (3 named people) for attempted theft and criminal damage to a motor vehicle.
I understand that the Beck Theatre is a place where, whilst performances are ongoing, vehicles are broken into and property stolen and recently there has been a spate of such incidents. In order to combat this problem yourself and four of your colleagues changed their duties from days to 4pm to 12 midnight to deal with the problem. Working as part of a team in conjunction with 6 Area Dog Section yourself and the other officers were able to arrest the 3 suspects.

This was an excellent piece of team work. Well done!

A copy of this report will be placed on your personal file."

X.X.Xxxxxx, Superintendent.

- - - - - o o o o o - - - - -

Memo from Xxxx Xxxxx, Chief Superintendent, Hillingdon Division
24th February 1993

"Dear Sid (sic),

*Whilst others have made mention to you of your continual good work, I am
very pleased to be able to add my own thanks. Your efforts are an example to
us all.*

Thank you very much." X.Xxxxx, Chief Superintendent.

I Took a Right Ribbing

On Hayes there was a secure unit for some of the worst female juvenile
offenders, all of whom were awaiting their respective trials for some
very serious offences. One evening, upset at some perceived injustices
(ironic, I think), some of them decided to barricade themselves into a
room and police were called. The staff knew which girls were in the
room so I suggested that a police officer was allocated to each social
worker and if, or when, we managed to get in they would target their
respective nominated girl. In the meantime I was trying to negotiate.
One girl decided she was desperate to go to the toilet so it was agreed
that they open the door slightly to let her out. There was a sofa
jammed behind the door.

As the door became ajar two burly officers decided to shoulder charge
it. Unfortunately I was between them and the door and they hit me so
hard that I broke two ribs. Not exactly rib-tickling. I ended up with
rather watery eyes, clutching my chest and missed the real fun of the
evacuation. It gave me some R & R (Rest and Recuperation) with a
month off work. I didn't complain or sue anyone. It was part of the Job
and I feel that there is too much compensation paid out for frivolous
injuries. One cannot expect to join the police and not receive some
minor injuries.

Run Along There

'Chalkie', the driver of the Jaguar police car, and I were called to a suspect in a large retailer's shop in Hayes. We arrested a man who had tried to deceive the store by buying a highly valued item of plumbing and who had retained the receipt. He would buy something then return later in the day, steal the identical item and, if challenged could produce the receipt. This was his Modus Operandi (MO). However the store detective was aware of his deception and called police. We placed the suspect behind the passenger seat of the car for safety reasons and I sat in the back. 'Chalkie' went to make arrangements for statement taking. The rear of a Jaguar does not have much leg room. It must have been a cold day as our car coats were in the back and I was trying to lay them across my knees with other paraphernalia so became encumbered.

The suspect suddenly opened the passenger door and decamped. I struggled to get out shouting to 'Chalkie', although he did not hear me, and chased the fugitive. I did not appear to be fit and was struggling for breath after a short distance. I was unaware at the time that I had a serious heart problem. The man ran into a large industrial estate and a greyhound, in the disguise of my driver, overtook me and, with directional help from some factory workers, detained the escapee. I was plumb tired. If you read this, 'Chalkie', you will remember this.

Thank you.

Deputy Sherriff

A friend of mine (RIP) wanted to come out on patrol with me to see how the police operated. Having received the appropriate permission, I took him out for four hours one night duty in the van. I was called to a Turkish kebab take-away where there was allegedly an illegal immigrant working. As I entered the premises with my friend, who, of course was in plain clothes, there were three men behind the counter each with long carving knives which were being used to carve the doner kebab. After establishing who the owner was I asked about the suspect. From the non-response and the sideways glances between them I had that 'inkling' again. I suspected that the wanted man had gone out the back way so I ran out of the shop and into the alleyway and, sure enough, there was the man trying to hide. I arrested him and put him in the back of the van. My friend joined me and we drove off.

"Never do that again," he entreated.

"'What do you mean?"

"You left me in the shop with three men with knives and they thought that I was a police officer. I have never been so scared in all my life."

"Now you know what we have to deal with."

Hay There

I arrived at the scene of a trailer which had shed its load of hay bales onto the footpath edging of a roundabout. The driver and witnesses were standing around oblivious to the fact that there may have been a pedestrian under the bales. We swiftly removed them but, thankfully, there was no Jack Straw to be seen.

What is a CAD

In October 1993 I was posted as a CAD (Computer Aided Despatch) operator and then controller, as acting sergeant, in the control room, another busy and pressurised position.

I had previously been on an intensive course and became a CAD (Computer Aided Dispatch) operator and then controller. The staff consisted of two operators (usually civilian) and a sergeant or acting sergeant controller whose job it was to ensure that events were dealt with expeditiously. They dealt with all incoming calls, whether mundane or urgent, and were responsible for dispatching foot or motorised officers to deal with any situation job involved receiving calls, assessing them, grading them and then dispatching officers (most were mobilised) to deal with the incident. Advice was rendered with great wisdom (or so we thought) to diverse and sometimes perverse enquiries from members of the public.

The task was varied and required an all-round knowledge and the capacity to work quickly and efficiently with tact and good humour. The civilian staff members, with whom I worked, were excellent and well-trained. This made life so much easier.

It could be very stressful when it was busy (which it usually was) where swift and/or protracted decisions had to be taken. It was not unusual that there were insufficient officers to deal with the calls.

No(t) PC

A Member of the Public (MOP) rang the control room and said that he had made a citizen's arrest of a man for attempting to steal from his van. I explained to him that there were no officers available at Hayes/West Drayton to assist and we would not be able to assist him for about an hour. He told me not to worry as he would take the culprit direct to the charging station at Uxbridge. I warned him that this may be dangerous but he assured me that he was very capable and happy to make the transfer. I completed the incident report on the CAD with all the necessary details and immediately forwarded it to the Uxbridge Control room so that they would be forewarned.

About an hour later the Duty Inspector stormed into the CAD room and, in front of the staff, berated me for my action. He said I should have forwarded it to either Southall or Hounslow (adjoining stations) for them to deal. I gently pointed out that I doubted that either would be pleased to deal with such a relatively minor offence. I asked him if he had found someone to deal and, when he replied that he had, I pointed out that we still did not have an officer available and that under the circumstances I felt it expedient to take the action I had done. He calmed down but was not best pleased.

Best Foot Forward

One day a man rang to ask us to be aware that his house would be empty for some time as he was selling up and moving to Scotland because his wife had been there the previous New Year's Eve and had fallen in love with Moffat, a border town. He said they had 'first footed' from house to house and then she began running up and down the Edinburgh Road in the snow in her wellies. I suggested that next time she put some clothes on as well. He roared with laughter.

'First footing' is a Scottish tradition whereby a 'dark handsome man' knocks on your door just after midnight bearing a dram of whisky, a piece of cake and a lump of coal. The latter resonates with the expression:-"Lang may yer lum reek," which translates as – "Long may your chimney smoke" or, liberally implying, "I hope you live for a long time."

Back to Back

A serial complainant continually rang up about his neighbour. On one occasion one of the civilian operators said there was a call for me and I fell for it. It was our friend with a complaint.

"He has gone too far this time. He has reversed his car into mine and the bumpers are locked together."

He didn't seem to understand when I suggested that he throw a bucket of water over them. (Another 'shagging' doggie story?). The two operators were listening in and couldn't stop laughing. The solution, I suggested, was to stand on the lower bumper until it was free.

The work that Cad entails was not usually acknowledged but the following letter was sent to:

Mr X.X.Xxxxxxx,L.B.H. (London Borough of Hillingdon) Highways Dept. on 18th October 1993

"Dear Mr Xxxxxxxx,

I wanted to formally record the thanks of myself and all my staff for the sterling work performed by you and your team on 13/14th October during the floods.

Both my Control Rooms reported excellent liaison with your staff and the enthusiasm of our team ensured that the police could largely attend to their other functions.
I am very grateful for the prompt and professional response to all of you. Well done.

Yours sincerely, X.X.Xxxxxx Superintendent."

A copy of the above was sent to all the operators who had been involved in the incident over a considerable period of time.

- - - - - o o o o o - - - - -

One More.

It didn't end there though as can be seen by the last accolade dated 18th August 1998 –six weeks before I retired at the age of 55 after 33 years' service. Still at it – as they say.

PC 519XH Scott, West Drayton.

"Dear Sydney,

A Quality Service Report has been completed by Inspector Xxxxxxx in relation to involvement in the arrest of a female for possession of controlled Drugs on Friday 1st May 1998. I take this opportunity to thank you for your professionalism. (Several others were also mentioned).
A copy of this letter and a copy of the Quality Service Report will be attached to your Personal File' (NB – This was only 5 months before I retired).

Yours sincerely, Xxxx Xxxxxxxx, Divisional Commander."

Heart Breaking

I was due to retire on my 52nd birthday on 30th September 1995. Two weeks beforehand I had severe chest pains on my way to work but carried on regardless. Needless to say, that night, I had a major heart attack at home and ended up in hospital where I was detained overnight. The following day I had another major attack and was lucky that that the nurse was in the room at the time and that 8 doctors were doing their morning rounds outside the door of my room: otherwise you would not be reading this riveting epistle. One of the doctors later said that I had had only 2 minutes to live.

∾

The Time of My Life
(Or Heart Beats by the Number)

B.P. = Blood Pressure.
P. = Pulse.

Here I lie, all alone
No TV or telephone
'Where am I', I ask myself
'Am I really on the shelf?'

Surrounded by a curtained wall
God, could I be ten feet tall?
To know what's what and where I be
Please pull them back so I can see.

A 'rasping' sound, the curtains slid
The Doves revealed on either side
All dressed in white with dazzling smile
'How are you Syd?' with Irish guile.

'Do tell us all your sorry tale'
My brain with questions they did assail
Well then I thought and thought it well
And to you all I'll surely tell.

The Tuesday was a busy day
To work I went – but on the way
A burning feeling in my chest
Did drain me of my usual zest.

But by the time I'd broke my fast
The searing pain had vaguely passed
Although throughout the passing day
The feeling did not go away.

Then to a meeting we did go
My wife and I – I did feel slow
A visit to a mutual friend
To drink a whisky we did wend.

Returning home I then did watch
The football – but without the Scotch
Asleep I fell before the close
To wake, but when – God only knows.

Upstairs I went but oh so sore
The pain I felt 'No more, no more'
To hospital we drove so fast
To A & E the die (ha, ha) was cast.

So on the trolley I was laid
By caring staff – all underpaid
The questions came – the questions flew
The Nurse and Sister – Doctor too.

B.P. 130 / 90 P. 82

A pricky here a pricky there
The needles they were everywhere
Treatment fast. The pain went down
But here I am now, in a gown.

My wife was there, my good friends too
'Never fear, they'll pull you through'
'The ache has gone, can I return?'
Doc Whittaker was very stern.

'Stay here my lad till you unwind
While we seek out and surely find
The reason for this episode
You then must stick to West Mid code'.

And there was I, all in a fix
Carted off to MD Six
A side ward – oh what luxury
A basin, toilet and TV!

A needle here, an E.C.G
(Where do you think I'd rather be?)
Machines did buzz, the counter count
The numbers they did mount and mount.

Patches, 'lectrodes, wires and things
The monitor it hums and pings
'Please do not move, just sit and rest
You're in here now so be our guest'

So there I lay, but did not sleep
And now and then the nurse did peep
Throughout the night and all next day
The staff did come and have their way.

Of visitors I had a few
And with their help, the day soon flew
But then the night, oh what an ache
Despite the drugs I kept awake.

Sitting up for hours – seemed days
The pain did work in funny ways
The Doctor – summonsed - did his check
But even so I felt a wreck.

B.P. 150 / 80 P. 76

More needles and more medicine
The wandering girl she caused a din
Shouting. Screaming, non-stop grind
Surely she was out of mind.

Waiting, waiting all the morn
Callers came and then were gone
Resting, sleeping then awake
I cannot see for goodness sake.

The sweat did pour, the sweat did run
The Doctors came – it wasn't fun
Surrounded by the coats of white
More pain, more pain, 'Please do not fight'.

B.P. 90 / 40 Brady Cardiac

And then the peace, the pain had passed
'What was the fuss – it did not last?'
To CCU I then was taken
So here I am - 'Fried egg and bacon?'

*B.P. 113 / 68 P. 51 **

An Irish voice an Irish smile
'With us you'll have to stay a while
We have a saying here you know
It's not the usual – 'Go Man Go'

My names is Bernie, how are you?
And this is Liz, she's your nurse too
Off into bed and do not move
And in our hands you will improve.

And so my friends if I should die
You'll never need to ask me why
The answer true is in this ditty
Far too long – but very witty.

To be continued (I hope......)
by Sydney T. Scott

~

May the Force Be With You

After a quadruple by-pass in January 1996 and subsequent convalescence I was sent to be assessed by a Force doctor. He asked me what I wanted to do. He was astonished when I said I had decided not to retire and wanted to go back to work. (More lucrative than trying to find another job in my condition).

"Do you know that there are two Gods - one up there and one across from me?" I said to his very glum secretary,

The doctor said remarked, "Mr Scott, you are a fitter man now than you were last year."

He signed my papers and I returned to work and served another 3 years. What else was I going to do? Initially, I was back on the streets as a Permanent Beat Officer (PBO).

Uniform v NATO Jumper

A Permanent Beat Officer (PBO) had a designated area and basically patrolled alone. I always wore my full uniform jacket and helmet of which I was proud. Most officers at that time were wearing NATO jumpers without even a flat hat. A Panda car driver gave me a lift to an elderly woman whose house had been burgled.

As I entered she proffered, "You look smart".

"Yes, you do," agreed the officer, to my surprise.

I reminded him he also had a full uniform. It was also more impressive when visiting schools, entering hospitals or going to court. I felt that there was more respect and I am afraid that the current uniform (2021) does not impress me although the dangling accoutrements are probably necessary. Oh, I thought my rants were over.

Unusual and Unexpected Accolade

Students who are nearing the end of their formal education are sent out on work experience. One such girl, who had an idea to join the police, attended the Sector Office, West Drayton Police Station, where I was ensconced. (See next chapter). She later wrote:

Dear Everyone,

"Thank you for allowing me to complete my work experience at West Drayton Police Station and thank you for making it such an enjoyable, interesting time for me. I learnt a lot about the Police and am still interested in it.
A special thank you to all the people in the Sector Support Office who made sure I always knew what I was doing and made me feel very welcome.
It was certainly a very big change from sitting in classrooms day after day and I had a great time.
Thank you once again."

Unsigned and undated.

CHAPTER 41
THE END IS NIGH

Almost Over

My last posting was as the Sector Clerk at West Drayton Police Station where my previous experience of CAD, (Computer Aided Dispatch), PNC (Police National Computer) and MSS (Message Switching Service) and as a Divisional trainer of such, was supportive of patrolling officers. During slack periods I volunteered to reorganise the Station Archives which had deteriorated into a shambles. (One couldn't even open the storeroom door fully because of the piles of confidential waste bags blocking it). Who cared? No-one really, but it kept me occupied during my last year of service. A Quality Control Inspector was inspecting the station including the archives. She was making appraisals and happened to check my work. Much to my surprise, she mentioned me in her final report.

"I was particularly impressed with the main archive store at West Drayton. So often when Divisions are forced to resort to a remote storage area weeding takes low priority or ceases altogether. Since April PC 519XH Scott has taken charge of the Archive Store and it is in excellent condition with the various categories of records filed together in a chronological order."

As a result, Insp. Maguire wrote a Quality Service report:-

"In May 1997 PC Scott transferred to XE (West Drayton) Sector and was employed as the Sector Clerk. He was also responsible for the maintenance of the Divisional Archives. On commencing duty in this post, together with PC Scott, I made a thorough check of the Archives which were in a disorganised state. There was a poor system of booking in or out work. The records were not in any order. PC Scott was tasked with organising the archives. He undertook this task with great enthusiasm and vigour. After several months of very dedicated work the archives were brought up to an excellent standard with proper systems in place for monitoring booking in and out and keeping the various categories in chronological order A recent inspection by Christine M. Thomas of Qpp3 (Archives) concluded with a very complimentary paragraph on PC Scott's good work. PC Scott deserves high praise for his dedication and organisation skills."

(endorsed by A/Ch. Insp.)

As a consequence, on my retirement, I received a framed Divisional Commander's Commendation for, '**dedication and commitment in reorganising the Divisional Archive System to provide one of the best examples in the service**'. Another unique and unexpected accolade indeed.

HILLINGDON **DIVISION**

Operational Command Unit

Divisional Commander's Commendation

Awarded to

Police Constable Sydney Scott

For

'dedication and commitment in reorganising the Divisional Archive System to provide one of the best examples in the service'.

8th October 1998

Divisional Commander

P41. Archive Commendation

CHAPTER 42
AND SO TO... THE FINAL CURTAIN

The Cover is on the Typewriter

I Am No Longer a Prisoner.

My mug with 'I'm not a number, I'm a free man', thereon, is in my bag. (True)

Whistle, Chain, Torch and Truncheon hung out to dry.

I listen to the click of the gate as I tiptoe away into obscurity into the gathering gloom.

Metropolitan Police

This is to certify that

Sydney Tulloch SCOTT

joined the Police Service, as Constable,

on the

25th October 1965

and retired on the

29th September 1998

The officer's conduct was

Exemplary

Given under my Hand and Seal

Commissioner of Police of the Metropolis

New Scotland Yard
Broadway
LONDON SW1H 0BG

P42. Exemplary commendation

I received a birthday card with 'Legend' thereon from an ex-Special Branch (SB) Officer, who, when we first met me many years after I had left the Job, said that I was a Legend in SB. The same appellation was given by a Notting Hill PC and a DC who wrote: "I recall you being

the simply the best collator in the business" and the other wrote, "'
Even though I was at Chelsea and Kensington I did a tour on the Area
Q car and spent a lot of time at BH. Syd Scott was one of the best
collators in the Met."

P43. Legend card

In October 2016 I had occasion to write to the Borough Commander
at Hounslow Police Station who had been a probationer PC at Hayes
(XY) when I was there. His opening paragraph in reply was:

*"Of course I remember you – you were a legend and I have fond memories of you
from my time at XY. I remember the banter you and Xxx Xxxxxxxx had 'back
in the day' – I think her nickname for you was "Fossil"? Those were good and
memorable days for me."*

(I was even called Legend by one of my sons and one of his best mates)

What accolades indeed!

I received a message from ex-Commissioner, Sir Ian Blair, who is invited to our annual BH reunions:-

"In a 35 year career in many places, I only spent one year at Notting Hill. I have very fond memories of that time as a Detective Sergeant. What I want to tell you, however, is that nowhere else in many places where I spent time in my career, whether inside the Met. (27 years) or outside (8 years), am I contacted by a group of former colleagues who have clearly stuck together through thick and thin. It endorses my decision to give my first press interview on my first day as a Commissioner from BH: there is something about the place."

I whole heartedly agree with the sentiments of the recruitment officers in Edinburgh and Aberdeen - I joined the best police force in the world and did not regret it.

It was an experience, which, as you can tell, I shall never forget.

Ergo Ego or Not Ego, that is the Question.

I will let you be the judge.

Goodbye or Good Buy?

!.......... W O O S H ....!

Curtain Call

P.S. A year after leaving The Job I was employed at Richmond upon Thames tertiary college (There lies another book) but when I left after 10 years I received the following certificate from the OCU Commander at Richmond Police Station. I think it and the one regarding the archives are unique in the annals of the Metropolitan Police.

Richmond-Upon-Thames Borough Commendations
RFU Stadium Twickenham
2nd December 2009

P44. Presentation of RUTC commendation

P45. RUTC commendation

PPS. I can tell one story from the College as it relates to Notting Hill. I was interviewing a witness regarding a theft and I asked him for his address.

"Cambridge Gardens in Notting Hill," he replied.

I asked him the house number and he said 43. I then said, "So you go up Ladbroke Grove, go under the railway bridge, take the first turning on the right and you live in the third house on the right."

He looked flabbergasted. "How do you know that, he spluttered?"

"I know everything," I replied hoping he would spread this message to the other students. I did not tell him my previous profession or posting.

Originally, streets in London emanated from Charing Cross, numbered with the lowest being closest to Charing Cross, Even numbers were on the right and odd numbers on the left. Three streets that crossed Ladbroke Grove did just that and the split was c. No 50 so it was easy for me to guess his address. This information was useful when looking for an address, especially on emergency calls. **Not a lot of people know that...** (a phrase mistakenly attributed to Sir Michael Caine)

The Thin Blue Line

———————————————————————

So endeth my police career but not my episodes with Lighthouses.

CHAPTER 43
THE LAND OF MY MOTHER
SHETLAND LIGHTS SHOW THE WAY

Sumburgh Head

P46. Sumburgh head

On Monday 2nd June 2014 flying in to Sumburgh Airport was an emotional experience. My mother came from Unst. My father was stationed at the Muckle Flugga light (or North Unst as it was then called) where my eldest brother, John, was born and named by semaphore. He was then posted to Sumburgh Head where my eldest sister, Norna, was born. Place names of which I had heard throughout my life but had never visited. Now was my opportunity. An unexpected invitation to the opening of the Sumburgh Head Visitor Centre was the reason. I had supplied some material, photos etc. for the exhibition. Another guest? HRH The Princess Royal, Princess Anne, who, as the Patron of the Northern Lighthouse Board, had been selected to conduct the Opening and Unveiling Ceremony.

I hired a car and checked in to the Sumburgh Hotel (featured in the dramatic BBC series 'Shetland'). The receptionist was related to an ex-keeper. I headed for the bar. Two or three local men who either worked at Sumburgh Head or who had lighthouse relations, propped it up and we exchanged relatively interesting stories.

Nearly midnight and the 'simmer dim' was apparent. A lonely evening stroll to the lighthouse beckoned so I wandered along the west footway of the headland in the moonlight. A couple of ponies lifted their heads from their chewing and glanced nonchalantly at me then bowed their heads again. The sound of the waves gently massaging the rocks in the geos below kept me company. A steepish climb through the fields and over the dykes brought me to the eerie confines of the deserted lighthouse grounds. Various interesting areas were identified by several strategically planted information boards. Not a soul in sight. The sea views through the muted light were magical. I wondered if I was being watched bearing in mind that Princess Anne would be here the following day. I doubt it. Peace reigned.

A gentle downhill saunter along the road took me back to the hotel. The native sheep and their lambs eyed me with suspicion and sidled away if I approached too closely. No fences: - this was their domain. How dare I disturb their breakfast.

Next morning there were several buses to take the invited guests to the rendezvous point below the complex and then a steep winding climb to await the arrival of her Royal Highness. It was a gey dreich grey day with a fresh wind and squally showers. We huddled in a large marquee, suited, booted, coated, gloved and hatted – you get the picture. And so did those with the many cameras, iPads and mobile phones. There, I met many ex-lighthouse keepers and their wives and their names sprang out of the darkness of my memory. The Tullochs, the Eunsons, the Watts and the Blacks were there and, I am sure, several others.

Princess Anne, in her hooded raincoat, and her entourage toured the several buildings pausing now and again to chat to the assembled crowd who waited patiently despite the weather. Speeches were made and then HRH unveiled a commemorative plaque by pulling off the Shetland flag with the off-set cross typical of Nordic tradition.

Wine and nibbles in the warmth of the beautifully designed observation room overlooking the Sumburgh Roost, was most welcome. I met Brian Gregson, the Chairman of the Shetland Amenity Trust whose members were responsible for the amelioration of the buildings and the design of the wonderful, interesting and informative exhibits. I presented him with a mounted glass etching of the Muckle Flugga and Sumburgh Head which had been part of a larger plaque that my late brother had created for my mother's 90th birthday. (Don't ask....) – This may explain it.

P47. Glass etching of the Muckle Flugga and Sumburgh Head

Sea the Lights: Replicating a Piece of Lighthouse History (or Lights of our Life?)

by Classic Miniatures, 8 Heathlands Close, Twickenham, TW1 4BP

In late 2013 we were approached by a new customer, Mr Scott, after a large glass plaque, measuring 60cm x 28cm, which he owned, accidentally fell from its display area and smashed. It was extremely precious to the Scott family, holding great historical and sentimental importance. It was etched by Mr Scott's brother, Sigurd, and given by him to their mother, Rose, as a gift for her 90th birthday. Etched onto it were eight Northern Lighthouse Board lighthouses, each one representing where the Scott family had lived and moved to throughout their lives whilst their father, John, worked as a Lighthouse Keeper. Beneath the etched lighthouses were engraved the full names of John and Rose, their five children and their dates of birth, making it a truly personal piece.

After the tragic, accidental damage of the original, Mr Scott, was left with the desire and need to have it replicated. When he contacted us it was the first time we had ever received such an inquiry. Whilst we had received inquiries of replicas in the past, the magnitude of this piece weighed upon us heavily. Of course, we were apprehensive at first as the task at hand was huge. Could we copy it exactly? Would the customer be happy with the end result? How long would it take? These were questions we pondered before making the final decision to be a part of such a fantastic project.

The piece of glass meant a lot to the family. It was an immense undertaking for Pritesh, our product designer, who was given the task of accurately replicating the Scott family plaque. To begin, he gained access to the photographic images that had been used to create the original as well as using the remnants of the plaque which had been taped together by Mr Scott. These were then etched onto a new, large piece of glass.

This took time and effort, carefully and delicately drawing each lighthouse and its surrounding buildings using digital technology to the correct size and digitally laying it out onto the glass to ensure each lighthouse fitted and was placed in the correct position.

The entire process lasted around three months as there was much planning and preparation to do, as well as communication to be made, but it was entirely

worth it for everyone involved. Mr Scott believed we had done a magnificent job and was beyond pleased with the outcome. Pritesh learnt a lot while working on such a piece and was glad to have had the opportunity, as did the whole team. Mr Scott kindly rewarded Pritesh for his hard work by using a piece of the original glass that was undamaged (in that it still held an entire lighthouse, Stroma, within the piece), cutting it down, sanding it and placing it into a wooden plinth with the words "Pritesh – Master Craftsman' engraved thereon and presenting it to him.

It was one of the greatest things we have ever done as a company – to restore a piece that meant so much to a family and to get it spot on, when we hadn't had experience in replicating something of that size, entirely from scratch before. It was a great achievement.

The glass plaque was mounted on a wooden base and has been retained by the Scott family as an heirloom. Another two original images of Shetland light-houses - Muckle Flugga and Sumburgh Head - were together and also undam-aged. That sheet of glass was also mounted and was donated by Mr Scott to the Heritage/Visitor centre in Shetland at Sumburgh Head as part of an exhibition which was officially opened this year by The Princess Royal, HRH Princess Anne.

The following day I wandered around the superb interactive information centre and I was not disappointed. The displays and the accompanying texts were enlightening and instructive and it was obvious that much work had been carried out by knowledgeable and dedicated staff. I climbed the foghorn where there were stupendous views over the cliffs with many varieties of sea birds swooping and diving. Visiting the radio rooms was a revelation. They were crucial during the Second World War by giving early warning of the approaching invasion of German aircraft intent on destroying the British fleet sheltering in Scapa Flow in Orkney. Their importance turned out to be immense.

Any visitor here will be imbued with the natural beauty and variety of the fauna and flora on a rugged headland jutting out into the North Atlantic and pounded or tickled by the incoming waves.

There are many other interesting observations of which I could write but this was just the start of a fantastic adventure throughout Shetland.

(Mikla Flugey - Norse for Large steep sided island)

P48. Muckle Flugga

Strangely I have always known it as that name but it was not officially so called until 1964 having previously been named North Unst.

This was my father's first substantive posting. It is a steep sided pinnacle of rock off the northernmost tip of Unst. The next stop is The Arctic. Lashed by the North Atlantic rollers, saturated by the rain and incessant spray born in the grasp of westerly gales hurtling across an empty ocean, it sits proud and defiant. To get a good view I tramped with other sightseers across the desolate and windswept Hermaness. It was a gorgeous day but one had to be aware of the ever changing weather patterns as thick fog can quickly obscure the head-land. But what a delight, accompanied by a very enthusiastic guide, to trudge across the moorland and duck boards strategically laid to preserve the environment and keep a straggling vagabond on the right track.

Bonxies. These are Great Skuas which have flourished with no predators to cull their numbers and have now exceeded 2,000 nesting pairs. They are a protected species but no-one has told them that humans should be a protected species – from them. They nest within feet of the path but if they are disturbed they will dive-bomb an unsuspecting passer-by so an umbrella or walking stick is advisable to ward off their vicious talons. Onwards to the edge of the western cliffs where myriads of sea birds, especially gannets, fulmars, guillemots and razorbills raised a deafening sound as they clung precariously on the ledges or swirled and dived in graceful flight. One or two rascally, comical and curious puffins popped up their heads from their underground lairs but I suspect that most of them were out at sea.

Offshore several large white encrusted rocks hove into sight. Why white? They were covered in gannets and their guano. A hardy trek down and up the sides of a small valley, dissected by a gurgling little stream, brought me into a panoramic view of the Muckle Flugga Light – a lone sentinel on a barren rock. It was built in brick, rather than the granite interlocking blocks that would have been the norm. The Stevensons, who designed it, realised that they were unable to lift such blocks up the steep rock face. The outcrop is only a mile from Unst but, as you can imagine, the crossing though the treacherous seas by hardy lighthouse keepers was, nevertheless, not for the faint hearted and climbing ashore was dangerous. A signal station was built on the top of Hermaness and its circular stone base is still there. My eldest brother was born at the shore station of Burrafirth whilst my father was on the rock and he had to be asked by semaphore what name he would give to his son. I think several other keepers' sons and daughters were so named.

The boathouse at Burrafirth still stands and is habitually in use as is a wee bothy which contains many interesting seafaring items some of which, I am sure, were there when my father used to have a cup of tea there in the 1920's as he awaited his lift(s) on the swell to the island. A married couple still use it as their base before launching their small fishing boat into the Firth. With true Shetland hospitality they made me a cup of tea. Surreal, eh? A visit to both the wonderful Unst Heritage Centre and the Unst Boat Haven in Haroldswick is a must for anyone wishing to know the history of the lighthouse and the island as a whole. Ancestry records are not only on the computer but also the original documents can be studied. The staff at both are very welcoming and informative. I had the fortune of staying with my cousin in Haroldswick where I met many of my relatives. We went to the village hall and were thoroughly entertained by the local worthies with fiddle music, dance and very funny sketches.

Esha Ness[1]

P49. Esha Ness

Over the hills and far away.

.   .   .

I do not have an affiliation to this light but it was another name which stirred up my little grey cells. A trip back from Unst to the Mainland (as the largest Shetland island is called) and a long drive through sparsely populated hills,

moor and glens took me to the end of the earth. The first glimpse of the buildings reminded me of Lego. A square tower surrounded by square buildings. Unusual and unexpected.

To describe the surrounding scenery as spectacular would do it an injustice. Very high cliffs with sheer drops into the turbulent sea below were dotted with the ubiquitous seabirds each one intent to out-screech its neighbours.

When visiting this outpost it is recommended to visit the wee but very delightful museum of Tangwick Haa where you will be welcomed by the most hospitable curator and offered tea/coffee and biscuits. I discovered that she was a distant relation of mine through marriage. A lady visitor was from New Zealand where one of my sons lives and another said she was from Wick, in Caithness but when questioned further it was established that she was born on Stroma – an a small island between Caithness and Orkney. My other brother was born when my father was stationed there.

Just a glimpse into the saga of these extraordinary islands. If you ever have the fortune to visit Shetland do not forget your stout walking boots, your walking stick and your waterproofs. May the Norse Gods be with you and keep you safe.

———————————————————

1. If you ever visit this magnificent archipelago I recommend that one Googles: Unst Heritage Centre, Unst Boat Haven, Tangwick Haa Museum.

CHAPTER 44
STROMA CALLING

The following are extracts from a longer narrative which I had written in August 2017 called 'Northern Adventures'.

Stroma is a small island, c. 2 miles x 1 mile, in the turbulent Pentland Firth close to the confluence of the mighty Atlantic Ocean and the shallower North Sea. Their rivalry is unparalleled causing very dangerous rip tidal races twice a day.

P50. Stroma

The Viking name means 'The Island in the Stream' and there is no
doubt that these seafaring adventurers were respectful of the power of
the surrounding waters. The successive male inhabitants became the
undoubted masters of pilotage through the Firth with their vast
knowledge of the prevailing winds and tides. After many years of nego-
tiations a new pier was constructed but instead of being the panacea
for the islanders it became a means of escape from the arduous life-
style and a non-stop exodus occurred whereby the island was
completely abandoned in 1962 apart from the lighthouse families who
left in 1997 when the light was automated. The emigrants left most of
their goods and chattels behind, in situ, and sought a livelihood on the
Scottish mainland. The Simpson family who were born and bred on
Stroma purchased it and it is now used for the grazing of sheep.

My father had been stationed on this rugged but semi-fertile low lying
parcel of land in the 1930s. The lighthouse and its associated buildings
e.g. two foghorns, living quarters, engine room etc. is situated on the
north point of the islet overlooking the narrow strip of water dividing

it from its nearest neighbours, the island of Swona and the Orkney archipelago. It is now fully automatic and meticulously maintained by the Northern Lighthouse Board artificers and contracted workers. The immaculate white coated dazzling exterior is in graphic contrast to all the other drab stone built buildings on the landscape.

The foghorns, however, had been left to the ravages of the elements, their white lime coating had been stripped and their red horns dismantled.

My brother John and sister Norna went to school on Stroma and my other brother, Sigurd, was born on this wee patch of land. My mother, Rose, said her years there were the best times she had had in the lighthouse service: hence my desire to set foot and explore this outcrop. My parents had been great friends with James and Chrissie Simpson, since deceased, and their son, James, went to school with John both also now deceased. At this time I was fortunate to acquire the telephone number of James and his wife, Lena and she gave me the contact number of their son, William, who is now the boatman and shepherd. He agreed to take me across, weather permitting, on the Sunday. I duly arrived at Gill's pier, the springboard for the short (half an hour) sea trip and, with eight others (one man) we set sail in his small open decked motor boat – Boy James.

I did not know it at the time but he only takes bona fide visitors, family, friends and ex- Stroma relatives with pedigree because, on previous occasions, casual visitors, who may have camped on the island, had indiscriminately destroyed much of the infrastructure and burnt a considerable amount of the furniture and priceless paper work and photographs to use as heating material.

Curious to find out who my fellow seafarers might be I spoke to the woman next to me. Although she said her surname was Bremner, which was a common name there, she believed that she was not related to anyone but had come as a guest of others on the boat. Much to my surprise she said her first name was 'Sydney' spelt with a 'Y'. (The first coincidence).

She pointed to another lady whom she said was an ex-resident. When I spoke to her and told her of my connection, she said that her father had been the relief or occasional keeper at the lighthouse. These men would stand in for someone who may be sick or on holiday. She said her name was Marjory McKinnon nee McGaughey from Dunbeath. I asked her if she knew an author called Catherine Byrne who was born on Stroma and had written a love story book – Follow The Dove - based on Raumsey (as she called it). I had been in email contact with Catherine and I had intended visiting her in Wick. Marjory said, 'She is my sister'. (A second coincidence). I then remembered that Catherine had said her maiden name was McGaughey.

The sea was fairly calm with a bit of a swell and we landed safely at the pier. People broke up into small groups. The climb up from the harbour is quite steep through mounds of grass. We stopped at the original dwelling of the McGaughey family which is now a ruined shelter for sheep and nesting pigeons - as are most of the old 'but and bens'. Facing south there are unrestricted views of the Firth, the north coast of Caithness and the two lighthouses on the Pentland Skerries were clearly silhouetted against the bright blue sky. Bleak in winter I should imagine but those inhabitants were hardy people. I took a photograph of Marjory and Sydney Bremner outside the House.

Tramping on I met up with Meg Telfer nee West who works at Northlands Glass, Mission Hall Gallery, Melvich, Sutherland. She stated that she was an artist. I later found out that most of the party were artists of one sort or another and were known to each other – hence their presence. She said she painted scenes, painted and etched on glass and was also a sculptor. I asked her if she had heard of my cousin, Ian Scott from North Ronaldsay who was a well-known sculptor who had been commissioned to portray lifeboat figures in commemoration of those who had lost their lives in the disasters of 1969 (Longhope – all crew lost) and 1970 (Fraserburgh – 5 out of 6 crew lost) and also the statue of John Rae, the Arctic explorer who had discovered the North West Passage during his quest to discover the fate of another explorer, Sir John Franklin. Again, to my surprise she said, 'He was at Art school with me in Aberdeen 50 years ago'. She also said that she had been taught English by a Miss Scott at Girls High School, Aberdeen. I said, 'That was my Auntie Mary'. (Coincidences 3 and 4).

Some rusty discarded farm equipment was nearby – a familiar feature throughout.

Several of us went to the old tiny school—now a sheep shearing shelter—and to the communal hall where the dilapidation was ever apparent. Dust and cobwebs covered the remaining artefacts which included a piano or organ where Marjory 'attempted' to play 'Oh Flower of Scotland'. I videoed her. Old magazines, postcards, bibles and school books – some with the pupils' names thereon – were scattered around. There was a variety of chairs, tables, two cookers and, incongruously, a new rubber dinghy sitting on a plastic covered mattress. It would seem that the hall was still being used for gatherings or shelter. There was a stuffed stag's head with 10 tines mounted on the wall. Apparently this deer, not yet fully mature, had allegedly swum across from the mainland and was on the island for a number of years.

Meg did not come any further as she wished to do some sketching but some of the party stopped in the shelter of a house to have their sandwiches. I carried along the long straight downhill gradient road towards the lighthouse where, for sentimental reasons I suppose, I proposed to eat my lunch. I passed sporadically spaced derelict houses with rusting farm machinery nestling in the overgrown grass and nettles. The sheep in the fields looked balefully at me and scampered away if I ventured too close. I noticed two skuas arise from the moorland about 500 yards away and fly towards me. One of them swooped down, narrowly missing me. Continuing I heard the wings of another as it also came close and when I looked up there were three of them. They obviously decided that I was of no threat and they flew off and dropped down in the distance whence they came.

Onwards I pressed to my goal. As I approached I could hear the swishing and splashing of the waves as they broke against the gneiss-like rocks with spray being borne on the freshening wind. Out to sea the ever changing line where the two heavyweights met was evident –

roughish seas on one side and placid seas on the other with small whirlpools and eddies punctuating its border. I did not see the dreaded whirlpool of the 'Swelkie' which has devoured men and boats who have dared or accidentally entered its gravitational and unforgiving downward spiral. I sat on a rock and had a light lunch during which I was joined by some of the others. A small, roofless, dilapidated shelter or storage shed was close by containing a bounty of discarded multi-coloured flotation buoys and other redundant fishing paraphernalia. A lone orange net or lobster pot buoy bobbed just off-shore and I wondered with admiration how these brave seamen would venture out into that maelstrom to harvest crabs or lobsters.

A long trudge, and I mean 'trudge' as I was flagging, back up the sloping road gradually being left behind by the others. I veered off, to my regret, into the fields to take some photos. The others had taken a right hand detour to find the 'Gloup' which is a natural large hole or ravine in the landscape with an underground passage into which the tide ebbs and flows and in rough weather throws up spumes of water and white foam. It resembles a sink hole. I cut across diagonally towards them stepping wearily or jumping from grass or heather hillock to avoid the deep marsh land.

We met up with a tractor and trailer on which William's sister, Chrissie, her husband and daughter were sitting and to whom we were introduced. They had been staying in the schoolhouse which The Simpsons family had ameliorated and used for accommodation when any of them stayed on the island. They were on the way to the pier.

We rested for a short time and I took photos of the outside of the desecrated church, the smashed phone box and the scattering of more rusting farm machinery.

Others in the group were Christine Scheuerl, who is a friend of Marjory and Maggie Sinclair who had been brought up by Christine. We wandered back to the pier and a couple of seals, as is their want, popped their heads up and stared curiously and unconcernedly with their doleful eyes at us before dropping down and reappearing a short distance away.

A packed cruise ship nudged its way into the entrance to the harbour before reversing out and heading for the Pentland Skerries and Duncansby Head. We embarked back to Gills harbour. Extra on board were Chrissie, two dogs, members of her family and a woman called Helen Simpson / Sinclair but I cannot remember her relationship but she had worked at Crossroads school where I had attended.

The next day I visited relatives of my mother in Thurso who ran the Station Hotel. I asked them if there was an art gallery nearby and they stated there was one in the library behind the hotel. Image my surprise when I walked in and the lady looked up from her desk and declared, "I know you". She was Maggie Sinclair who had been on the Stroma trip the day before. (Coincidence 5).[1]

---

1. In the book 'Stroma' ISBN 1 871704 07 3 there is reference to two Stroma men who joined the Metropolitan Police. Sinclair Bremner from Bagway (House name) served from 1910 to 1935 in which year he was awarded a silver Jubilee medal and Walter Simpson who joined on 16th April 1894 and resigned on 14th September 1919.

CHAPTER 45

RETROSPECT OF ERRAID

Having left Erraid at the age of 2 months in 1943, I decided to return in 1997 with my wife, Phill and youngest son, Philip. We drove south from Fionnphort along the west coast of Mull but were unsure how far, or exactly where, Erraid was. We spoke to a lady, Ann, who was walking her dog and asked her the way.

She said, "I'll show you. I was just going there myself."

I said I wanted to go as I was born there.

She said, "So was I." (Coincidence 1)

I asked her if her father was a lighthouse keeper.

"No, he was the shepherd and my mother happened to be on the island when she went into labour and I was born in the bothy."

I said, "I thought that my sister and I were the only people born there."

(I have subsequently found out that there were several lighthouse bairns born on Erraid).

We parked in the small car park at the end of the road and walked to the edge of Mull. Before us lay the 'drained' stretch of sand and

pulverised sea shells which separated Mull from Erraid. The rays of the
sun were glistening from the almost pure white panorama. Ripples of
sand transgressed the breach interspersed with residual pools of sea
water - no doubt hiding those tiny crustaceans and small fry which
linger there until the incoming tide releases them from their watery
keep. Onward we trudged – well, tiptoed - between the pools and
clambered onto that magical island where David Balfour, the hero of
'Kidnapped', written by Robert Louis Stevenson, was marooned – or
thought he was.

A well-worn path led from the sandy beach across the scrub and
heather, by-passing a wee white painted house. Arriving at a gate in a
high stone wall we noticed a compact structure which our guide
informed us was the chemical toilet which must have been about 50 -
60 yards from the row of lighthouse houses which constituted 'The
Street'. One wonders what were the delights of having to brave the
elements on a dark windswept (gale-swept) snowy night just to relieve
oneself. (Buckets and po toilets come to mind). 'The Street' consisted
of, I think, nine granite-built terraced cottages. Six of these would
have been for the keepers of Skerryvore and Dubh Artach lights. One
other was the washroom. Deep white porcelain sinks, wash/scrubbing
boards and lozenges of yellow carbolic soap would have been the only
facilities here. The hardy women would probably have had their
specific allocated days to use these, now antiquated, washing aids.
Another provision was the school where the lighthouse bairns, of
whatever age, were taught all together by the lone teacher. My brother,
John, was 15 and still attending when we left.

"How will I know which was our house?" I had asked my brother,
Sigurd, before embarking on our exploits.

"Our father was the Principal Keeper so the doorstep is bigger than
the others."

Sure enough! When we reached the end of the path, there it was. We
were greeted with a warm welcome by the then current occupants –
two ladies from the Findhorn Foundation. They were delighted to
meet someone who had been born there and conducted us on a 'tour'

of our small cottage. Apart from an American style fire complex which replaced the open hearth, I imagined that it had changed little in the intervening years. There were high-up shelves to deter the imagined vermin. The ubiquitous, and still used, clothes pulley was hanging from the ceiling. I think there were two bedrooms in one of which I was born (as was my sister, June). Outside there was an enclosed paved area on which stood a water barrel and an oil barrel. Steps led up to the drying green with its row of metal poles standing as straight as soldiers, with the ropes drooping, awaiting to be adorned by the signal flags of shirts, socks, underwear and other apparel.

"Dar'st thou hang them upside down for all the neighbours to gossip about?"

I have a photograph of my parents taken from this vantage point sitting in the paved area. It could have been that day – not 54 years or so previously. Nothing appeared to have changed.

As we exited through the front door, my son, Philip, pointed out a small Royal Navy Warship in the Sound of Mull which I thought may have been a frigate. Two large gated pillars interjected into the high stone wall which was designed to keep the ravages of the weather from destroying the necessary home grown vegetables cradled within its bosom. A woman in a large 'Indian Coolie' wide brimmed sun-hat was sitting among the very large cabbages and seemed to be either talking or singing to them. Incongruously, to my mind, there was a George V (I think) letter box set into one of the pillars. The postman, who I think had a house on the island, would have had to collect the mail from there before transferring it to Mull by either walking across the sand or rowing a small boat. That he couldn't just knock on each door seemed to me to be a very Victorian influence. Progress? He/she probably still has to retrieve the mail that way.

We started to hurry back before the tidal race threatened to cut us off for 8 or 10 hours. My wife happened to mention to our 'Good Shepherd' that I was a police officer. (Coincidence 2)

"So am I," she replied.

"I am in the Metropolitan Police in London," I explained.

"Oh, I am an officer at the Royal Mint in Cardiff," she proffered.

"We know people in Wales." said my wife (as one would!),

"Where"

"Llantrisant," was the response. (Cardiff is about 13 miles from there).

"I live in Llantrisant. Who do you know that lives there?" (Coincidence 3)

We couldn't immediately remember the surname but I said, "The boy's name is Matthew. He is about 12/13 years old."

Just then, out of nowhere, appeared her two sons on their bicycles riding on the sand.

She called them over and said to the older one. "Do you have anyone one called 'Matthew' in your class?"

"Matthew Wilson. I now remember," I said.

"'Yes." he replied,

"Do you play rugby?"

"Yes, and Mathew is our captain."

"'Who is your coach?"

"'Mr McLoughlin."

I had been involved in running Mini and Youth rugby at London Irish for many years and Matthew had attended coaching lessons. Gerry McLoughlin was an Irish International (who famously dragged six Englishmen over the line at Twickenham to score a try). He had been in our house only a few weeks previously and he lived in Gilfach Goch (6 ½ miles from Llantrisant) where we used to visit on our way to Ireland whence my wife comes. (Coincidence 4) We knew the Wilson family when they lived in London because my wife, who was a child-minder, used to take the children to school, pick them up again and feed them until one of their parents collected them later after their work. We also called on them on our way to Eire.

I asked Ann how old her parents were - thinking they may have gone to school with my brother, John.

"They are in their early seventies, 'They live over there. Why not ask them?" she suggested, pointing to a farm (Knockvologan) across the inlet.

It was a hot summer day but, as we entered, her parents (Hugh and Bella Cameron RIP) were sitting either side of the inglenook with the fire on. Ann introduced us by saying that I was Mr. Scott and that my parents had been on the island.

Both together they said, "That will be Jock and Rose," (my parents)

"They were the best dancers that ever came to the island," Bella added. "Did you know they had five children? They were (in the correct order) John, Norna, Sigurd, June and Sydney."

"Well, I'm Sydney." I would never have guessed her next words.

"I was in the room when you were born." (Coincidence 5)

Knock me down with some heather. I never saw that one coming. Bear in mind this was 54 years after we had left. What memories they had. Unfortunately we could not stay for a chat as we had to drive across Mull to catch the ferry from Craignure back to Oban. I had taken many photographs which I would have loved to have shared with you but not one of them came out. Scary, eh?

Following the road from Fionphort back through Bunessan, we again saw the naval ship. What was it doing there? It was escorting HMY Britannia on one of her last voyages and on board was the whole Royal Family including HM The Queen Mother and another Philip - Prince Philip. My father had met her several times, once in the Isle of Man when stationed at Douglas Head, and also at Dunnet Head where she had been introduced to my sister, June, and me. (Coincidence 6)

. . .

Sydney T. Scott 12th June 2016

CHAPTER 46
SKERRYVORE LIGHTHOUSE

The loneliness of a Lighthouse Keeper's life, whilst stationed on a rock far out to sea, can only be imagined. Three men are stranded for a month or more depending on the vagaries of the prevailing weather. As previously mentioned, Skerryvore was automated and now stands alone on a sliver of rock in the wild Atlantic battered and pummelled by the relentless and often tumultuous waves. The men had no TV so listening to the radio, (if they had one) reading and the pursuit of their individual hobbies were their only recourse to remain relatively sane.

Swept Off their Feet

There is a metal landing stage built across the frequent wave-swept rocks at the base of the tower where the small tender would lay alongside to deliver the necessary goods, including fresh water in barrels. Standing on it would be hazardous depending on the volatility of the surrounding sea. My father and another keeper were standing there when a rogue wave swept them off. My father managed to grab a stanchion and was rescued by other men. The second man was swept underneath and when he was rescued the arms and upper thigh parts of his oilskins were the only clothing he still had on. The sea and the rocks had stripped everything else off. They were very lucky men. The lighthouse tender, Hesperus, had to be diverted to deal with the incident.

A few years ago I heard of a Crowe family that lived in Crimond which is near Fraserburgh. It being a familiar name within the lighthouse fraternity I decided to visit them – Alan and Irene. Whilst recounting my father's narrow escape on Skerryvore I was dumfounded when

P51. Skerryvore landing

Alan stated that the second man had been his father. I never knew that that they had served at Skerryvore at the same time.

A look-out post was constructed on Erraid. In the early days, each morning between 9 and 10 o'clock, a ball signal was raised at the lighthouse signifying that everything was alright. If this did not happen a schooner would be sent out immediately to ascertain the reason. There was no other means of communication. (Maybe semaphore was introduced later). I do not know when the ball method was discontinued or when radio transmission was established.

I wrote, and reproduce here, a trilogy of poems to mark the human abandonment in 1994 of this magnificent structure which I hope reflects the sadness of a building completed in 1844. After 150 years of selfless service to the safety of mariners and occupied by men of courage, tenacity and loyalty, it is now hollow and reverberating only with the mutated sounds of the ghosts from the past. However, there is no doubt that it will continue, with the dedicated organisation of the members of the Northern Lighthouse Board, for at least another 150 years.

I shall repeat the NLB motto: 'In Salutem Omnium' ('For the Safety of All')

CHAPTER 47
SKERRYVORE POEMS

Lonely Skerryvore
Tall Tale 1

My lighthouse name is Skerryvore
Rising fourteen miles from shore
But now I stand here, all alone
Now the keepers all have flown.

The waves keep pounding on my sides
Like tears the water down me slides
But I stand firm, as firm can be
Defiant of the angry sea.

The rocks above and down below
Many of them did not show
Lying in the ocean deep
The secrets below the waves they keep.

Many ships had fallen foul
You can almost hear the sailors howl
From desperation and the fear
As into the brine they disappear.

A light was needed to save lives
So no more sad and grieving wives
A plan was hatched to build a tower
To Stevenson they gave the power.

He landed to survey the scene
Where few men had ever been
He measured, sounded, thought it through
And sketches, plans and drafts he drew.

A barrack structure was erected
But through the storm it was dissected
It disappeared without trace
Another was to take its place

I was born in thirty nine
Surrounded by the foaming brine
The weary workmen blew out a base
The building then began apace.

At Hynish the building blocks were cast
The gneiss was hard and made to last
By artisans who knew their craft
No strangers to the arduous graft.

The base complete, the granite came
Massive segments, none the same
They built me up to such a height
Now I'm dominated by a light.

The men had toiled through wind and sea
As they scrambled over me
To give them praise is not enough
They were strong and they were tough.

The furnishing of it then ensued
Stores for water, oil and food
Eleven rooms were built in all
Entombed within a curv'ed wall.

Keepers came and keepers went
I knew them all who e'er they sent
Many a foot has tread my stairs
Some would swear and some said prayers.

Nineteen fifty four was bad
And it made me very sad
The roaring fire it was so fierce
It reduc'ed even me to tears.

In fifty nine I shone again
Having recovered from the pain
In seventy two a helipad
Made the keepers very glad.

In ninety four they left for good
Now I'm in a dismal mood
I cannot hear their laughs and chatter
Many say it doesn't matter.

Composed by Sydney T. Scott 7.2.19

∾

Lonely Skerryvore
Tall Tale 2

Shipwrecks, sunshine and some showers
Sadly, not too many flowers
Solar Panels, ships and seals
Sometimes there are fishers' creels.

Kettles whistling on the stoves
Keepers buttering new baked loaves
Kelp washed up upon the rocks
Knitting and darning of the socks.

Evenings merging into nights
Engine turning for the lights
Eating, sleeping then on call
Every day I've seen it all.

Rainbows shining out at sea
Ripples on the waves I see
Railings on the landing grate
Ready for the welcome freight.

Reeling in the fishing line
Rock cod, so that they can dine
Running up the lighthouse stairs
Reading, writing on their chairs.

Years have pass'ed, one by one
Your work here is never done
Yesteryear I'll not forget
Yearning - but with no regret.

Violent storms have battered me
Vicious is the raging sea
Valiant men have all been here
Vowing that they have no fear.

Other people they arrive
Oilskins so that they survive
Officers with golden braid
Over here and underpaid.

Ranging out o'er twenty miles
Rotating lenses, flashing dials
Remind me of the tasks I do
Reliable and safe for you.

Every time the fog rolls in
Each time the signal makes a din
Eerie sounds are very rude
Ear defenders are no good

Composed by Sydney T. Scott 11.2.19

Lonely Skerryvore
Tall Tale 3

The background round me is austere
And sometimes it is very drear
But the architecture has been praised
When people see me, they are amazed.

Many birds around me fly
Gannets swirling way up high
Diving like an arrow true
Into the water - azure blue.

Puffins, razorbills and shags
Standing on the exposed crags
Resting, waiting for the tide
When into the briny they will slide.

A landing stage is at my feet
Railings round make it complete
Water barrels and oil too
Sometimes they were overdue.

Two men, once, were swept away
But they lived another day
Scott and Crowe near lost their lives
Then there would be grieving wives.

On the 'Street' of Erraid's isle
Lived the families for a while
The cottages there were very small
But they seemed to hold them all.

Granite from this barren place
Was also used to make my face
A signal box was there on top
To contact me if I should stop.

My tales are nearly at an end
Before I go, I'll tell you friend
Even I was near upstaged
When two people came and got engaged.

Composed by Sydney.T.Scott 12.2.19

⌇

Patrick and Joy Tubby, members of the Association of Lighthouse Keepers, were
engaged on the rock at Skerryvore accompanied by the skirl of bagpipes.

THE SMALL WORLD OF
LIGHTHOUSE FOLK

In Chapter One, 'In Memory of My Father', I mentioned that he and George MacKenzie were involved in the initiation of the first lighthouse keepers' union – The Scottish Lighthouse Keepers' Association - although they never served together.

Three ex-'Trinity House' keepers formed the Association of Lighthouse Keepers (ALK) whose purpose was to propagate an interest in lighthouses. Not only ex-keepers joined but word spread to the wider community and a global network of aficionados was quickly established. 2017 was the 30th anniversary of the forming of the organisation so a Members invitational gathering was organised. A trip on a river boat on the Thames was organised followed by a tour of, and dinner at, Trinity House, the regulator body of the English and Welsh lights.

Whilst having a pre-dinner glass of wine, I was approached by a man whom I did not recognise. He was sporting a Northern Lighthouse tie, as was I. I thought he must have been the NLB representative. He introduced himself by saying, 'Your father knew my father'. The inscription on his name tag was 'Lord Hector MacKenzie of Culkein'. He was the son of George and whom I never knew existed. Photographs were taken

P52. Hector MacKenzie

...and he invited me to lunch at the House of Lords during which he appraised me of his parents wedding which had taken place at the lighthouse on North Ronaldsay (NR).

George MacKenzie served at NR between 1925 and 1934 so would probably have met my father several times when my father had holidays in NR.

In 2018 I visited NR and related these circumstances to my cousin's wife. She took me to a room, pointed to a chair and said, 'George MacKenzie made that for your grandmother'. This was probably in the late 1920s.

P53. George MacKenzie chair

LEST WE FORGET

Reflections are dimming. The lights are fading. Thankfully I mean the Lighthouse families and not the actual lanterns which shine out as strongly as ever and, as I understand it, are becoming increasing in importance for the need for static and reliable warnings to those who 'go down to the sea in ships'.

I speak, of course, of the dwindling memories of Lighthouse folk following automation. I surmise that in another generation's time our reminiscences will have disappeared into the dusty annals of history. The words 'Lighthouse Keeper' will not generate stories of the trials and tribulations undergone by the men and their families or the humour and fun which were the emotional safety valves.

Hardly a day, and certainly not a week, goes by without the Lighthouse Service popping up in the memory banks. I have photographs of Douglas Head, Dunnet Head and Kinnaird Head in my office. I have a very large framed photograph of Skerryvore in our sitting room – a reminder of the hardships endured and the dedication and unstinting duty that many families demonstrated. But the comradeship was never forgotten. Long live – and I mean it – all those of the lineage whose lives will one by one slowly dwindle away beneath the waves along with the setting sun.

Last one out, please leave the lights on.........

FINAL CURTAIN

!..........W O O S H..........!

(I have not mentioned, amongst other life experiences, my long association with London Irish Mini and Youth Rugby or my subsequent 10 years as security at Richmond upon Thames Tertiary College but they would be two books on their own. Someday...............!)